The Moving City

The Moving City

SCENES FROM THE DELHI METRO AND
THE SOCIAL LIFE OF INFRASTRUCTURE

Rashmi Sadana

UNIVERSITY OF CALIFORNIA PRESS

University of California Press
Oakland, California

© 2022 by Rashmi Sadana

Library of Congress Cataloging-in-Publication Data

Names: Sadana, Rashmi, 1969– author.

Title: The moving city : scenes from the Delhi metro and the social life of
    infrastructure / Rashmi Sadana.

Description: Oakland, California : University of California Press, [2022]
    | Includes bibliographical references and index.

Identifiers: LCCN 2021023170 (print) | LCCN 2021023171 (ebook) |
    ISBN 9780520383951 (cloth) | ISBN 9780520383968 (paperback) |
    ISBN 9780520383975 (epub)

Subjects: LCSH: Subways—India—Delhi Metropolitan Area. |
    Urbanization—India—Delhi. | City planning—India—Delhi. | Delhi
    (India)—Social life and customs. | BISAC: SOCIAL SCIENCE /
    Anthropology / Cultural & Social | SOCIAL SCIENCE / Ethnic
    Studies / Asian Studies

Classification: LCC HE4999.D45 S23 2022 (print) | LCC HE4999.D45
    (ebook) | DDC 388.4/2095456—dc23

LC record available at https://lccn.loc.gov/2021023170

LC ebook record available at https://lccn.loc.gov/2021023171

For Vivek

Contents

Introduction

When you get off at the elevated Mundka station, a line of small white vans waits for passengers at the bottom of the escalator. Young men call out place-names for destinations all across the Haryana state border. Cow dung patties dry in the sun to one side of the station escalator; jagged lines of cars and buses jostle on the other. Half-built Metro stanchions leading to future stations rise up in the distance. Leaving Mundka, Raveena, a slim woman in her twenties, gets on the women-only coach of the Metro. We start to chat, and she tells me that her father drops her off and picks her up at the station each day. She takes the Metro a few stops eastward to Paschim Vihar to attend college. She is certain that she would not be on the Metro at all if it were not for "the ladies' coach."

"After Mundka, it's good," she says, "but before Mundka, it's very bad, the crowd and all." For Raveena, "crowd" is about place, about where you are from and the attitudes you may hold. It is an imagined likeness and social reality but perhaps more a public than an actual crowd. It is also, of course, a manner of speaking.

"Haryana is not good, not good for girls. Men are not good, even boys. They stare at me, sometimes they vent at me. I can't do anything," she explains. "Vent" is typical Delhi-speak to describe when someone lashes out in a stream of verbal abuse erupting like a volcano. On the street they see her as a species rather than a person. What are they angry about? That she is a girl in public, that she moves with confidence, that she is protected, that she studies, that they don't have girlfriends, that they don't have jobs, that, ironically enough, there aren't more women around. On the Metro, the crowd is simply more "neutral," Raveena says, and I also see that it allows her to imagine, and perhaps enact, a future beyond it.[1]

Delhi has been notorious as a place where women not only get harassed on the street but also may be subjected to the grisliest of crimes. These stories and statistics feed into a larger narrative about girls' and women's safety and their proper place in the city (usually at home).[2] The safety discourse teaches women from a young age that it is their fault if anything happens to them and that they need male protectors and guardians to get through life—and public space. And yet on the streets and lanes of Delhi, you see women everywhere; they have places to go and things to do, from moving bricks at construction sites to leading the city as top-ranking public officials. As state-sponsored infrastructure, the Delhi Metro has given women in particular a new way into the city, as a site of purpose, aspiration, and pleasure. One out of four Metro riders is female, which is similar to the percentage of women who work outside the home in India.[3] As a street-level ethnographic view of the city, this book documents women and men in public places: how people flow into and out of trains and the new embodied experience of that flow; how they melt into the crowds yet emerge with individual experiences; how urban life comes to be narrated through the Metro. It recounts diverse experiences of the city and especially reveals what becomes visible through female gazes.

The arrival of the Delhi Metro—an ultra-modern, high-tech, and highly surveilled urban rail system, and South Asia's first large-scale, multiline metro—has become a touchstone for discussions of urban development, gendered social mobility, and India's increasingly aspirational culture. The Metro is also a set of places and a facet of everyday urban life. Even though it shares many of the same features and feel of metro and subway systems around the world, the Metro is forced to take up the city as much as it overlays its own concreteness on it. Inside the trains, many of the social meanings and distinctions of Delhi society are transported and sometimes transformed. The Metro may be a highly regulated system, and its riders may have specific purposes and destinations in mind, but it is also a new concentration of strangers in an expansive social space where people are learning new things about their own desires. At the peripheral edges of the city, where the Metro meets more rural sensibilities, ideas of the urban are created and contested.

The first line of the Delhi Metro, the Red Line, opened on December 24, 2002. Since then eight more lines (Yellow, Blue, Green, Violet, Orange, Magenta, Pink, Grey) and a total of 285 stations (and counting) have been built over three construction phases. A fourth phase is currently underway. The Metro covers close to 400 kilometers of Delhi's National Capital Region, extending into the states of Uttar Pradesh and Haryana, making it one of the largest urban rail networks in the world. With the now ubiquitous Delhi Metro map, the system offers a new and dominant paradigm for thinking about and traveling across the city. Both a visual rhetoric and abstraction of space, the map is part of the new surveillance that comes with the system. It orders the city not only for Metro riding but for governing as well.[4] And yet the Metro also unleashes a web of connections—social, economic, political—that are difficult to map or pin down. The system represents solidity and the mastery of time over space, even as it operates in a fluid, circulatory manner. It is a built environment and a moving one.

~

I first got on the Metro in 2006 at Central Secretariat station near India Gate, which was as far south as the Yellow Line went at the time. The train tilted and turned through dark tunnels. Inside it was like any metro system in the world: bright lights, sleek flooring, and the rhythmic sound of sliding doors. Announcers on the PA system spoke in Hindi and English to remind you about the gap. Known places—Chawri Bazar, Chandni Chowk, Kashmere Gate—became destinations newly lined up and ordered.[5] Unknown places become names on the Metro map, possibilities of knowing, of going to, of reaching like never before. It felt like a revelation. Seven stops later, at Civil Lines, I exited through a glass cube-like station. The trip felt more like a ride; it almost didn't matter where I was going. I was, like so many in the city, a first timer, a joyrider.

Figure 1. Civil Lines station, Yellow Line, 2006.

For some Dilliwalas, or Delhiites, the novelty of riding the Metro came from the fact that it was in India, and they could compare it to what they had only ever experienced abroad, in cities like London or Singapore. For most in the city, it was their first experience of high-speed underground rail travel. For still others, it was the first time they had ridden an escalator. For all, the system had rearranged city space and their experience of time. In this solid state-of-the-art structure, a new form of fleetingness took shape, a multitude of instances, a moving city.

Delhi is a desert city in a bowl, in the vast Indo-Gangetic Plain. The Aravalli mountain range lies to the southwest of the city, gaining stature as it breaks away from the Ridge, a monkey-filled, forested area in north Delhi where people stroll in the mornings and evenings, sticks in hand. With the Ridge and the city's many parks and green spaces, Delhi can feel both lush and dry depending on the season and where you are in the city. Delhi has the largest square acreage of any city in India, incorporating villages and wildlife, as well as diverse sensibilities, from rural mind-sets to middle-class aspirations and globalized consumerism. The Metro joins and cuts across these spaces.

Delhi has a population of twenty million, but it is not a crowded city in the way that Mumbai, Hong Kong, and New York are. Or at least it doesn't feel that way. It's not bounded by oceans or bays but rather crossed by a dwindling river, the Yamuna, that cuts through the city instead of creating a border around it. The city is spread out. And it keeps going. It has no natural limit, only other cities at its far perimeters—Gurugram (formerly Gurgaon), Ghaziabad, Noida, Faridabad, Bahadurgarh, and Sonipat.[6]

Landlocked, Delhi has always been at the crossroads of cultures and commerce as well as ideas and beliefs. Yet modern narratives of the city tend toward the historical, focusing on the 1857 war of independence from the British, the 1911 establishment of the colonial capital, and the range of events related to the Indian nationalist, anticolonial movement, leading to the nation's independence and the partition of the subcontinent in 1947. While informed and often moved by the historical, my curiosity about Delhi was spurred by what I was seeing and experiencing in the here and now and the everyday, a large part of which related to getting around.

The Delhi Metro has not only given new shape and definition to the ever-expanding megacity but also gives Dilliwalas themselves a greater awareness of those who live, and work in, and depend on it. Those who rush by and those absorbing the atmosphere at a slower pace, sitting on staircases, strolling to cafés, waiting on platforms. The different modes and paces I noticed across stations and hubs in my anthropology of the city enabled me to see the Metro as a place for transit and *flânerie*. And to see, at this intersection of concrete and crowds, how the Metro spurs new forms of sociality in the city. The Metro is a distinctive space, and it is also a set of new spatial dynamics and coordinates that reframe social life and the image of the city. A system in a set of linked, enclosed spaces, the Metro provides a kind of cohesiveness, even if it is illusory. These new pathways set the stage for repeated journeys, a deepening of grooves, the city as map, picture, place.

The central areas of Delhi have always been for the rich or powerful—politicians, bureaucrats, lawyers, and the like. These areas form an elite geography cordoned off by large roadways and roundabouts, big bungalows and imposing monuments. On the streets you see hawkers and office workers, but it's clear they are there to do the bidding of the more powerful. Older market areas like Karol Bagh or the lanes off Chandni Chowk in the old city are markedly different in that they teem with people, activity, and a vast array of specialized markets for spices, paper, cloth, and electronics—domains far removed from the office crowd. The Metro connects these two worlds: the older markets and the newer malls and offices. Riding it can be a revelation for not only who you see—the people, the crowds—but also how they connect to different parts of the city and the new cultural geographies that are laid bare.[7]

Delhi's most recognizable public spaces have long been its monuments, not just for their historical value or sublime architecture but for the kind of places they are in the everyday life of the city.[8] In most cases these are people-friendly places for all classes, ones that allure and create publics: the central vista from Rashtrapati Bhavan to India Gate to Purana Qila, Lodi Gardens, Jantar Mantar, Jama Masjid, Akshardham Temple, the memorial ghats on the Yamuna River, as well as more practical spaces for large public gatherings and conventions such as Ramlila Maidan and Pragati Maidan. I would add the Delhi Metro to this list, for it is not only the single largest set of public spaces in the city, a place to *be* as much as to journey through, but also a zone that is carefully managed by the state. It adds to the city's image as it connects existing structures and reframes them by overlaying its own structure on what was already there. The system has both a singular impact and an all-encompassing "renewing" effect on the urban landscape.[9]

In India, where urban transport is a site of status and contestation, the Metro is a place where "the people" come to be defined and molded. This kind of place is significant in the liberalized era, where public space has been shrinking as there are more and more paid social spaces in the city, from restaurants and eating parks to gardens and malls. These experience-heavy destinations aim at making Delhi more global and more exclusive.

The Metro offers a new grid and key to the city. Its platforms and stations provide a sense of certainty in a city where traffic times are hard to predict, and other forms of transport are not always reliable. There is a bus system but not enough buses. There are auto rickshaws and taxis, but you have to find one and then fix a price with the driver. Phone apps such as Ola Cabs and Uber have changed the taxi landscape, but even with global positioning systems, you often still have to negotiate last-mile directions: they still have to find you.

My interest in Delhi's Metro stems from what I saw as a seismic shift in how the city was being experienced and perceived from the late 2000s. I was living and commuting in Delhi at the time and taking the Metro most days. The Metro wasn't an integrated system then; it was in a state of becoming. It was the recognizable high-tech system you see in other cities, just as clean and ordered, often more so, just as fast and efficient; but outside, the seams were still showing where the stations and the city met.

I came to think of these seams as the interface between the city and the Metro, a system which I soon learned *was* built as a stand-alone artifact. To become an effective metro system, I also knew that the Metro would have to be integrated with "the city"—its roads, its people, and its other forms of transit (buses, vans, jeeps, cycle rickshaws, auto rickshaws, taxis). In a highly developed and densely populated city like Delhi, this process was both exciting and unnerving to watch. I started to contemplate the nature of "the urban" and to ask: When will these seams dissolve? And what is at stake in this transformation, this integration?

I used ethnographic research methods to study the Metro, meaning I rode the trains as much as I could, on all lines and to all stations, clocking over four thousand hours in all. I observed, interacted with, and talked to people on trains, at stations, and around stations, once I got over the strangeness of talking to strangers on public transport. Going around the city in this way helped me to focus on it as a gendered space; for instance, the way darkness signals when women should not be on the streets. In this case, the Metro's bright lights counter this gendered assumption and practice, since it's always daytime in the system; and in fact, many women told me that the Metro is the only form of public transport they feel is a legitimate urban space for them at night. But space is not only a physical location or set of coordinates; it is also a sense of possibility, a mental pose, a kind of social permission.[10] I also interviewed a range of Metro officials, planners, architects, bureaucrats, and politicians, usually in their offices or home offices. Moving between the spaces of transit and the office spaces of people planning transit, I found both connection and disconnection.

∼

The Metro began as a management structure in the form of the Delhi Metro Rail Corporation, or DMRC, set up in 1995. The DMRC is a half central government of India, half Delhi state government agency that built and manages the system; it is a management company and brand that links to five hundred private contractors. The Delhi Metro is an example of the public-private partnerships and transnational capital flows of the neoliberalized era. The system is a space produced by those flows. The majority of its workers are nonunionized and contractual, even as they have safer working conditions compared to other major construction sites in the country. In India this era was launched by the liberalization reforms of the Indian economy from the late 1980s onward.

The Metro has become emblematic of the new kinds of social mobility people imagine and plan for in this new economy. In this way, Delhi's urbanism speaks to the future as much as, if not more than, the grand cities of industrial modernity such as Paris, London, and New York.[11] This future includes the pleasures and powers of rising, consumerist middle classes, ethical questions around modernity and sustainable development, and the persistent inequalities of living, gulfs really, that point directly to the control of resources and infrastructures.

Even though the Metro only accounts for 5 percent of individual trips in the city (the majority are by bus, followed by motorcycles, scooters, taxis, and cars), the Metro's expansive network of stations and viaducts drives the city's property development and is a new site for the production of dreams, tastes, and desires. The Metro is not reducible to the new middle-class consumer culture in the way that shopping malls or gated communities might be; it is a more complex and multifarious urban space.[12] Nonetheless, the Metro is most definitely a class-making space and an example of aspirational infrastructure for its three million daily riders.[13] The Metro offers a globally identifiable, middle-class experience, with its visible high technology, quick commuting times, and comfortable, climate-controlled ride, that is both everyday and embodied. The globalized aspect of a transnationally produced infrastructure elevates its aspirational quality. The Metro carries the moral dimension of middleclassness in terms of how one should behave but also what one should be aspiring to: certain kinds of jobs, education, and lifestyles.[14] Many see the Metro as an effective social leveler precisely because of the rules that people must follow to ride it. The implication in some of the discourse on the Metro is that the "unruly" and "unwashed" laboring classes will have to reform in order to blend in while riding the Metro. So the system is a social leveler by offering a relatively low-cost access to urban space and a new way to perform and be in that space. However, as urban infrastructure, the system creates more inequality by determining future property values and the city's financial obligations for its ongoing maintenance and operation. The system transforms urban space, and also takes up a lot of space with its stations, tracks, and viaducts, as well as offices, warehouses, workshops, plants, machineries, sheds, and depots—all fixed to the landscape. The system as a material object expands its own space of profit as a property developer, with kiosks, shopping malls, and thirty-year lease commercial and residential developments, as a way to pay for the Metro along with passenger fares. It is a capital project more than a people project, and its meaning and symbolic value lie in the contradictions inherent in this dual role.[15]

Delhi's Metro was made with enormous political will behind it; it is a joint venture between the Indian and Japanese governments, the latter of which supported 65 percent of the Metro construction in the form of loans. As one Metro consultant put it to me, "The Japanese have chosen to invest in India in a major way, whereas before they avoided it. Now it is 'less China, more India,' which reflects their political interests and history." The Metro is in fact one of many infrastructure projects funded by the Japanese across India. It is perhaps the shiniest and most "people-facing," but one where the viability of the project is not and was never up for public debate.

The Metro comes under the auspices of the central government's Ministry of Urban Development and operates under the Metro Act of 2002, giving it powers to acquire, hold, dispose of, improve, develop, and alter all kinds of properties and assets.[16] A metro system is the kind of infrastructure that creates a new relationship and promise between governments on the one hand and with ordinary citizens on the other. These citizens are "stakeholders" in the world of infrastructural finance schemes. Throughout this book I highlight instances of this citizen-state relationship (one of capital and knowledge flows) and the new kinds of "Metro publics" (new forms of citizenship) that emerge. In an era where the idea and practice of citizenship is being hotly contested and fought over in the streets, a study of urban citizenship in the space of public transit points to the everyday, often slight, nuances of belonging and not belonging.[17]

The Moving City is not a historical narrative of the Metro's making but rather an examination of points of connection between grand-scale planning and the thinking behind it, and the daily movements and activity of Metro commuters. How do people's miniature expanses—of thought, experience—connect to the mega-ness of public transport? What do people see through the innumerable new frames on the city the Metro provides, through station exits and entrances and windows in every coach? What does all this seeing do?

An anthropological approach to a metro system sees it as infrastructure—a physical network enabling transport—but sees infrastructure as more than the function it serves. Infrastructure is a "collective fantasy" that both reveals a particular constitution of the political and addresses a new set of publics. Infrastructures put matter, substances, and people in motion and in relation. High-speed urban rail transport—both a hallmark of the industrial age *and* a contemporary symbol of globalized culture and transnationally produced mega-infrastructure—is nothing if not a statement of social and technological change in the form of new habits and ways of being and thinking.[18]

This book is a consideration of what it means to study the urban in a twenty-first-century megacity—the kinds of crowds and compressions, expansions and possibilities, visibilities and invisibilities that come to the fore. The more I rode the trains and visited stations, the more Metro officials I talked to, and the more commuters I interacted with, the more I came to see that to understand the Metro's social impact was to see how the particular and the individual related to the whole ("the whole" being the Metro system but also the city of Delhi); how the system and ideas about the system impacted each station and each journey; how people were making individual journeys but also understanding their city and themselves in a new way. I was struck by the relatedness and connections on the Metro but also by its randomness and anonymity. The Metro as a system both draws in (people, places, ideas) and doles out (its own systematics).

To match what I was seeing, my research became radically multisited within a single city. To exit a station, reenter it, and go back from where I had come, if I so desired. To make triangular journeys in the city or quadrangular ones. To crisscross it and pass by hundreds of people at a time, in seas and waves and trickles. I gave in to my own randomized itineraries and embraced the contingencies of the ethnographic on an urban scale. At the same time, I started to connect diverse places (Metro stations as well as places where Metro riders told me they were coming from) with people's everyday experiences and ideas. And I started to see the growth of existing lines not only in terms of construction but also in terms of the changing idea of the urban in Delhi—from the perspective of those living in the city, people planning the city, and also those coming into the city. The connective thread of my study and this book is the Metro in all its concreteness (trains, viaducts, stations) but also in its symbolics: what it means and represents as a global emblem of technological modernity and a master urban plan.

The Delhi Metro is also one of the few spaces in the city, and certainly the largest, that offers a measure of equal access across many lines of social division. It is one of the cheapest metros in the world to ride, with one-way fares ranging by distance from 10 to 60 rupees (14 to 84 cents), in a city where the per capita monthly income is 25,256 rupees (334 USD), but where nearly a quarter of the population lives below the poverty line.[19] The Metro is a space where no one technically benefits from having a higher social or economic status, even if riding it does not erase what people feel inside (though at times it might do that); it is a space where social differences subside from ticket entry point to exit gate. It is an accessible space in a highly uneven city, uneven in terms of one's footing on the road and one's social status. This semblance of equal access makes the Metro an especially potent symbol in a city of stark social and economic divides. The idea of public transport as a social leveler is nothing new, but how the leveling out happens and doesn't happen in particular instances and situations reveals much about a place. The access, the equality is ephemeral, it comes and goes like the trains. Yet the repetition has some substance to it, some weight.[20]

There are multiple constituencies served by the Metro, but the system has been especially consequential for women. The ladies' coach of the Metro has become a site of social and political significance, not only for the coach itself but also for how it structures the rest of the train and the larger discourse on women's safety and mobility in the city.[21] It is a women-only car, usually the first car of the train; pink signage on platforms designates where women should wait to board it. Women travel in the ladies' coach a few feet from and in full view of the men standing or sitting in the open pathway between the ladies' and general (or mixed) coaches. The space is fluid even as the very categories of "women" and "men" come to be reinforced. The Metro is a response to an urban space that is already experienced differently based on one's gender, and the ladies' coach further shapes that space, beginning with its very name. This divide is present in other cities in the world that have women-only cars on their metro systems, such as Rio de Janeiro, Cairo, Tehran, Guangzhou, Tokyo, and Mexico City. The circulation of ideas about gender relate not only to Delhi but to a broader circulation between cities, enabling us to ask: To what extent do these segregated spaces reconstitute patriarchal norms even as they may increase women's mobility in cities?[22]

When a women-only coach was instituted by the Delhi Metro Rail Corporation in October 2010, many women in the city were against it, saying it countered the idea of women as equal citizens with the right to be treated respectfully in public places. The Metro was supposed to condition society into a new gender equality or at least peaceable recognition. I agreed with those arguments at the time and still do; there is something to be said for enacting the change you want to see. In the early years of riding the Metro, before the ladies' coach was instituted, I remember marveling at the shared male-female space of the trains and sensing a kind of commuter kinship that seemed to outweigh anything else. However, in the years since then, I have met so many women who tell me that they started riding the Metro *only* because there is a ladies' coach that I am glad it exists.

The ladies' coach is not only a "safe space" away from unwanted male gazes and physical contact but also a porous space. There is no hard-and-fast "gender line" between the ladies' and general coaches, since the Metro's design is one long snaking train with no barriers, only open connectors that bend and curve with the movement of the train. Men in the adjoining general coach can look in as they stand on the threshold of the ladies' coach, but these looks are different from those given on the street.

Figure 2. The ladies' coach, 2019. The first coach of every Delhi Metro train (and on one route, the last coach) is reserved for women passengers.

The aggression and intensity of the street seems at a remove. The Metro environment is taming, and this is what women on the trains appreciate. The gender line is one under constant construction, modulated by the looks women give to men who enter the coach or stand at its borders. It is a space where female gazes match male ones, where women are given credence before the fact, even as they are subject to the perceived necessity of a ladies' coach. The availability of the Metro, as many told me, gave them more license, and made Delhi seem like more of an open city.

~

The Delhi Metro is an infrastructure that requires immense capital and planning, an agent of urbanization. Seeing how the Metro was planned and built is to see how a certain kind of top-down, government-instituted urbanization works, the processes behind it and the culture of technocratic management that it instills. Delhi's Metro, like most mega-infrastructure projects, represents capital interests in the city that favor property owners and the already upper class and upper caste. These larger structural issues have become more entrenched with the coming of the Metro; the Metro does not shake up this order. Economic analyses showed that a fraction of what it cost to build the Delhi Metro (11.3 billion USD for the first three phases) would have been more effectively spent on making a world-class bus system, serving more people, especially poor, working-class, and lower-middle-class people traveling to more intermediate destinations.[23] But that was never the point. The government and technocratic class wanted a Metro, they got it, and now they are building more systems like it, though with fewer stops and fewer lines, in cities across India. These cities will also "have" metros, in the sense of possession and emblem. There is an undeniable "love" for the Metro, which is also an indelible part of its success.[24]

Still, there is something that happens on the trains, a new kind of experience, feeling, and set of relations being piled up—and distributed. The Metro encapsulates the idea of urbanism as a way of life, discernible in people's attitudes, ideas, and personalities.[25] The Metro brings a different kind of knowingness about the city to its people. It is in this space of knowingness that Dilliwalas reconcile the system's extravagance with the everyday necessities of getting around. The Metro contributes to their identity formation and their claim to citizenship in a highly diverse city. It relays a moral claim of middle classness by offering access to new consumer spaces and vistas but also with the idea and promise of mobility itself. The Metro symbolizes a global culture its riders are a part of, even as the Metro marks a contrast within the city itself, where other infrastructures—water, sanitation, roads—are in need of such capital input and care. In this way, the Metro "addresses" the public. It is a kind of text that circulates in the city and "speaks to" those riding it and living in its midst. By addressing a public, the Metro also creates one.[26]

Metro and subway systems, along with airports, are increasingly sites of protest, not just because they symbolize the state but also because they highlight the relation between the everyday and the extraordinary. This was the case in Brazil in June 2013 when countrywide protests against corruption were sparked by an increase in bus, train, and metro fares in São Paulo, what came to be called the "free fare movement." Similarly, the October 2019 protests in Santiago, Chile, came after a 4 percent subway fare hike. The social contract of public transit can be damaged but also can symbolize and enact a much wider set of issues around inequality, described by one Chilean activist as "life itself."[27] During the nationwide protests against India's Citizenship Amendment Act that began in December 2019, the Delhi Metro Rail Corporation had to continually update which stations around the city were being closed, numbering as many as sixteen on some days. The closings gave a sense of what was happening where—outside the Metro, on the streets, as well as the state management of the city's circulatory flows. At Jaffrabad station in northeast Delhi, hundreds of people filled the road space between the Metro's pillars, chanting slogans and lighting candles, as if under a concrete umbrella. The moving city was stopped in places, but it was not curtailed.[28]

The Metro is a constant reminder of government power and resolve, and this book shows how the state intersects with people's everyday experiences and imaginaries. I describe aspects of this top-down story in that at times I "study up" by talking to Metro officials, architects, urban planners, bureaucrats, and politicians.[29] However, I mostly do what I would call "study across"—across the city, across platforms, across a broad spectrum of working- and middle-class people who I saw, heard, and interacted with on the Metro over many years. Studying across reflects my interest in the growing global middle classes and what they signify.[30] Studying across is also how people recognize and engage with one another on the trains. Each coach of the Metro is lined with benches. People sit and naturally look opposite, when they're not looking down at their phones.

~

Histories of metro and subway systems around the world, taken together, say much about the role of the engineer and architect in society as well as the politics of urban planning and design.[31] An ethnographic approach aims to understand the social life of infrastructure, how people engage with the technology and in the process remake themselves. In the field of anthropology, the first ethnography of an urban metro rail system was Marc Augé's 1986 study of the Paris Métro, *Un ethnologue dans le métro* (*In the Metro*).[32] A form of auto-ethnography, the book is foremost an evocation of things past, of well-worn itineraries and the long-term entwining of city and metro. In his telling, the city *is* the Métro. Augé's approach is particularly fitting for the Paris Métro, whose first line opened in 1900. The Paris Métro was a revelation for what a city could be and do in the industrial age. Paris has long been a center for the study of capitalist modernity and the production of urban theory, with its wide boulevards, shopping arcades, and Métro as its defining features and experiences: reverie, *flânerie*, profundity. In the era of European colonialism, Paris was a political and cultural center from which many of the world's divisions were mapped out. The city is also a hallmark of the kinds of class and racial divisions mapped onto city spaces, a city of centers, peripheries, and *banlieues*, or suburbs. Augé's work—a philosophical reflection, a musing on correspondences, a dwelling on memory—is an inspiration for and counterpoint to my own study.

The animating feature of Delhi's Metro is precisely its newness amidst the ongoing transformations of a megacity turned metacity, diffuse and polycentric.[33] In Delhi's story, the significance of Metro stations is sometimes for what they erase, but more often for what they suggest—and to whom. The connections Delhi commuters are making between stations and their lives, the Metro and their worlds, are happening in a digital, globalized age, in a rising economy. Delhi's Metro is a symbol of a hypermodernity, and it is a modernity that people can step into. Whether a "hypermodernity" or a "hypercity," as these urban agglomerations are sometimes also called, the implication is something that is over and above, but that could also be concerning in the sense of being high-strung or keyed up. Delhi's increasing speed and ongoing expansion pushes interior and exterior limits. The Metro is seen and experienced by many as a system that manages and negotiates the city by plotting it in a new way. And for this reason, the Metro becomes a site of personal transformation through the very idea of collectivity and in the space of public transit.

Delhi Metro stations recall heritage points in the city, at Red Fort, Qutab Minar, Tughlakabad, and elsewhere, but the vast majority of stations mark and initiate new processes of place-making.[34] New places and names have sprung up everywhere. New juxtapositions and rearticulations of what was there before. Riding the Metro becomes a new way to write the city.

The Delhi Metro can certainly be compared in size, scope, and impact to London's, Paris's, New York's, Tokyo's, Moscow's, or Mexico City's, but it is also of a piece with more recent systems in Cairo, Taipei, Hong Kong, Seoul, Singapore, Shanghai, and Beijing.[35] To integrate a massive, multiline transport infrastructure in a densely developed city, with already existing networks of monuments, roads, built forms, people, customs, and histories, is an engineering feat but also a feat of the imagination for the makers and riders of the Metro alike.[36]

In India's postcolonial period, a metro rail system for Delhi was first proposed in 1969 in a study by the Delhi-based Central Road Research Institute. The idea dovetailed with Prime Minister Jawaharlal Nehru's series of five-year plans to modernize the new nation's industries, technologies, and cities.[37] The Metro was an urban plan, not a national one, as it was meant specifically for the nation's capital. It never got off the ground.

Meanwhile, on the eastern coast of the subcontinent around the same time, Calcutta began building its own metro system. After tearing up that city, the system first opened seventeen years later in 1984. It was fully completed in the early 1990s, as a single line with sixteen stations. Delhi's eventual metro system was planned and financed differently, but its construction benefited from technological advances in the intervening years. Whereas in the 1970s Calcutta workers had to dig up the entire stretch of the metro corridor, in 2000s Delhi a tunnel boring machine enabled workers to use a cut-and-cover method, whereby they could make one large hole and lower the machine in the ground for underground construction. In the Delhi Metro Rail Corporation's own origin story, the Delhi Metro was meant to be distinct from Calcutta's as well as from the national Indian Railway system. Delhi's Metro was to mark not only a new system of urban transport but an entirely new way of doing things.[38]

Nevertheless, Calcutta's metro symbolized the city's and the nation's modernity in the 1980s and 1990s. News reports from the time talk of people marveling over the cleanliness, the mix of people on the trains, and the escalators.[39] It wasn't just the technology and concreteness of it. It was how people moved through and on the metro, the feeling of being modern that resided within them and in their bodily movements.[40] Calcutta had always been seen as being ahead; it was the first colonial capital under the British and a meeting ground for Indian and British ideas and cultural practices. It was a city used to absorbing the new and making something of it. Calcutta's modernity was matched only by the bustling port city and financial capital of Bombay, where the railway commuter trains were packed to the gills, but Bombayites were arguably the most forward thinking in India, men and women moving with confidence and nonchalance through the city. Delhi has always been cast differently, as a less agile city, a city laden with its heavy Partition past—of violence, sorrow, and division—and its bureaucratic stodginess.

In the 1990s, after the liberalization of the Indian economy, changes started happening in the city and in people's lives—greater consumer choices, different kinds of urban spaces, new forms of desire. On Delhi's roads, flyovers (overpasses) sprang up to ease the flow of traffic, while also having the effect of bifurcating neighborhoods and dwarfing street life with concrete pillars. Foreign-made cars in every color began to populate those flyovers as the upper middle classes came to see and understand the city through their cars. By the end of the 1990s, the percentage of people using public transport in the city dropped by almost 15 percent.[41]

With the influx of new cars, roads became contested spaces, with ever more accidents and incidents between drivers and the machines they

Figure 3. Near Laxmi Nagar station, Blue Line, 2012.

operated. The road could be menacing but also had a carnivalesque flavor to it. The road elicited new personalities and ways of being and feeling. People were paid off. Others died on the spot. There was a psychic element to road crashes and road rages, what urban theorist Ravi Sundaram describes as a meeting of "private trauma" and "public tragedy," whereby the road was "a reference point of constant dread, and everyday stress," even as Delhiites were becoming part of "a new commodity world."[42] There was a speeding up, he seems to say, of availability and automobility, and this heady mix led to more blood on the road.

In the years before the Metro, the city's then privately owned Blueline buses were in direct competition with the state-owned Delhi Transport Corporation buses, which only numbered 3,500. Blueline buses were ubiquitous and got you places but were also sometimes referred to as "killer buses" that were driven "in a hurricane manner." They claimed more than a hundred deaths per year, usually when buses struck pedestrians in their path. As one bus driver put it, "If you saw the kind of traffic on Delhi roads—no traffic sense, no lane driving, two-wheelers crisscrossing lanes—you wouldn't be surprised at the number of accidents."[43]

And yet the road was also a space of status-making and display. By the 2000s, India had a veritable "aspirational culture," where having a four-wheeled vehicle soon became the mark of being middle class (earlier it had been a refrigerator and a scooter). What had once been seen as the purview of the rich—the best goods, technology, education—became possible for more people, widening the landscape of desire.

The Metro has a dialectical relationship with the road. The road is everything the Metro is not: congested, potholed, weathered, and host to a variety of vehicles, pedestrians, animals, and carts. Piercing horns, sputtering diesel engines, barking dogs, the rip of a motorcycle, a dainty ringing bicycle bell, and deep-voiced pushcart vendors calling out their wares punctuate an elongated din of traffic, more avant-garde than orchestral. Time gets stretched out in the road's soundscape. When it's hot, what you hear is amplified by your own sweat and prickling skin; it's a relief to enter a station and get off the road. Firecrackers launched at Diwali celebrations each year leave a smoky residue for weeks; then the city becomes enveloped by gauzy, white skies as people huddle around coal stoves on the road, and the sun appears to squint at the city, a yellow smear in the sky. The Metro, by contrast, is smooth, singular, and climate controlled; you are at once at an acoustic remove. When you enter a station, a kind of quiet settles in as the regulated coolness seeps into your pores. There's also a different configuration of lightness and darkness compared to outside. You quickly adjust. The sound of the trains coming and going is more of a shuffle than a steady beat, modulated like a sleep machine. Even the gongs that alert you to a coming station have a rhythmic quality to them.

The Metro is contained the way the road is not, its entrances clearly demarcated by security checks, ticket booths, and automated gates. Once you enter a station and buy your token, you have to go through airport-like security; for men, this means going under a wooden-framed, electronic metal detector and then being "wanded" by a male security guard; women enter a small curtained security booth, where they are wanded by a female security officer. Between the lines of men (always much longer) and women entering the bodily security checks is a baggage scanner where everyone drops their stuff. Once you pass through security and collect your belongings you go through the electronic turnstiles, either with a token or travel card. Despite all the steps, the whole experience takes a minute, unless it's rush hour at a busy station and you're a man who is waiting in line to be scanned.

Delhi's Metro shields you from the outside, with its dangerous traffic and often harsh weather. From November to February, the fog becomes thick with pollution as particles get frozen into the air-scape, making for a still, heavy cold. From April to October, it's the heat that swallows you, first hot and dry like an oven, sometimes accompanied by a blistering wind, the infamous *loo*, that sweeps over the north India plains, and then wet and sticky as the monsoon arrives in July, a glorious relief, as kids play in the streets and potholes fill with water. The Metro captures neither the savory or unsavory aspects of the seasons; the system pulls you into the trains and then you forget what it feels like outside.

The Metro is considered a safer mode of transport than buses or auto rickshaws because of the system's surveillance mechanisms, its regularity, and its mastery of converting inside to outside and outside to inside. The Metro is a space of high surveillance, where freedom of movement is doled out as you move from the security check to the electronic ticketing gate, and then down or up to a platform. The cameras can be comforting, even if you're not sure if they are switched on or working; they are the global installations of modern life.

The Delhi Metro viaducts, now ubiquitous across the city, loom above the road, often alongside flyovers, crossing over traffic or the Yamuna River, and sometimes emerging from underground tunnels, leading to elevated stations. People watch the approaching train, moving seamlessly across a low sky.

∼

Writing about people (a basic definition of "ethnography") is not only the description and analysis of ways of life but also an immersion in a particular place. Ethnography is a form of engagement, interaction, and documentation, a precise set of acts, a doing in the world, and also, a way to perceive. But as much as ethnography can be planned, it is an idiosyncratic and contingent form of research. The Metro is scripted, a story of transnational finance, government protocols, and bureaucratic norms. And yet the Metro is not a linear narrative but rather a multiline, episodic one. It goes round-and-round, out and back, this way and that. This is the story of the Metro that I privilege in these pages. I offer an orchestrated series of vignettes that reflects how I came to see and analyze everyday experiences in light of this type of mega-infrastructure in a city such as Delhi. The Metro makes connections for us, for all time, but its plotting of places and stations, the new proximities it creates, do not stamp out the randomness of the system or the arbitrariness of getting around.

The vignettes that make up *The Moving City* are based entirely on ethnographic research, including interviews, observations, and a long-term engagement with a place and the people living there. However, my use of this form is not only meant to relay stories. The vignettes are also "studies" in the senses of portrayal and experiment, an examination of small parts leading up to a whole. Each vignette represents a world of its own, which connects to the Metro in some way and intersects with the city. Each vignette is a kind of magnification. For this reason, they are not uniform in approach or even style; each contains its own ethnographic strategy, which I see as the way in which tone, scene-setting, dialogue, and other features highlight meaning and argument.

The vignettes, with their brevity and perhaps ephemerality, mimic the flow of the Metro with its starts and stops. One cannot dwell anywhere for too long. These micro-ethnographic encounters are contained, like the journeys on a metro train, and yet bountiful and endless in a modern-day megacity.

The Metro is an emergent whole, a vast technology and system that has redefined the urban landscape; yet with its numerous stops, the Metro also signifies the fragment, the partial journey, the unexpected meeting.[44] You can know where you are going but not exactly who or what you will encounter. Included in the idea of stops are the Metro stations themselves and how people's lives become organized around stations, the stops and starts, flows and stoppages of various kinds of circulation and new forms of value in the city, having to do with everything from styles of dress and the transport of goods to language and social attitudes. In my rendering of the impact and meaning of Delhi's Metro, the vignettes take center stage.

They forefront the urban experience of people, the lives and itineraries of Delhiites whose paths crisscross the city.

The vignette has long been part of the presentation of anthropological research, in chapter openings, for instance, or as a way to divide and pause between chapters. These slices of life are technically evidence of something, crafted into stories or scenes. It is where a writer meets her method, where the seams show. It is also where the gap between experience and representation can be explored and probed. "The gap" is also an intrinsic feature of the Metro's built environment, between trains and platforms. It is an audible reminder on the trains and an embodied experience of getting on and off them. The gap lies between the train and the platform but also, in an interpretive sense, between the Metro and the city. Writing about the Metro is a practice of containment and definition. I rode the Metro in all its expansiveness, as researcher, commuter, interloper, but then purposefully pared it down, chiseled it away. The resulting form of this book is a way to show how things, people, places come in and out of view but is also a recognition of not always knowing how things leave off.[45]

My use of the vignette form is the message I want to convey about the experience of the Delhi Metro as an affective realm and transport assemblage.[46] The Metro highlights the city's beauty and possibility. The Metro forges and destroys. The Metro is the everyday. And is also yesterday, today, and tomorrow. I see the vignettes as a way to showcase but also mull over the disparate scenes of the Metro. As on the Metro, there are different ways to connect.[47]

There are multiple plots at work here. The Metro enables a new circulatory flow where one did not previously exist. It is in constant circulation but is also a permanent, fixed presence on the urban landscape. The system stops at night, but even then, trains are being washed and serviced. This flow is part of a particular kind of social contract that public transit represents.

~

This book is arranged in three parts: Crowded, Expanding, Visible. These are the three principles I see at work on the Metro, in the city, and in people's lives. The Metro collects, defines, and disperses the crowd; it expands the borders of the city as it contracts the time to travel to those borders; it makes things, people, ideas, visible in new ways, whether to individuals, communities, or the state. Crowds have long symbolized urban life, as anonymous collectives and physical pulsating masses. They represent an uneasy movement between states of being as much as identifiable social markers. Borders, as they expand or contract, gain meaning depending on which side of them you are on. Creating them is an act of mythmaking. Crossing them can redefine the self. Visibility is not just about what we can see but is also an act of recognition, even if slight, even if momentary. In the midst of the crowds interchanging at Rajiv Chowk station, under the stone columns of Connaught Place, this visibility is also a reminder of all that goes unseen, in the blur and rush of the crowd, as individuals go through turnstiles and up the escalators at the largest station in the system. Similarly, the photographs that appear in this book, which I originally took as part of my field notes, gesture to what can and cannot be seen just beyond the frame.[48]

The book's triptych structure reflects the Metro's three main construction phases. Part One introduces early stations and changes to the urban landscape and details the new kinds of embodied experiences riders have. It asks what kind of development Delhi's Metro actualizes. Part Two recounts the expansion of existing Metro lines and the appearance of new lines. It dwells on what differentiates the Metro from the street. And it shows what kinds of social mobilities are enabled by the Metro and to what extent urban design and mass transit can be vehicles for change. Part Three incorporates the new lines completed in the Metro's third construction phase, lines that circle the city and enable a host of new connections. It documents some of the new visibilities made possible as riders survey and experience a mostly elevated urban rail system. It shows who becomes visible because of the Metro.

The parts and vignettes in this book can be read in or out of order. The Metro is an act of ordering and arranging, in the most concrete terms. It is a lasting imprint on the city. And yet the millions of individual journeys on it each day continually shuffle this deck of stations, these lines and layers of travel.

In order, the vignettes offer a more chronological sense of how ideas about the Metro entered the public consciousness, how the Delhi landscape changed over time, how lines were extended, how construction remade roads and areas. But if you were to shuffle the vignettes like a deck of cards, the experience may be more arbitrary but still connected, offering a cumulative portrait of this city, in this time, and how some of its people inhabit place. Out of order, the stories of people, from slight interactions to formal conversations, stand as secular parables or urban chronicles, a set of small impacts in these years of great infrastructural change.

PART I Crowded

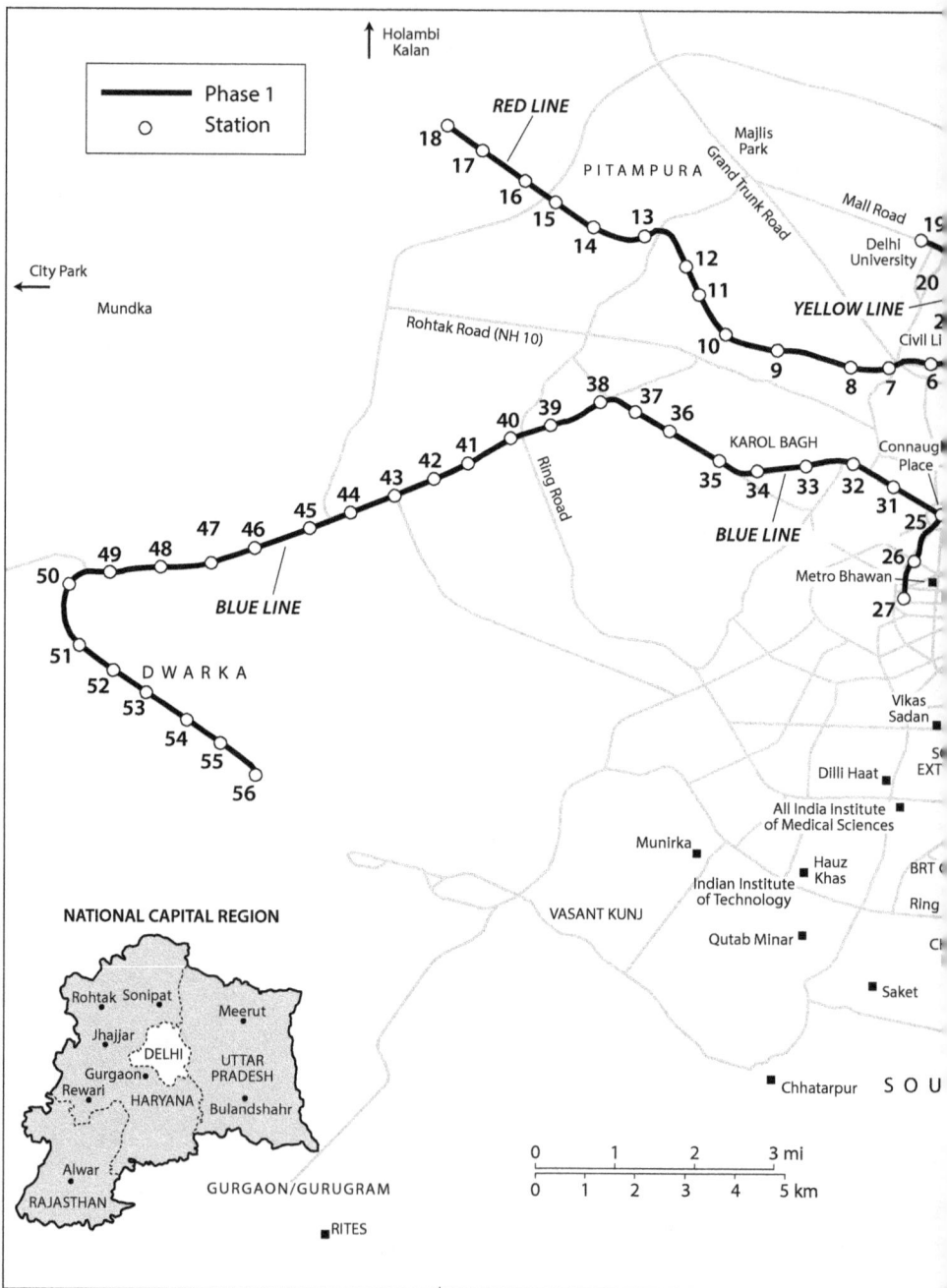

Holambi
Kalan

Phase 1
Station

RED LINE

Majlis
Park

PITAMPURA

Grand Trunk Road

Mall Road

19

Delhi
University

YELLOW LINE

2

Civil Li

20

City Park

Mundka

Rohtak Road (NH 10)

18
17
16
15
14
13
12
11
10
9
8   7   6

38
37
36
39
40
41
42
43
44
45
46
47
48
49
50

35
34   33   32
31

KAROL BAGH

Connaug
Place

25

BLUE LINE

26

Metro Bhawan

27

Ring Road

BLUE LINE

51
52
53
54
55
56

D W A R K A

Vikas
Sadan

S
EXT

Dilli Haat

All India Institute
of Medical Sciences

Munirka

Hauz
Khas

BRT

Indian Institute
of Technology

Ring

VASANT KUNJ

Qutab Minar

Ch

Saket

NATIONAL CAPITAL REGION

Rohtak   Sonipat

Meerut

Jhajjar

DELHI

Gurgaon

UTTAR
PRADESH

Rewari

HARYANA

Bulandshahr

Chhatarpur   S O U

Alwar

RAJASTHAN

GURGAON/GURUGRAM

RITES

0   1   2   3 mi
0   1   2   3   4   5 km

N

RED LINE

GHAZIABAD

4   3   2   1

al Quila-Red Fort
ama Masjid
Chandni Chowk
Chawri Bazar
School of Planning
and Architecture
Vikas Minar
28   Akshardham

PATPARGANJ

al Gallery
odern Art

TRILOKPURI

MAYUR
VIHAR

GPURA
ce
y

NOIDA

AT
AR   Kalkaji
Temple

OKHLA

Botanical
Garden

Nehru Place

Yamuna River

npuri

L H I   BADARPUR

FARIDABAD

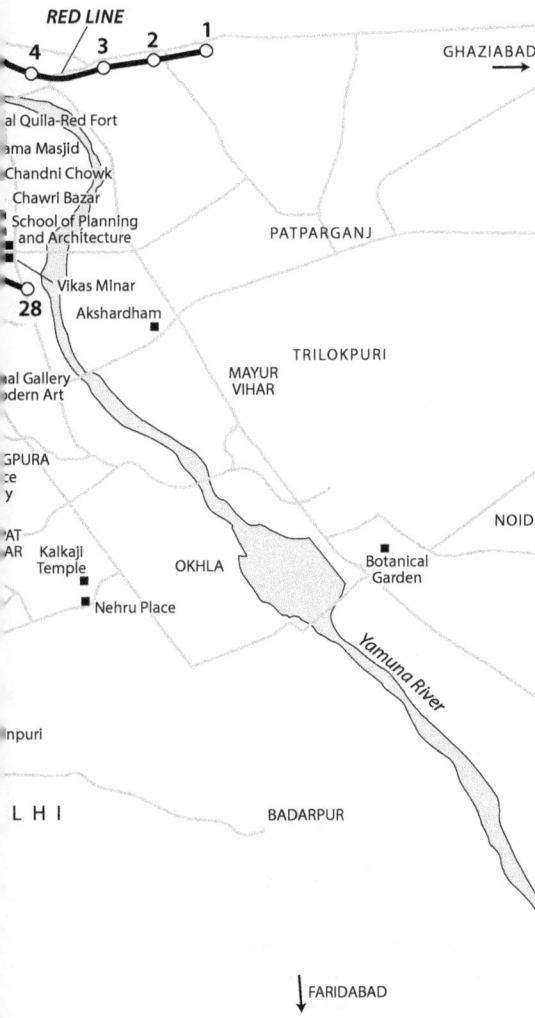

Metro Stations

1	Shahdara	29	Pragati Maidan
2	Welcome	30	Mandi House
3	Seelampur	31	R.K. Ashram
4	Shastri Park	32	Jhandewalan
5	Kashmere Gate	33	Karol Bagh
6	Tis Hazari	34	Rajendra Place
7	Pul Bangash	35	Patel Nagar
8	Pratap Nagar	36	Shadipur
9	Shastri Nagar	37	Kirti Nagar
10	Inderlok	38	Moti Nagar
11	Kanhaiya Nagar	39	Ramesh Nagar
12	Keshav Puram	40	Rajouri Garden
13	Netaji Subhash	41	Tagore Garden
14	Kohat Enclave	42	Subhash Nagar
15	Pitampura	43	Tilak Nagar
16	Rohini East	44	Janakpuri East
17	Rohini West	45	Janakpura West
18	Rithala	46	Uttam Nagar East
19	Vishwavidyalaya	47	Uttam Nagar West
20	Vidhan Sabha	48	Nawada
21	Civil Lines	49	Dwarka Mor
22	Chandni Chowk	50	Dwarka
23	Chawri Bazar	51	Dwarka Sec.14
24	New Delhi	52	Dwarka Sec. 13
25	Rajiv Chowk	53	Dwarka Sec. 12
26	Patel Chowk	54	Dwarka Sec. 11
27	Central Sect.	55	Dwarka Sec. 10
28	Indraprastha	56	Dwarka Sec. 9

Map 1. (overleaf) Phase 1 of the Delhi Metro opened in stages between 2002 and 2006 and consisted of three lines: Red, Yellow, and Blue. With Phase I, Dilliwalas became accustomed to torn-up streets, blocked entrances, and blue corrugated-metal boundary walls that lined city roads, especially in central Delhi (Yellow Line), northwest Delhi (Red Line), and west Delhi (Blue Line). Phase I was the opening salvo in the Metro offensive. It was the time when the interface between the Metro and the city was first felt and negotiated. City residents and business owners had been and were still being moved out of the Metro's way. As station names and places took hold in the imagination, those displaced by the construction were permanently relocated to places far from the city (and the Metro), such as Holambi Kalan in northwest Delhi.

The train to Dwarka is crowded even on an early Sunday afternoon. Central Delhi may be more still, and the road traffic-less, but inside the Metro throngs of people are going places. At times they crush into one another.

A creation of the Delhi Development Authority, the sub-city of Dwarka has risen up along the Metro corridor with hundreds of low-rise housing colonies and scores of "international" schools, business centers, sports clubs, and malls.[1]

A few men in their early twenties sit cross-legged on the floor, talking and laughing. Three younger boys, thirteen or fourteen years old, stand in front of them, doing pull-ups on the high bar, joking, trying to get the attention of the other men by entertaining them with curiosities pulled from their pockets. One says he has Afghan currency and is parading it around. It is a scene you might see almost anywhere in the city, an approximation of the street below, and yet completely removed from it.

Many people are hooked up to music players or talking on their mobiles. Men carry goods in tightly packed cartons; toddlers lie on the seats or stand on them to look out the windows, delighting in their own reflections. My arms rub against the women sitting on either side of me. In the space between the coaches, a man squats talking on his mobile. People mostly sit quietly; they do not eat or drink or spit. Most noticeable is what is missing: heat, sweat, filth, food, trash, odor, aroma. The stick in the air. Inside, the elements have been reordered, enabling a different view of this city-region of thirty million. Curiously, people look but do not stare, even the multiple packs of young men in slim jeans.

At Rajiv Chowk station commuters line up in neat rows waiting for the train to Dwarka, only to dissolve into a mass once the train arrives and the doors slide open. The logic of entering and exiting the train is whichever side has more people wins, like a scrimmage. People collide head-on as they push past each other. The spoils are there for all to see: for those coming in, a shiny seat; for those going out, their destination in record time and comfort.

The Metro has no ticket collector to complain to if something goes wrong or if someone gets out of line, for this is an automated environment. Many people were shocked, when, early on, a contracted Metro worker directing people to board a train got his hand stuck in the door as it was closing and was dragged to the next station while clutching the outside of the train. Passengers on board watched in amazement and horror but didn't know to hit the emergency bell.

As the train heads west, aboveground, the city opens up and peters out into a landscape of circling birds, low-level dwellings, institutes of knowledge, health, and beauty, and the occasional shopping mall. This east-west line is for commuters; the trains go aboveground soon after Connaught Place, and people tend to stay on for more than a few stops. There is time to relax and settle in.

A wiry young man I'm standing next to, Pranjal, is studying at the National Law University. He shares an apartment with another student near Delhi University and regularly rides the train. When I tell him I'm studying the Metro, he says, "I don't know if you're looking at the economics of it or issues of marketing, but I have some thoughts." He feels the need to teach, tell, persuade, or command people to follow certain rules, he says, like the one to let other passengers off the train before boarding themselves. He describes being in the crush of the crowd one day, alongside a young mother carrying a small child. The crowd hadn't made way for her but had pushed her aside. He couldn't understand this, nor do anything to help her; he ended up ensnarled in her bangles and left the train with bruised arms.

On the platform people rush to the escalators, forming a wide circle at the bottom of each one. It slowly shrinks as people move up. A smaller group waits for the elevator. "Stay Fit, Use the Stairs" signs are posted at each exit, placed there, it turns out, not to keep the populace in shape but to encourage the able-bodied to leave room in the elevators for others. Once upstairs (or downstairs, if at an elevated station) everyone passes through the electronic gates once more to leave the station. Some walk, others look for a bus or an auto or cycle rickshaw.

One afternoon I wait for a train with Sunila, a commuter from Dwarka in her mid-twenties. She is going to Uttam Nagar East, on her way to work. She didn't talk about the city in the same way when she used to ride the bus, she tells me. Then, her route was not direct and not as fast. It was not, as she says now, "Delhi up-down."[2]

MANDI HOUSE

Mandi House station first rose up in 2006. It was a mirage then, stylish, compact, and somewhat disconnected from the traffic circle around it. The station's pale gray stone façade was meant to blend into the landscape, which it eventually did; but in 2006 it still had a curb, a crumbling set of stones at its perimeter that pointed to its newness, a place, a line really, where the station and the city met. This line in the stony sand represented the city's becomingness in the sense that the urban is always becoming, always in process. The line also made the city visible, in the sense that it came into being in a new manner, a new framing. There was more to see, to apprehend, in the new angles and fixtures.

This line demarcating the station was an invitation, or at least an announcement. It announced that there would be a before and after the Metro. It announced that people in the city would be circulated in a new way. A circulation through the crisscrossing of perpendicular lines rather than roads and roundabouts. The line demarcating the station was one of the many new visibilities that the destruction and construction of the Delhi Metro unearthed, enabled, instituted.

During the first phase of the project, numerous neighborhoods that the Metro would soon pass through first became construction zones piled high with dust, corrugated metal sheets, cement, and cranes. Traffic was rerouted and city dwellers in many areas suffered from what one urban planner called "a tidal wave of physical destruction and social disorientation."[3] Then these same areas were restored and embellished, even as dislocation became relocation for hundreds of families and businesses moved out of the Metro's way. It will soon be hard to remember what the city was like before the Metro.[4]

In daytime the sound of traffic on Delhi's roads is constant; it pierces,

Figure 4. Mandi House station, Blue Line, 2006. The area would go on to be remade again in Phase 3 of the Metro's construction when the station became an interchange hub for the Blue and Violet Lines.

whistles, and demarcates outsideness. Sounds indicate motion in the city; they expand the space of the road and become something you not only hear but feel. Ambient sounds are everywhere, creating an "interlocking soundscape."[5] With sirens and the ringing of temple bells in the mix, you could be in a video arcade. Then an airplane hums overhead; you can barely hear it, but the sight of it somehow trumps the sound on the road.

The Metro system takes people out of circulation at first, of sight and sound, then reprocesses them inside through the ticket line, security check, and platforms to join another type of circulation. Mandi House station's sixteenth-century moniker, the Raja of Mandi, has no place or purpose in this new urban reckoning. Mandi House had already become a general urban designation for this place of establishment arts, communications, and culture. It originally referred to a building, then to a roundabout, and now to a Metro station. Names also travel in cities, they circulate and designate; they are signs, both arbitrary and meaningful, perhaps meaningful because of their arbitrariness. A name can gain momentum over time.

Kamala, who works as a beautician in south Delhi homes, first went on the Metro when her husband took her and their three children for a joyride. Her husband used to go "up-down" on the Blue Line from Mayur Vihar to Mandi House. He worked as a cook at the National School of Drama. "He cooked for those kids learning how to act," she tells me.

Kamala's husband died earlier in the year, making her a thirty-eight-year-old widow. "He took too many medicines from the chemist and had a bad reaction," she explains. "His lungs failed." The youngest of her three children thinks his father is still in the hospital and sometimes asks why he's been there for so long. Her husband was good, she says, "he showed a lot of love."

Kamala describes the Metro as being *"andhar hee andhar"*—enclosed, encompassed. When it's hot you escape the heat, when it's cold you escape the cold. One afternoon we ride to Mandi House together; Kamala gets in line to buy a token, and I follow suit. We take the Blue Line toward Noida. From there the train goes aboveground at Pragati Maidan. Kamala points out the window of the train to the light blue and white World Health Organization building just beneath us in the close distance and tells me that this is where they set the nutrition guidelines for India. We get down at Yamuna Bank station to meet her cousin, Alok, on the platform. He is taking her to a government office to deposit her widow's pension papers. We take the next train and get to Mayur Vihar, and she and Alok go off to look for an auto rickshaw. Before leaving, Kamala points to the half-done Metro line overhead; "This one will come to my house," she says, "then it will be even easier."

VANITA

When Vanita and I meet at Dilli Haat one afternoon in 2009, she tells me that she's had a "generally protected life." We are sitting at a food court table in an open-air artisan market in south Delhi, but she's describing 1960s Calcutta, where she grew up. "Someone was always taking me, I always went with someone—a grandfather, an uncle. Just to take a bus, you had to get down at the right stop."

I got in touch with Vanita through a friend of a friend, who, on hearing about my interest in the Metro, said, "I know someone you should talk to." I called Vanita and we arranged to meet.

Vanita is a college lecturer and came to Delhi in the 1970s when she finished her postgrad education and got married. She doesn't tell me anything about her husband other than "he knew how to drive." He bought a secondhand car for them, and soon she couldn't think of being in Delhi without one. They lived in east Delhi, and after some time they got a better car. They had a traditional middle-class division of labor: she looked after the children while he focused on his profession.

"He tried teaching me how to drive, but I was a late starter, I couldn't deal with the traffic. I became more and more dependent on him." Then they hired a driver, which Vanita came to understand as "this other dependence." If her husband and the driver were not around, she'd call a taxi. They lived in Vasant Kunj by this time, which was badly connected to central areas of the city. "Autos always charged extra," she says.

Not knowing how to drive and becoming dependent on a driver—first her husband and then a hired driver—framed Vanita's relationship with the city for over thirty years. In 2004, her husband gifted her a new car, an Opel Corsa. She thought, "Since when have we become so rich? It used to be that you got a casserole as a gift. I only ever traveled in the car with him on a few special occasions."

The idea of going anywhere alone, without the driver, didn't cross her mind. It only changed with the rude and painful experience of her husband leaving her after twenty-seven years of marriage. Her husband suggested they sell the Corsa and buy her something small. He soon moved out of the house, and she continued to travel to Pitampura in the northeast of the city from Vasant Kunj, in south Delhi beyond the Outer Ring Road. She had a driver and took the other car, the "poor" Zen.

Several years on, the divorce proceedings were getting messier. Vanita got a stay order to keep the house but not the car. "My husband came with a key and took the car one day. My neighbor saw him." She contacted the police, but they laughed at her when she told them the car registration was in her husband's name. "That's when I realized he used to take care of everything, even the mobile recharge. I had reduced myself to a complete state of dependence."

And then a friend suggested she start taking the Metro, even though it required her to take an auto rickshaw until Central Secretariat, almost half the distance. The commute wasn't really practical, but she did it anyway. "The Metro became part of my day-to-day," Vanita says. "You have to walk fast; you can't waddle along. You can get jostled a bit. But within several days, riding it made me a different person. It was a novelty, but it also took my mind off things. I had lost my trust in anyone."

Vanita explains that she used to have a family and she used to have a family car. "One had been living in that kind of illusion," she tells me. Suddenly, she was left without anything. It was then that the Metro gained importance in her life. She got a Metro card. "Whether I use it or not, it's a great psychological support for me. I'm someone who's not been abroad. When you see the Metro, you think, my god, you seem to be in a foreign country. Indian trains are so different, grimy. The Metro is so different. You feel a very small portion of what it's like in other countries."

Vanita not only started taking the Metro to the college where she worked, but to Tis Hazari Court as well, which happened to be on the same line. By then she was involved in three cases against her husband and had to make regular trips to the court for proceedings.

"I could see it from the train," she says, "My god, have I reached here? It was a wonder. It gave me a different angle on my life to see the court from there, and to be getting there by taking the Metro. My husband's absence, earlier it used to disturb me, but not now."

THE IMAGE OF THE CITY

For Delhi architect A.G. Krishna Menon, the question of the Metro was one about investment—"They've thrown gold at Delhi, but were there other options? Yes, the loan is from abroad," he says, referencing the Japanese financing of the project, "but it is the government who is backing the loan. The Metro is a manifestation of India's image, the India shining bit."

Menon, who has had leading roles for several decades at the Indian

National Trust for Art and Cultural Heritage (INTACH), the Delhi Urban
Arts Commission, and the Heritage Conservation Committee, is not only
a practicing architect but someone invested in the broader picture of the
city and how it gets imagined. He believes that the Metro was a bad economic decision but also concedes it might do some good: "People might
begin to see this megacity as a city, which would be a good thing, binding
the city. The image of the city is going to change."

According to Menon, the Delhi Metro Rail Corporation (DMRC) had
shown the Delhi Urban Arts Commission a "conceptual proposal" of the
Metro lines, though not the actual thing. On that basis, the group lodged
their complaints and requests: to protect an old cinema façade in Chawri
Bazar was one, with the reasoning that the memory of the street it was
located on should remain; the second was to change the route of the
Yellow Line so that it didn't obstruct the view of Qutab Minar, one of the
city's oldest monuments and tourist sites and a defining feature of its skyline. The DMRC got rid of the cinema façade in Chawri Bazar but changed
the route of the Yellow Line at Qutab Minar at a cost of 300 crores [USD
40 million].

Besides the issue of protecting heritage, what concerns Menon most
about the Metro lines spreading across the city is the five hundred meters
of densification—what gets built and developed—along each line. The
Metro routes were chosen based on land acquisition and travel surveys.
Now, Menon says, the DMRC must justify those routes and the master plan must be changed to fit the increasing densification along those
routes, an example, he says, of "the tail wagging the dog."

The Metro in this sense has become the de facto plan, but without committee or consultation. Delhi's first master plan, with the help of the Ford
Foundation team in India, was formulated in 1962 and laid out a decen-
tralized city even as it sought to integrate the development of the city. The
point of plans, though—whether this one or the two that followed for 2001
and 2021—is that they are available for public scrutiny and conceived of by
multiple stakeholding agencies, even if issued by the Delhi Development
Authority.

In a 1997 article in *Economic and Political Weekly*, Menon had argued
that planning in India was dominated by Western models, and for him
this meant that urban planners were not only working on behalf of the

middle class but were entrenched in their beliefs, in their idea of the city. For Menon this is both a practical problem and an ethical one.

We talk about the New Delhi Municipal Corporation's plans to beautify and pedestrianize Connaught Place. Their plans are to change the iconic stone pillars from sandstone to marble, to create standardized signage for all the shops, to change the windows. "The planners want it to look new and clean, not to look old, which it is, eighty years old." Menon thinks that things can look old *and* good. He unrolls plan after plan on the large worktable we're sitting around in his home office in south Delhi off the Outer Ring Road. Menon believes that conservation is not and should not be reduced to beautification, but he feels he can't communicate this point with any kind of effectiveness across the many platforms he has in the city. He can't argue, he tells me, against the aspiration people have to beautify.

Another example is Gole Market, which was the "native" market in the colonial period. Here they want to gentrify what is still a working market, and this vision is for outsiders rather than for the people who come to the market and work in the market. "They want to add a glass dome; they want to change a market into a museum," Menon says. "Who is this conservation for? Conservation in India can't be an elite activity; you have to be thinking about the local sentiment, of the fishmonger, the grocer, etc. The neighborhood is made up of low-level clerks; the market must serve their needs. The problem is that conservation is equated with backwardness. It's seen as dragging people back. Instead, you must make everything development-oriented."

Menon is not against beautiful architecture, and in fact he tells me he thinks most of the Metro stations are ugly, a lost opportunity. What he opposes is "the march to beautify" and destroy the authenticity of what was there before. Heritage is not merely to be protected but also understood. The more we talk, the more I come to think of his idea of authenticity as being about integrity—whether the integrity of neighborhoods and their composition, or of building materials, the very elements of the built environment. How, he seems to be asking, can we preserve the relationship between the built environment and communities in its midst?

The larger problem, in Menon's view, is "the dearth of an urban discourse." He tells me that his friends don't know and don't care what he does. And then he shares this image: of people sitting in Vienna in a café at 11 p.m. arguing about a new building that is going to be built. He relishes this scene of critical discussion and laments what he sees around him as a disinterested public. "Here in India, regarding architecture and city planning, the poor suffer it, the middle class enjoys it, and the elites couldn't care less. The public is profane. The rich can follow the master plan, the rules laid down by it, but the poor are forced to break the law."[6]

Menon doesn't give in to his own cynicism. He remains active, central even, on panels, with nonprofits, and at a host of writing and speaking engagements. He has hardly given up. For him, architecture and the role of the architect is a social practice as much as a creative or technical one.

Before I leave, Menon reminds me that the seventy-third and seventy-fourth amendments to the Indian Constitution mandate power to the people, *panchayat raj*, the local self-governance councils across rural and urban India. The law says, "bottom up," he tells me, but Delhi is "top down."

METRO BHAWAN

The headquarters of the Delhi Metro Rail Corporation (DMRC) are located in Metro Bhawan (Building) on Fire Brigade Lane off Barakhamba Road. It's a radial road extending from Connaught Place, one of the city's core commercial areas. The wide, shiny building anchors this area filled with office workers and looms over them. It's far from being a skyscraper; it only has eight floors, but its exterior is made of concrete, steel, and glass and projects both industrialized modernity and corporate culture.

Once you cross the building's manicured lawns in front, you pass through security, which, like getting on the Metro, includes multiple electronic security gates, searches, and, unlike the Metro, identity protocols. The lobby by contrast is an empty, open space, with a light-filled atrium. Floor-to-sky ceilings create a dramatic entrance, with offices on multiple floors in the recesses of the building. The gray stone interior is warming, even as glass elevators move up and down the height of the building. Riding in one you feel like you are part of the technology.[7]

Metro Bhawan relays a message of efficiency, cleanliness, order, and grandeur. It's not meant for the public; it is a workplace. And yet it also introduces a new historical form to the city, a distillation of the new Metro system crisscrossing the city. It is an architecture that stands apart from the Mughal, colonial, and even postcolonial, with an exterior that suggests movement, even locomotion, via its gleaming, sun-reflecting surfaces, curved front, and diamond-shaped cut-outs. It does not blend into the surroundings but rather dominates them. The building is reflective of the Metro system rather than the city. And like the Metro system, Metro Bhawan marks out the idea and feeling of inside as outside and outside as inside, from its façade to its elevators. It is a headquarter building in the center of the city, yet one that symbolizes the myriad new connections the Metro forges between center and periphery, and the creation of new city centers in the form of interchange stations. Metro Bhawan's disjuncture with its surroundings is not about postmodern fragmentation and dislocation, but rather a new centering that is imposed on the city, plonked down. For the good of the city, the DMRC would say.

Once inside I'm directed to the public relations office. Sushma, a senior officer, tells me that the Metro was required, otherwise "the city would collapse." This idea of collapse, the city on the brink, is one that gets written into the origin story of the Metro across DMRC publications. Sushma chalks up the Metro's success to three principles: leadership, guidance, and massive training sessions. Four thousand people work for the DMRC and go through a rigorous three-month training program. The project is built on public-private partnerships with some five hundred contractors. It is the cheapest metro ride in the world. A poster behind Sushma's desk reads:

DMRC—A PROFESSIONAL WORK CULTURE WITH

1. Accountability

2. Transparency

3. Teamwork

4. Time-bound commitments

Driven by passion

Sushma takes me into the office of Anuj Dayal, the chief spokesperson for the DMRC, the face of the organization after its project managers—first

Figure 5. Metro Bhawan, DMRC headquarters, Barakhamba Road, 2008.

Elattuvalapil Sreedharan and then Mangu Singh.[8] Dayal asks me what I want to know and where my questionnaires are. He is friendly, polite, and seemingly willing to help. At the same time, I never get access to anyone at the DMRC through him. When I ask him about the famed work culture and discipline of the organization, he invites me to witness one of the on-site yoga sessions at Metro Bhawan.

It's a late-afternoon class with a dozen Metro officials in regulation slacks and cotton polo shirts and one yogi, a small taut man in a yellow kurta pajama. We are in an auditorium off the main lobby; they are all on the stage and I am in the audience of one. The yogi leads the class in Hindi through a number of sun salutations, seated asanas, pranayama, sivasana. Feet circle in the air, heads bob up and down. I feel relaxed just watching them.

Here in this sleek building in central Delhi it's hard not to see this yoga practice, these familiar postures, as a kind of "postmodern transformation of culture."[9] This is yoga for a purpose, a kind of solution to the problem of the modern workplace and the very timings and pressures that the DMRC demands of its workers. The sticking to the clock. But the yoga also aims to be spiritual guidance: How will Indians build and run a world-class Metro? How will this city remain Indian with a Metro? How will people's insides match the outside? The solutions almost seem to be in the poses themselves, ones that began in India, traveled the world, and then came back as global products for the body and spirit. The Metro and the yoga poses seem to have been destined to meet on this stage.

SPACE AND MATTER

A new space is a new set of boundaries. The most obvious of these for riders are the entrances to the Metro—the security check, ticket booth, and automated entry. These areas are bounded by physical objects: electronic gates and doors, uniformed security guards, metal detectors, stairwells, potted plants, glass dividers, and metal handrails.

At the Dwarka Sector 9 station, I notice a sheet of paper posted at the security-curtained area on the side of the metal detector, listing what cannot be brought on to the train: dried blood; human corpse; animal carcasses; any part of human skeleton; manure. I wonder if this has something to do with this station being at the end of the line, reaching out to the hinterlands, an external boundary. These materials are listed not as being dangerous but as "offensive."

RED LINE

On the Jangpura station platform, a portly man in his thirties asks me in Hindi which train goes to Kashmere Gate, by which he means, which side of the platform should he be on. I tell him it's the side we're on and point toward the train that has just gone into the tunnel, the one we've just missed. He goes back to his two friends, they confer, and then the three of them come and ask me how to get to Rohini. I tell them to go to Kashmere Gate and then change to the Red Line toward Rithala.

There's no one gathering point in the Metro, no plaza per se; instead there are these new bits of street knowledge, spatial approximations, and outright information that people have built up since riding the Metro. This gets shared, this new calculating of time and space. How to get somewhere in relation to a Metro station or how to get to a place by some combination of Metro lines. Finding one's way becomes a group pastime like never before. Finding one's way is part of the new time pressure of the Metro, timed transport, and the timed subject.[10]

At Kashmere Gate station, tall escalators descend to glossy platforms and wide staircases in what resembles a huge warehouse or a down-market mall. This station has more food on offer than any others. You can eat *momos, idli sambhar, chole bhature*, a burger from Burger King, and a range of snacks at Kingdom of Food.

At station exits, just beyond the electronic ticket turnstiles, Central Industrial Security Force (CISF) officers are positioned behind sandbags, with only their heads and half torsos visible, their rifles pointing out. On the platform toward Dilshad Garden, a blind man, neatly dressed in a gray safari suit, with a collapsed white walking stick clutched under his arm, is being escorted by a Metro staff member to the train.

Packs of young men watch the moving colored lights and squiggly lines on the wall-size Metro map on the main concourse. This map is more of an exhibit and draws in passersby to see the Metro lines in their geographic context. But people are already underground at this point, already in the domain of the hand-sized Metro map, where all stations are equidistant and all lines cut straight through the city. The men seem to be caught up in the wonder and order indicated by the lights and squiggly lines traversing the city. This map in the station is not meant to be a wayfinder so much as an energizer; it shows rather than gives directions; it is a summary of the city, a moving installation.

Crossing Old Delhi on the Red Line, men enter the train through the ladies' coach and then hurry along. There are more sari-clad women, more *salwars*. Two young women sitting on opposite sides of the coach recognize one another and excitedly say "Hi!" before going back to their phones. Two women meet on the train, one watching for her friend from within the ladies' coach, the other coming onto the train at Kashmere Gate station.

Riding out to Rithala, my eye grazes the tops of small-storied residential buildings; I can see onto people's roofs and into some restaurants. The billboards get increasingly specific about the lifestyle I should be imagining. This is especially true from Keshav Puram station onward. The stations themselves are much wider as compared to those on the Blue Line. As I notice this, I remember Sushma from the DMRC telling me that was the case. They had realized they had wasted space on the Red Line and that the stations could be much smaller.

Some CISF officers get on the train. They, not the local Delhi police, are responsible for Metro security. They are young men in fatigues and heavy black boots, with automatic rifles slung over their shoulders. An older policeman, also with CISF insignia on his sleeve, sits on the other side; he isn't with the other three but slowly moves toward them after a few stations pass and free seats become available. They all chat. This older man, much older, has sunken, pock-marked cheeks and an empty gun canister.

RESIDENT WELFARE

When Metro construction began to reach middle-class "colonies," the name for planned and sanctioned neighborhoods, cracks started appearing in people's homes. Metro officials were contacted, they came for surveys, and the problem was fixed. But colony residents were not only concerned about damage to their property. As the Metro moved out from central areas of the city, its viaducts, trains, and stations went aboveground. Some feared Metro riders would actually be able to look into their homes, and that with more traffic to and from the station the exclusive nature of their colony would change.

By the time Metro's Violet Line was being built aboveground in south Delhi in 2010, there were campaigns against it. It wasn't just that the car-owning classes didn't see personal value in mass transit; rather, it was the material imposition of the system that was concerning. As the bureaucrat P.K. Tripathi, who worked closely with Delhi chief minister Sheila Dikshit's government at the time of the Metro's initial construction, told me, "If the initial line of the Delhi Metro had been planned in south Delhi, as the failed Bus Rapid Transit corridor had been, it might also have failed."

To get to south Delhi's Defence Colony main market you pass a small (by Delhi standards) Mughal monument surrounded by a lawn and fence. The structure had long ago served as a rest stop for horses on the way to Red Fort. Today it is an office for the colony's Resident Welfare Association (RWA). I would sometimes see members gathered on chairs in the lawn. I knew they had been the vanguard of the movement against the Metro entering their colony. One morning, Romela, the general secretary of Defence Colony's RWA, explained to me what their concerns had been:

"We were not happy about the Metro going overhead; we would have preferred it going underground; we just had no experience of it. We thought the houses in D-block would feel the Metro's vibrations, that there would be noise and no privacy, that you would open your doors and be *into* the Metro. That was the great debate. We never thought people *wouldn't* use the Metro. We had another doubt, that if you have the Metro here and you don't have a parking lot at the station, people would come from outside and park on colony roads, leading to congestion. We were worried about that—how would it affect entry into the colony?"

"So, how did people come together on these issues?" I ask.

"Through email messages, we decided 'let's get together.' At first there was one meeting, then two meetings, and then a delegation formed. We were scared about the aesthetics of the Metro and the sound issue. Then the DMRC told us they're putting those sound barriers, which work, so sound has not been an issue.

"Every house in this colony used to have two floors, now they have five floors," Romela explains, referring to the renovations and additions people were making on their own houses. She chalks this up to "people's aspirations" as they accrue more wealth. She continues, "If I earn more, I need a bigger car. So, parking is an issue, obviously. Though now the houses with five floors have stilt parking, which is very, very good. The entire demographics of the colony has changed; earlier it was defense personnel who were very judicious about their expenses. Many of them had lived in small towns, so the concept of one family having four cars was not there. They had small families with small homes, with one or two floors.

"Now the entire colony is being redeveloped. A lot of business community, trading community, everybody has come in, and with that, more money has come in, expendable money, a lot of expendable money has come in; that had to happen, we are one of the most central colonies in Delhi, we have connectivity to south Delhi, to Noida, to every place, very central, so having said that, more and more people are wanting to come to an area like this. Aesthetically, it's a very great colony."

"It was, it was," Veena, another RWA member sitting with us, chimes in.

"This is an old colony," Romela continues, "you see, the roads and streets are so well laid out, so wide." She goes on to explain how the older colonies were better planned with service lanes to keep the congestion at the backside of houses rather than the front, where you have nice wide streets.

"See GK [Greater Kailash], all these new colonies that have come, I don't know how they've made these newer colonies. Kailash Hills, you *cannot enter*!" Romela also notes a difference between gated and ungated communities. The infrastructure in gated communities is better, she concedes, as is the possibility of developing more infrastructure. "A lot of people from this colony are selling out and going to those areas. All the facilities in one: security, parking is taken care of. But the openness you get here, you won't get there."

"And being so central," Veena adds.

"The gated communities offer a different lifestyle," I conjecture, thinking of the gated communities at the southern end of the Yellow Line in Gurgaon, which are cut-off oases of convenience and high-end infrastructure.

"It's a different lifestyle that a lot of people are deciding to go for," Romela replies.

"Would you consider it?" I ask.

"No, I wouldn't. I wouldn't because I am a person of Defence Colony; since before marriage, my maternal home is in Defence Colony. So, a person like me would not."

"That's why we're fighting to keep it at least under control," says Veena.

"At RWA, there's a constant battle to get things done," Romela explains. "The upside of all the protests and *dharnas* [sit-ins] we did with the DMRC was that the Green Park line [the Yellow Line, which runs about parallel to the west of the Violet Line in south Delhi] went underground. Here it was already planned, and once so much money gets put in and infrastructure is done, they're not going to agree with us. We knew that it was a losing battle but then, yes, later on for all those congested colonies [on the Yellow Line] they've gone underground—Hauz Khas, Green Park. The protests must have had some effect. Look at East of Kailash colony [Violet Line], the Metro is literally in their homes; we were lucky the station came on that side [Lajpat Nagar]. Lajpat Nagar is a commercial area, more of a business area. The fact that the station is named after that area is better for us, too."

"Do you ride the Metro?" I ask.

"I, for one, I have my own car, but if I have to go for a meeting, like now, I won't take my car, I'll call a cab because there's no parking. But then you're stuck in traffic. Every earning member of the family has to have a car, otherwise how do you get to work? That is one reason why Delhi really needs a good public transport system. If the Metro would go directly, then I don't mind, I would take it. Connectivity has to be there. Not only do you have to change twice, but there's no last-mile connectivity.

"All said and done, look at our country, our weather eight months of the year is not conducive to walking. To get to Lajpat Nagar, I go over the bridge. I'm very happy to do that. But look at the infrastructure, it's not for walking. You can't just have these cycle rickshaws; there has to be something streamlined, organized."

A line of cycle rickshaws greets passengers as they descend from the station on the Lajpat Nagar and Defence Colony sides. They offer convenience but make for jolting, bumpy rides. The cycle-rickshaw drivers themselves are the lowest on the transportation totem pole, toiling for hours at twenty rupees a ride, making between 500 and 800 rupees a day, depending on their luck. The Metro brings them a steady stream of passengers, but they still must line up and jockey for them. For car drivers, cycle rickshaws are a nuisance on the road, bulky and slow, as they maneuver alongside vehicular traffic.

"We lost our fight with the DMRC because by the time we came to know," says Romela, "it was too late; the pillars were there. But in a way they [the DMRC] are doing a great job. We were convinced; they explained everything well. Protests were happening at the same time against the BRT [Bus Rapid Transit corridor]. Look what happened there. BRT was such a disaster."

OKHLA STATION

The curve and arc of the Metro line forms a necklace around Okhla industrial area, dividing Okhla from the locality of Harkesh Nagar. Okhla started out as "old canal housing and land authority"—more of a designation than a place; it has the Yamuna River to one side and the wealthy colony of New Friends to the other. In the lanes down from the Metro station, fabric sellers offer reams of black, brown, and gray cloth stacked high on bicycles. Local boys sit eating bananas. One thirty-year-old man, Dharanvi, stands next to two circular clothes racks of trousers and shirts, alongside the *pakoda* (vegetable fritter) sellers. He confirms my suspicion that he must be outfitting the workers in the various industries around us. He takes the Metro from Old Delhi where he lives to work here every day. It's more expensive, he tells me, but has made his commute faster and easier.

I learn from the residents living in informal settlements around the station—where it's common for a family of four to share a single room—that the Metro is a talisman, albatross, and jewel. The station itself is a big yellow box, warehouse-like, with escalators at the front and cows grazing out back in the muck. People go up and look out, the new surveyors of the land and environs. Some things have stayed in place: the grape seller, with the station to his back, the bicycle fixer who regards the Metro with suspicion.

A group of women sit on a set of concrete steps where a narrow lane of the *mohalla* meets a wider path. Nearby several men congregate near a fruit cart. A white BMW SUV honks down another lane in the distance. The men tell me that they wish the Metro "would just go away." They don't ride it, and it's too expensive compared to the bus. One of the men says, "Many houses were destroyed to make the Metro." Everyone watches the Metro line above, but despite its proximity it seems more like a distancing mechanism.

An Aircel ad looms over the area. A leading mobile phone provider, its ad speaks to both constituencies here—those riding the trains and those living in the informal settlements just below the Metro viaduct.

Meenakshi, a woman who lives in the area, tells me that she *wants* to be relocated to a metro colony, where she knows that those whose houses were displaced because of the Metro have gone. I tell her it is far away

Figure 6. Violet Line train approaching Okhla station, 2012.

from the central areas of the city and that the so-called metro colony is not accessible by the Metro. She doesn't seem to care; she is concerned with the quality of the housing—if it is *pukka,* firmly made, or not. Her housing, as it is now placed next to the Metro, appears more fragile, while it has also become more visible, more legible. The Metro at once dwarfs and draws attention to. To see the elevated trains each day overhead is to be reminded of the possibility of good construction and of the will of government.

This "will" becomes a subject of debate among residents here. On the roads and alleyways around the station, a narrative about *bade* and *chhota aadmi,* big and small men, emerges. Those living in the settlements next to the Metro line see the object as having been built by the government for those already working for the government. It is for people who park their cars and then get on the Metro. There may be some *chhota aadmi* who ride the Metro, but really, they tell me, the Metro is to increase the power and mobility for those who already have some.

NAIPAUL ON THE METRO

A documentary on V.S. Naipaul features footage from a trip he took to Delhi, one that included a ride on the Metro.[11] What does the man, a UK–based writer of Indian origin born and brought up in Trinidad, and infamous for having expounded on the filth and disorder of Indian cities, have to say?

"Very, nice, very nice," he can be heard muttering as he passes through the electronic gate.

Naipaul's response to the Metro is akin to countless others I had heard, and to what I myself had experienced. Who could not be impressed? The ordered space and gleaming surfaces are nothing if not a crucible of the city's modernity. The Metro is a marvel, something to marvel at for anyone who visits Delhi, but also, and especially so, for its residents. It goes against everything they know. It is shiny, cool, and clean, but it was also built on time, within budget, and without the scale of corruption that stalls or derails so many public and private sector projects.

When Naipaul exits the Metro, chatting with the filmmaker, he remarks on the "endless announcements" in the trains, and how people are "behaving with great dignity"; they were "following the rules." And then he speculates that the experience of riding the Metro will, over time, "make them more civil." Here he seems to be back in Naipaulian territory: To what extent do bodily actions and repetitions make the man or woman? It was the distinction he made long ago in his 1964 book, *An Area of Darkness*, on watching a sweeper at work: There was the act of sweeping and there was the condition of being a sweeper. In the latter, Naipaul saw the social ills of a deeply hierarchical society and went on to make his pronouncements about Indian stagnation among other things.

One day as I pull into Ramesh Nagar station, a man pushing a wide broom moves slowly across the empty platform. He is not a sweeper, but a uniformed Metro worker who works for a company to which the DMRC has outsourced its housekeeping. Perhaps the uniform makes him part of the system. Perhaps the bodily comportment gets concealed by the uniform.

About the Metro Naipaul makes the following observation: The passengers are trying to match the Metro with their own behavior. It's an old postulation, and one I have continually heard in relation to the Metro, about how new forms and ways of being are taking hold in society, and how the environment of the Metro makes people "more sophisticated." What is it about the Metro that makes people act in certain ways? Are Dilliwalas proud of the Metro and so of themselves? Are they in fact more civil because the surroundings are new and clean, and full of security and CCTV cameras? And who would be a better spokesperson for this grand neoliberal vision—of individuals who gain autonomy as they "freely" subject themselves to new rules and regulations—than Naipaul?[12]

NUKKAD NATAK

Hindi actor Naresh Goswain explains to me one early evening how people started throwing stones at the Metro when the first line, the Red Line, entered their communities. Then they cut the wires surrounding the stations. The Metro was not a gleaming symbol of speed and comfort, but rather a beast of a machine trampling over their known ways of getting around.

"They didn't want to lose their other ways of conveyance, bus lines and local trains. Many people were used to traveling in trains, getting on and off without buying tickets. On the local train there is no reason to buy the ticket. You can enter from either side. But with the Metro you can only enter with the token and then must know how to use it."

Naresh and I are standing outside the Shri Ram Centre for Performing Arts at Mandi House, drinking tea from a nearby stall. Birds chirp overhead about as loudly as the honking horns we try to speak over. Naresh, in his mid-fifties, with a round face and figure, has had numerous small roles in Hindi films but his background is in theater, from the time he was a child in Delhi. He heads a theater troupe, Drishantar, meaning, he tells me, "what is behind what you see." The troupe's "bread and butter" is work in films, TV serials, and commercials "to survive," but the members are also involved in theatrical awareness campaigns across the city—street plays or "nukkad natak"—working for different organizations that they feel are worthy of support, including the DMRC.

"We used to go into many interior villages in Seelampur to perform our skits, to educate people. We start with a man and woman fighting in the street to get people's attention; then as they start to surround us, to gather and look, we start a skit. We told them, please do not throw stones or cut wires as you can hurt your own relatives traveling inside. We create an emotional drama about it and tell them, if you're caught and sent to jail, your career will be finished; your life will be ruined as your whole family will be affected.

"Our skits are performed with seven to eight actors. We perform at different Metro stations to educate local people on different subjects, like the benefits of using the Metro, the basics of how to use the Metro. We make them aware about security cameras. They are afraid and believe that the police are watching them through these cameras and that they will come get them. We have to tell them that the cameras are for their own safety. Then we do awareness about cleanliness, that inside the Metro they must put paper trash in their bag and throw it outside the station. Ninety percent of the public is aware of keeping Metro clean; everybody watches others; there is a fear of public condemnation, so they wait to throw papers outside Metro stations.

"We do street plays in front of contractors and their migrant workers against drinking wine and whiskey. We don't tell them not to drink, just show them the effects of what can happen if you drink and hurt yourself in an accident; what will be the impact on your wife and family? Your wife may go astray; your kids may have to beg on the roadside. Do you want your family to have to do such kinds of things? Then we joke by offering to join the contractors for a drink; they say 'no, no' after watching the show. We show them that if something happens to you, your survival is affected, and your whole family will be ruined. We use the workers' language; we use the high society language for some shows or just change according to the audiences."

I watch one of these plays, a "safety natak," on YouTube. Naresh and his troupe are performing a skit for Metro construction workers. Dozens of young men in hard hats are assembled, sitting on the ground, cross-legged, watching a skit about a worker who takes his hard hat off while he is still on a Metro construction site. The skit dramatizes the worker's nonchalance about the need to wear a hard hat at all times, as well as what happens when something falls on his head. They are also reminded to put construction scraps in the scrapyard, to avoid falling over what's been left behind. The play has some of the same themes as what Naresh had described to me. A message that says: If you stay safe, your family will stay safe. It also reminds the workers that they are part of making this "nice Metro." There's a lightness to the whole thing, bordering on slapstick, and everyone laughs, at which point, Naresh admonishes the audience, "You're laughing because this is a natak, but if this were real, would you be laughing?"

There is a common theme to these Hindi-language plays aimed at low-income communities and construction workers, as described by Naresh. They link caring for the Metro, even protecting the Metro, to family duty and notions of shame. The style and message are different from the puppet characters, Chintu and Pinky, who are featured in DMRC videos aimed at the general Metro ridership, with jingles like "*Sundar*, safe or beautiful, Dilli Metro cool cool, My metro, your metro, *sabki* metro." These Hindi-English videos shown in stations are also pedagogic—they tell people to wait patiently for trains, how to deal with crowds, and how to give people the chance to exit the train before entering—but they feel more like public service announcements and less like admonishments.

This moral slant to some performances ultimately serves the state's infrastructural interest. Naresh says, "We performed for the people being displaced by the construction of the Metro line, telling them it is for the good of their family as they were being paid to move, and that they are providing a service for Delhi. We also encourage people to go to see the Metro Museum, to see how it all works, man and machinery.

"Sex workers wait on the side of Metro stations for the migrant workers who are here mostly from Bihar and U.P. We used to perform awareness about AIDS to the Metro workers. We also performed at Tihar Jail. No condoms are given in the jail as no sex is allowed. If the jailers provide condoms, they feel they are giving permission for sex. But sex in the jail happens. Most people know about AIDS but do not have awareness of all the precautions. We worked with a foreigner lady, Isabel Madam, who was very bold and spoke in pure Hindi. I really adored her. She taught AIDS awareness in the jail to the prisoners in their raunchy language. Sadly, she is no more.

"I enjoy doing these for social change. We're not getting so much money for it. But if we can influence one person, and one person understands my points, like in the case of AIDS, we save not only one person but a whole family and community. Our social cause is for the masses."

MUMBAI

The day after the three-day terrorist shooting and bombing spree on the streets of Mumbai, the whole country has come to a stop, as if in a collective gasp. In Delhi, security officers pat down each and every passenger entering the Metro. I wonder how long this will last.

URBAN HAZARDS

The Hazards Centre on Outer Ring Road is several circles removed from the power center of the city. It is a small, multidisciplinary group that takes community requests for help on various issues and projects. For the people who work there, "community" is another way of saying the marginalized majority. The organization expressly does not represent rich and middle-class interests since it sees those sectors of society as already having representation elsewhere. By contrast, the Hazards Centre works for communities who can't afford professional help.

Dunu Roy, the white-haired wizard of the organization, proclaims they have a "poor bias" and that their constituency is the poor. It is from this position that the Hazards Centre views the city—from the bottom up. Roy is a former professor from the Indian Institute of Technology, just down the road. Like many social activists in Delhi, Roy sees the city as having become an arena for the commercialization of virtually everything. He describes a kind of spatial struggle in the city. The poor are punished for having to live in slums, for instance, while the rich take up more road space with their cars. Delhi's development is geared toward the middle classes and rich, rather than the working population, which is the vast majority. He sees the working poor, from waste-pickers to cycle-rickshaw pullers, as doing the most and hardest work in the city, effectively providing for others. Delhi as a global and world-class city aspirant, meanwhile, celebrates and rewards consumers and wealth creators, whose numbers are small but whose voices loom large.

Roy not only sees this spatial struggle in economic terms; it is also a question of values. Europe, he tells me, develops public spaces for culture and for the people. India, he suggests, does not. As a result, Delhi is simply "up for sale."

The first time I came to the Hazards Centre was in June 2009. I had just given a lecture about the Delhi Metro at the India International Center. The next morning on page two of the *Times of India*, there was a story about the lecture, characterizing it as a celebration of the Delhi Metro. Roy had the newspaper on his desk when I walked in, and after he clicked his tongue in disapproval at how I had been co-opted, we discussed how the Metro had the unequivocal support of the press. Any Metro news was good news or was made to appear so. The Metro as a public good went unquestioned.

Roy, on the other hand, sees the Metro as a real estate project and emblematic of the new social divisions of the city. "A conversion is going on," he says, "whereby value addition is shifting from manufacturing space to service space." In other words, the real value of things is not based on production but speculation. What he describes is the neoliberal economy of self-employment geared toward the service economy and the creation of a huge informal sector, which India is known for. Roy's concern is not the mere economics of it all, but rather the social and cultural reproduction of life that goes with it—"how relationships are built."[13]

"Earlier, conservation was the idea, now it's about 'clean and green,' which is a different kettle of fish. The change in language is significant though. The unclean class are those seen as being unsanitary and unwashed. It has nothing to do with nature. A whole range of sections of the underclass get moved off the map. This is a peculiar inversion of the reality of city life."

In this schema, or inversion, the Metro is "clean and green" while the bus is "dirty diesel." Transport gets mapped onto urban space and becomes class-specific in the process. What disturbs Roy is that the city is being made for the middle and upper classes, and here he echoes questions around the values and ethics of building the city in a particular image posed by architect A.G. Krishna Menon.

"The city," by which Roy means courts, ministers, politicians, and the upper class, "pretends to be metropolitan, secular, inclusive," while "intellectuals reserve some space in their discourse for the poor. Before, the poor were marginalized, now they are illegalized.

"One thousand poor families were displaced due to the Metro routes, maybe more. To Holambi Kalan and elsewhere. They don't get the land for free; they pay 7,000 rupees for 12.5 square meters; they take out loans and must pay more than the cost of the land. They get a five-year license for the land and may have to pay more later. They've had to resettle in multistory flats. It takes five to ten years for a family to recover from shock, save money, invest. And where they are, there is no infrastructure, no electricity, sanitation, water, schools, transportation."[14]

For Roy, the construction of the city is nothing if not the construction of imagination. For him, who is visible to and recognized by the city's planners is key to how the city is imagined and what gets done, planned, constructed. The Metro is on the "rich" side of the dichotomy, according to Roy, and reveals who the city is ultimately for.

RAMLILA MAIDAN

In August 2011 the Delhi Metro lived up to its promise as a social engine when it became the people's gateway to the corruption protest site at Ramlila Maidan. Large groups of mostly young men wearing *Main Anna Houn* (I am Anna) caps and singing *Vande Maataram* (an ode to the motherland and India's national song) rushed in and out of stations on the Yellow Line. The caps showed solidarity with rural social activist Anna Hazare, who had started a hunger strike a few days earlier, demanding the passage of a new bill to curb corruption. Many protesters were also carrying little Indian tricolor flags.

The men came in a head-turning rush; all of a sudden the banal corridors of the Metro station took on energy and urgency. The anonymous, atomized atmosphere of the Metro changed in an instant as a large group of people connected to one another and bolstered by one another took center stage. These people were not only going somewhere but also had something to say. And this was all being circulated on the Metro. While changing from the Violet to Yellow Lines at Central Secretariat, I came across one of these tricolor-bearing Anna groups and quickly moved to the side to let them pass. Were they, I wondered, a spontaneous, mobile public, a Metro public, or just a paying crowd?

They were identifiable as a group having a cause and set of beliefs, and this was partly because their physical presence in the city was simultaneously being discussed and broadcast on every television news channel. Seeing them in the Metro changed my view of the Metro itself; all of a sudden it *became* a public space.

The media backstory formed part of my perception. I knew that the Anna organizers had to fight and negotiate with the government in order to gather legally in large numbers in the city. Their presence in the city, anywhere in the city, took on greater meaning as a result. Moreover, the Metro itself had been heralded by anticorruption activist Arvind Kejriwal as being a model of governance. Kejriwal said that it was a *system* that worked and that individuals had to conform to it. (Seven years later in 2018 he would lambast the DMRC for raising fares and decidedly not being "for the people.") Seeing the Anna activists that day in the Metro made me think of Kejriwal's statement and whether metro publics could have a broader association, a way of creating a new kind of urban identity, and possibly, an ethical stance to go with it.[15]

A few days later, on my way to Ramlila Maidan, I observed how, at the New Delhi station, protesters came up the stairs and escalators from the station onto the street. Then, I watched as another mass of protesters poured into the Metro and got stuck up in swirls in the space between the ticket counters and security, and then in the even smaller space between the security and the electronic gates. It was as if the energy and exuberance of the street suddenly had to fit through a keyhole.

The Delhi Metro is a distinct environment, cut off from what lies above it, and yet the Metro and the street also form a contiguous space. Once through the gates, some of the momentum from the street was regained as people headed toward their trains. They became exuberant again, chant-

Figure 7. New Delhi station, Yellow Line, 2011. Protesters during the Anna Hazare–inspired anticorruption marches move from the Metro to the street.

ing and singing. The Metro became a public stage, and I watched the drama. Then I saw large signs with "Ramlila" and a big arrow leading me to the right exit and onto the street.

Once outside, I followed the crowd. There was a constant stream from the street to the Metro and from the Metro to the street. In the station itself the energy of the protesters was palpable before I even got to the street, let alone to the *maidan*, or field. Along the way, women and their children sold flags and tricolored wristbands. Young men offered to paint faces with the tricolor flag for ten rupees each. It had rained the day before, and there was sludge everywhere, but there was freshness too. I felt buoyed by the energy of the protesters on the street.

On the tenth day of Anna Hazare's fast, news broke that "they" had closed four Metro stations (Khan Market, Race Course, Udyog Bhawan, and Jor Bagh) in order to stop the movement of people to a protest site—not Ramlila Maidan but the prime minister's residence at 7 Race Course

Road. In the case of the stations being closed, the Metro as a frictionless conveyor allowing passengers to travel seamlessly across the city came to be seen as a problem for the authorities, something to be stopped.

The Metro is more easily controlled than the streets above. Police may barricade the street, as often happens when a VIP needs to use the street as his or her personal motorway. But there are still ways of getting around barricades, cajoling policemen, ducking behind bushes, and emerging on the other side of the street. The Metro being the "system" it is—a concrete edifice with bounded, shuttered exits and entrances—can be more fully closed and sealed off as compared to a city street.

When might a Metro crowd be recognized as a public? Indian Railway trains and platforms by comparison have long been famous for being sites of political gatherings and also specific protest actions. The space of the railways is more porous in its relationship with the Indian street, and it also operates on a national scale and intersects with a much broader set of publics.[16] The Metro is more limited in this way, as an enclosed set of technologies in urban areas. It is less a space of political communiques and more a space of travel to other sites of political action.

The day the stations were closed, the flow of people stopped as if a faucet had been turned off. Only the *Asian Age* got the story right by not merely stating that "stations were closed," as other newspapers blandly reported in the passive tense, but by headlining the story with "Cops Get Metro Stations Near PM House Closed." No matter how automatic their entry gates, the Metro stations do not close by themselves.

FROM BADARPUR

A group of eight or nine women get on the ladies' coach at Badarpur. Wearing simple *salwar kameez* suits in cotton fabrics, their heads are lightly covered, some are barefoot, some have small children with them.

Two young men, perhaps husbands or other kin, get on the ladies' coach with the women, settle them there, and then exit the coach and run along the platform (as if they were on a regular train platform) to enter a general coach. They do not—like most men who enter the ladies' coach—

simply walk through the invisible divider between the ladies' and general coaches, the in-between accordion space or gender line as I sometimes like to think of it. They seem to want to respect the ladies' coach being for ladies. This is what first makes them stand out.

A few minutes later, once the Metro is moving, one of the men enters the ladies' coach and walks purposefully down the length of the coach to his female kin and says in Hindi, "You're sure you know where to get off?" He says the name of a station and then quickly retreats to the general coach. Again, his movements are more of someone on an Indian Railways train than a Metro train.[17] Head a little stooped, walking tentatively with the sway of the coach. Soon these women with their bare feet and lightly covered heads become less conspicuous as more and more women enter the coach. Women in dress shirts and skirts or black pants going to office, students in sneakers, women in *salwars* or *churidar* pajamas with kurta tops of varying lengths. Fitted clothing with straighter lines begins to out-number the loose cotton flowy fabrics.

These women and their clothes and habits get absorbed by the crowd in the ladies' coach, but I can't figure out what will happen to the gait of their male kin, if over time they will move differently, as they walk the length of a Delhi Metro train, or if for them the Metro will always be a kind of Indian Railways train, one where they settle their women kin and check on them and make sure they know where to get off.

YELLOW LINE

On the Yellow Line a woman sits nursing an infant not more than twenty days old. We are not in the ladies' coach but in a mixed one where, on this morning, the ratio of men to women is about twenty to one. A glass panel with a map of the Metro system is all that separates me from the woman. I can tell she is not poor but also not well off. She has dark, chipped nail pol-ish on her toes and wears a nondescript sari with a frayed, light sweater. It's summer, and it's cold inside the train. She looks like a first-time mother to me, awkward in her feeding technique; she has the baby wrapped in a blanket on her lap. I feel protective toward her but keep quiet and start to make up a story in my head to explain why she is taking the Metro. I look around to make sure no one is looking at her, and yet, I also don't want to invade her privacy, even as a well-wisher or a would-be protector. There are two men who seem to be with her, but they are stern and silent, and I find this off-putting, maybe even a little distressing. Then my stop comes, and I get off.

At Patel Chowk station, there is a new display board at the Metro Museum on the main concourse. The display lists about a dozen cases of Metro train drivers stopping just in time to save a passenger who either jumped or fell onto the tracks. The display is meant to honor the drivers for their nimble life-saving responses, ones that stopped the trains just in time. The information is presented as a grid, including the cause of the train stoppage. One entry details that the person who had fallen onto the tracks was drunk. Another describes how a man and child were walking along the tracks. This list, I soon realize, is also meant to tell people what they shouldn't be doing on the Metro. I wonder what this man and child were doing, perhaps looking for a place to sleep or following the tracks to find a destination. It's a scene you might see on railroad tracks on any given day or hour. But the Metro is not amenable to this kind of improvisation, this kind of *jugaad*.

In the ladies' coach, Manasi tells me, "There are so many girls working, we need more women's coaches. If I'm a girl wearing a short dress I might not prefer the general coach. I don't know what kind of person I'll meet in that coach. It is like that." Her friend, Ekta, chimes in, "The Yellow Line is more civilized. The Blue Line, people are weird." Ekta, who like Manasi is in her twenties, thinks of herself as a child of the Metro generation. "People in buses are more friendly," she says, "there's more adventure. In the Metro, it's boring, sophisticated, but not friendly. There's no color, you can say." I wonder if she means that her generation shares more qualities with the Metro as she describes it, but before I can ask her, she and Manasi are off the train.

Rajiv Chowk station is jam-packed on the platforms. The flow of people at this central interchange beneath Connaught Place is akin to a tidal wave. You have to move with the wave in the direction it is going and hope that is where you want to go. It is a festival, a *mela* of movement. I step aside where there is a large sign hanging from a low railing that no one seems to notice, about escalators and elevators and how to use them. Families pass by carrying big plastic blanket bags filled with household items. Three middle-aged men wrapped in beige shawls and bright yellow turbans follow them. Dozens of young women and men in their twenties, wearing jeans and Converse-like sneakers; they all sport earbuds, and are glancing at their phones, rarely talking on them. One young woman wearing a short top and green leggings with tan ankle boots stops to ask me how to get to Malviya Nagar. Take the Yellow Line toward Huda City Centre, I tell her.

At the northern end of the Yellow Line, a dusty path traverses block after block of low-income housing. I walk for an hour and see nothing resembling central Delhi. This is a working-class community that all of a sudden feels included in the city, connected to this gleaming train. Women living here have stated that they feel safe to venture on the Metro alone, and for the first time will go to India Gate without their husbands. And as I sit outside the station one afternoon, I see these women coming and going, with suitcases and parcels, or just with each other. Some of them use the ends of their saris to cover their heads. A cycle rickshaw-wala outside the station tells me that now most of his trips involve ferrying people to and from the Metro. It has been good for his business, though he has yet to ride it himself. "Where would I leave my rickshaw?" he asks.

DRISHTI

One winter morning at Nehru Place station, I am absorbed by Drishti's description of the crowd. She has come from Vishwavidyalaya station, in the north of the city. She studies at a college in Noida to the east and takes the Metro there each day with her sister. They want to be designers, and Drishti wants to design kitchens, specifically. It has been her dream since childhood, she tells me. On this day she has come here on her own to buy thread and materials. We have just come off a crowded train in the mid-morning rush and are sitting outside on the station premises, on a small ledge near a landscaped lawn where people sit eating from tiffin boxes, the aromas of home-cooked lunches occasionally wafting toward us. The Bollywood actor Deepika Padukone looms large above us on a billboard, selling a new brand of mobile phone. We are now, Drishti and I, away from the Metro crowd, but we still can't help talking about it. Drishti's Hindi gains speed and emphasis as she talks about the crowd. Hindi is already a language that relies on repetition for emphasis, and her speech plays up this feature by repeating whole phrases in quick succession. It is as if her words are running into one another, pushing up against each other, or maybe just spinning.

"Sometimes there's a big crowd there," she starts, "people don't give others the way to come and go, you don't get any space at all and no one gives you the right of way. In the morning there's such a crowd that people don't let people get off. First they push; then the safety guard who is there tells them that they have to stay behind the yellow line, and they say this announcement so many times, but however many times they say the announcement, people don't stay behind the yellow line."

There is a kind of desperation and plea in her voice by this point, but also a sense that you do not *not* ride the Metro, you don't give up, you endure it. "Sometimes people bang into each other," she continues, "and sometimes someone even gets hurt. They don't give people space to get out at the station they need to get out at. They don't let you go forward; they say, 'Stay behind, Stay behind. You have to stay behind the doors.' They tell people to stand behind the doors, but what they don't understand is that people can get stuck behind it. People will say, 'Let us out first,' but no one lets the people on the train out first."

The way she describes it, there is a back and forth between speech and movement, what people assert through speech vis-à-vis the limits of what their bodies can do. "In the evenings," she concludes, "when people get out of work, there is such a crowd and they don't stay behind the line, when the doors open, everyone pushes; they don't stop, then they push."

At the end of the description, Drishti is out of the crowded space of her own language. She becomes more relaxed and her tempo slows as we move on to other topics—her college, her sister, her uncle. Anyone who rides the Metro in Delhi knows what she is talking about when she describes the way people push into each other or push people aside when entering or exiting trains. In the Metro, the crowd is alternately rivulet, stream, and eddy; it collects, passes through, and disperses. It does so to the rhythm of departing and arriving trains and to the tempo of foot traffic during different times of day. The natural elements symbolize attributes of the crowd: the way a fire spreads, the river flows, the sea changes, or the rain discharges. The elements highlight a crowd's changeability.[18]

And it's this movement of the crowd from one form to another that is significant, I realize one afternoon while talking with Anuraag Chowfla, whose architecture firm designed some of the early Metro stations. This movement—allowing for it and predicting it—is what goes into the "science of sizing" in station design. "You have to create a scenario," he explains, "where there are three missed headways, meaning three trains don't show up on time, which means when the train is at full capacity—the crush load—there could be nine thousand people on the platform. The station has to be designed in such a way so that people can be evacuated in four minutes."

As in every metro system, a late train on one side of the platform means a crowd will collect, a kind of stagnant crowd, hemmed in by the train, the platform, and time. When the train finally arrives, the crowd still has no space to expand since the train will arrive with new passengers, some of whom will want to get off. This is when the push and pull begins and when space and matter will come into conflict, when bodies themselves will become part of the architecture of the station. But how much can people be pushed?

The crowd is a physical sensation, "a bath of multitude"; one is either in it or not.[19] Being on the edge of the crowd is to be out of it. Watching a crowd, as people often do on platforms as trains go by, is to regard the crowd, often with resignation, sympathy, and occasional longing.

A DEVELOPED COUNTRY

In 2002, Gustavo Petro, Bogotá's mayor at the time, spoke about the success of his city's Bus Rapid Transit corridor, a system that had separate lanes and tube-like stations. Unlike metro systems, which were exorbitant to construct, and once constructed were fixed in place, BRTs were cost-effective and flexible. They also, Petro argued, foreshadowed an urban transformation.

Petro's oft-repeated phrase—"A developed country is not a place where the poor have cars. It's where the rich use public transportation."—is one you hear even now, from Delhi bus proponents but also from former Delhi Metro project manager E. Sreedharan. This phrase, which has become an international transit mantra, is aspirational in and of itself. The phrase is not just about the type of transit options available in a city, it is also about how they are regarded. The phrase gets to the heart of how a city is imagined, the direction people and planners want to go in, and the goal or outcomes of what society should be and feel like.

"Developed" in Petro's meaning is based on ideas of inclusion, the common good, and excellence in public works; it also imagines a change in attitude whereby the wealthier sections of society come to see that their own well-being is invested in public transportation. This change comes about, in Petro's view, when the public system becomes more efficient but also when it is nicer and more enjoyable than private means, when people of all income levels instinctively choose the public option over the private. A kind of social magic.

In Delhi, it is the separation of classes of people that has been the goal of elites, not their merging in public spaces. The city has a strong VIP culture that lauds and flaunts this separation. And in a broader sense, the merging of caste and class-based identities is a function of the separation: In a more caste-ridden society, each knows their place as lower castes are punished for transgressing spatial boundaries, so general proximity is not a problem, especially when lower castes are serving upper-caste interests and needs. In a more class-based, liberal society, where equality is enshrined in constitutions, "public space" is no longer desirable since you never know who you'll be rubbing shoulders with; private spaces get prioritized. Money, meanwhile, becomes the new social regulator, especially in cities, taking over from "tradition," in this case, casteism. It's not that caste is eradicated but rather is passed along like a baton. The spatial dynamic of caste/class exclusion is first worked out in urban middle- and upper-class homes and neighborhoods, where domestic servants occupy designated spaces. The dynamic then moves outside to malls, cafés, gated communities, and other paid-entry leisure spaces.

Delhi's Transportation Research and Injury Prevention Programme (TRIPP), based at the Indian Institute of Technology, issued study after

Figure 8. Construction of the Pink Line as it intersects with the Violet Line in Lajpat Nagar, 2016. The busy Lajpat Nagar central market is adjacent to the rained-out road on the left, usually crunched with traffic all around.

study that showed the value of public transit and the need for a comprehensive bus system. Researchers argued that a state-of-the-art bus system could transport the most commuters to the widest selection of destinations at a lower cost than other forms of transport (such as the Delhi Metro). TRIPP was not so much anti-Metro as it was pro-bus.

Dinesh Mohan, a University of Michigan–trained civil engineer, was the face of TRIPP when it came to his advocacy of Delhi's first Bus Rapid Transit corridor. His goal was not only for more social access and equity on Delhi's roads but also for less car use overall. Although Mohan advocates policies that would require cleaner motor vehicles, he also argues that to reduce car pollution, using cars less will have the greatest impact on air quality. His is an uphill battle. The anti-BRT ire of south Delhi's car driving elite became so intense in the lead-up to the construction of Delhi's first BRT that he and members of his research team were pilloried in the English-language press and routinely threatened. Cars are aspirational for many, but for others they already define their propertied claim to the city and its roads. It is for this reason that many see the debate over Delhi's BRT as a class conflict.

Mohan and I sat at a Café Coffee Day opposite the main gate of IIT one morning. Mohan, with his signature sideburn-heavy beard, spoke with the resolve and resignation of a longtime scholar-activist. For him, the root issue of transport is the allocation of city space. Who is allowed to take up the most space in the city, and at what cost?

We talk about the actual size of cars and how many meters they take up, as compared to, say, a bicycle or the width of human feet. The city has been given over to cars and their owners, Mohan contends. This translates into a mentality and attitude whereby space itself gets managed by class interests. It is an attitude that comes to determine the direction of urban planning in the city and one that extends beyond transport.

Mohan sees Delhi's Metro as an investment issue, whereby the project gets land from the government. He questions the public good of the investment. Why doesn't society get to make those choices? He cites a Brookings Institute Report that says the Metro is not a social good. Then he avers that the Metro lobby—the Germans and Japanese—is very strong. Glancing at the Delhi Metro Rail Corporations' contractors and suppliers for phase one of the project, as detailed in DMRC publications, it becomes clear that Japanese and German but also South Korean, Swedish, Finnish, French, Spanish, Swiss, and Austrian companies had much to offer and gain.[20]

Mohan points through the glass window in front of us to the street vendors outside: a guy selling crispy *gol gappas* and a *mochi* seated cross-legged repairing someone's black shoes. There are those, he says, who want to "clean up" the city by regulating vendors out of existence. Vendors not only provide services but are also "the eyes on the street," Mohan says, recalling urban planner Jane Jacobs's dictum about safe cities being contingent on a robust and diverse street life.[21] The eyes on Indian streets are indeed plentiful, from the snacks vendor to the local security guards, the women who iron clothes, and vegetable sellers to shopkeepers, sweepers, drivers, and gardeners. Jacobs might have embraced Indian urban population density but recoiled from the towering economic divisions separating people. As for Mohan, he questions what it means to be developed: to grow, advance, construct but also convert.

SOCIAL SPACE

The disembodied Metro voice in the train keeps announcing, "Please do not befriend any unknown person." But I see various forms of befriending. People in an enclosed space who don't know one another but might like to.

SEELAMPUR STATION

Seelampur station opens out onto a wide esplanade, so wide that it's mostly empty except for a few planters near the station entrance where people are often sitting on the ledges, chatting on their phones or to each other. An intermittent stream of people flows in and out of the large, airy station. The wide space marks a contrast with the rest of the busy area, with its cramped dwellings piled one on top of the other, bisected by drains and railway tracks, a collection of interstitial spaces.

Outside of the station, forty-year-old Rakesh explains that he was born and raised in Seelampur. "The area was all fields before," he says in Hindi, when I ask him about all of the small manufacturing the area is known for. Rakesh's family had a wood workshop, but about ten years ago he decided to follow his childhood dream of becoming a magician. He used to work at Apu Ghar, an amusement park that was originally built for the Asian Games Village, and now he works at the Adventureland Park in Rithala on the other side of the Yamuna and the other end of the Red Line, so he takes the Metro there.

Seelampur is known for having been a resettlement colony during the 1974–76 Emergency imposed by then prime minister Indira Gandhi. Thousands of families from Old Delhi and parts of central Delhi had their homes demolished in an attempt to "clean up" the city and were offered

plots across the Yamuna. Sometimes they had to show certificates of having been sterilized to claim those plots.[22]

A newer narrative is that people across the Yamuna in east Delhi, in
places like Seelampur and neighboring Welcome, are now taking the
Metro back to the city. For these areas, buses, often running on irregular schedules, had been the main mode of transport connecting what had
been outlying areas to city centers like Kashmere Gate and Connaught
Place. People in Seelampur still take the bus for their short journeys, and
buses are their everyday lifeline; but for longer journeys, especially across
the Yamuna, it's cheap enough or at least "value for money" to consider
taking the Metro. As in most poor areas near Metro stations, the people
who ride the Metro regularly are the ones who have somewhere to go. A
school, a job.

Rakesh predicts that just as the local train is the "lifeline of Bombay,"
this will become the case for Delhi. He's also convinced that "forty percent"
of Metro traffic comes from "trans-Yamuna," or east of the Yamuna River.

An aboveground station, Seelampur is "at grade" rather than "elevated,"
so you don't have to descend a second set of stairs to exit the station. This
has the effect of making the station seem more connected to the community around it. Anuraag Chowfla, whose architecture firm designed this
station and several others, says that the firm's idea for the station was "that
it should be transparent."

Just beyond the esplanade, past the cycle rickshaws, vendors are lined
up to one side. An old man squats in front of a scale, offering to check your
weight; another man sells *paan*, others cold drinking water and assorted
fried snacks. The path adjacent to the Metro station parallels a congested
highway and leads to the new Carrefour, a French company meaning
"crossroads," housed in a characterless, air-conditioned box of a building,
now part of the Parsvnath Metro Mall complex,

Inside Carrefour, a wide range of products are stacked from floor to ceiling: from hardware, stationery, office chairs, desks, televisions, and print-
ers, to fresh fish, halal meat, and vegetables, to all varieties of *namkeen*
(salty snacks), chocolate, and biscuits. There are no French products, but
instead those known only too well in the Indian marketplace, from Maggi
to Usha, Eurolex to Dabar. Everything you'd find in corner shops or in the
bazaar, but here everything is on the same plane—flat-screen TVs alongside twenty-rupee packets of Bournavita. The ultimate ordering of things.

Price cards list the wholesale price, the MRP, and the profit percentage for the particular item. I see that more sizeable profits are to be made from plastic buckets, paper products, and copper pots as opposed to hair oil, teacups, and plates. Outside the automatic glass doors, large trucks, small cars, motorized and man-powered rickshaws are being loaded and unloaded with goods.

Outside, to the right of Carrefour, walking away from the Metro station, there's another kind of bazaar, selling borders, ribbons, fabric pieces, tape measures, and readymade garments in thin plastic wraps. There, at a tea stall, people sit and watch the mess of traffic in front of them. No one has ever heard of Carrefour, only *badee dukaan*, big shop, which is next door and within eyesight.

Continuing down the lane, a tunneled path leads under the Metro line to the area of Old Seelampur just behind the Metro station and alongside a *nala* (canal). Chowfla explains that his firm fought to have the tunnel leading into the neighborhood behind the Metro station. It was one of the few linkages to the community beyond the Metro station perimeter that the DMRC agreed to. I take the path and immediately notice hundreds of pairs of blue jeans hanging to dry. They hang from fences, walls, and awnings. They come in all sizes. White threads hang from the jeans. Walking further into the *galis* (narrow lanes), I see a young girl sitting on the step of her front door, pulling excess threads from jeans. Nearby a gush of blue water drains from a large pipe. Further along, cycle rickshaws stacked high with blue and black jeans travel to the Gandhi Nagar market where they will be sold at wholesale prices.

In one gali, Lucky and Dhruv, both twenty-five years old, explain that they are from the Gujjar community and were born and brought up in Seelampur. Unprompted, they give me the *jati* (subcaste) breakdown of the area, lane by lane. But it is clear that their point is to emphasize the cohesiveness of their community rather than divisions in it. By now we're sitting on red plastic chairs in front of Lucky's mobile phone accessories shop drinking Limca sodas. Lucky tells me he owns the shop and lives in the same building. There are very few items in the shop. Lucky sees Seelampur as a diverse, thriving neighborhood that "just wants to be left alone." By this he is referring to the time the government closed the small-scale factories in 2006. People lost their livelihoods and a few lost their lives when there were protests against the closings, or "sealings." The jeans hanging to dry all over this part of town are a reminder of the industry but also of the possibility that the government can intervene at any time.

Lucky and Dhruv think the Metro is *bhadiya* (excellent) and speak of people from their neighborhood who travel to Gurgaon on it to work in car factories. But they themselves only ride it on occasion, gesturing to the Metro and Northern Railway lines on the parallel elevated tracks just above us, crossing the nala. Between the nala, the edges of railway lines, and gutters of blue, we seem to be in the inbetween spaces of the city.

The Metro represents having somewhere to go, but for some it is also a place to be. Some women from Seelampur's low-income Muslim community now work at Metro station ticket counters. These jobs are considered safe and glamorous, even if women sometimes have to deal with rude and abusive behavior from men, customers toward whom they are only allowed to be polite.[23]

Upstairs on the platform, the slightly lopsided, low-level brick buildings of Seelampur are at eye-level. The windows are too tiny to see into but there are a few people on the rooftops. For people from Seelampur waiting for a train, it is a perfect view, a snapshot of where they live, and like a snapshot it allows them to be temporarily distanced from it.

PRESSURE COOKER

The pressure cooker is the steam engine of the modern Indian kitchen, the *rasoi*, the *bawarchikhana*, that place of darkness that has become increasingly light, even luminescent. It is the industrial transport mechanism of the kitchen, a remnant, reminder of how outside becomes inside. An everyday space-time compression, the pressure cooker famously and sociologically enables the modern woman and sometime working wife to compress her duties or watch over someone who will compress them for her, giving her satisfaction that the dal is done.

The pressure cooker has a secretive element to it. Its lid shuts tightly over food and water, with rubber washer precisely in place. The maneuver requires a firm handshake to seal the deal as metal hinge is flipped over a double-layered handle locking mechanism.

This instant of physical exertion ushers in a new way of thinking about the properties of food and the time it takes to alter them. What is hard—rice, dal, vegetable, meat and bone—becomes soft, tender, ready in a third of the time. With its steam of air pushed into the food and boiling over boiling point temperature, it is a daily defiance. You don't see the result, not even a whiff of it, until it's all over.

The cooker itself is the opposite of lightness or softness. It is heavy gauge and piston ready. It rattles over the gas like an incoming train. It is cavernous, with its wide inner ridge requiring skilled, angular cleaning. An old-fashioned efficiency.

The pressure cooker works in concert now with the microwave, but the two represent different kinds of technologies and ideologies. The cooker is obstinately unplugged, with no digital displays. It sits around in an ordinary cupboard. Next to the tiffin carrier or the steel plate and tumbler, it reigns supreme.

This is maybe, who knows, because it also carries within it a threat. With its washer and piston and necessary alignments, it can be high maintenance at times. It has been known on occasion to fell a *bua* or *biji*, an aunt, a mother.

More recently, in the twenty-first century, filled with nails, shards, ball bearings, the pressure cooker can puncture balloons and heads in a nearby market in an instant. The pressure cooker's chirpy whistle replaced by a blast cap, detonation by digital watch or mobile phone sends fragments in all directions at a thousand meters per second.

In these pressure-filled times, the cooker has come to have other uses, as TNT makes for an IED, in an always expanding and expansive modernity. This nefarious dimension of the most ordinary of objects lamentably but surely connects the home and the world of urban space in a new way, leaving a trail of bones, limbs, and trauma. Chillingly if not always precisely, it is also homemade.

BLUE LINE

On the Blue Line in the mid-afternoon, boys in school uniforms carrying backpacks get on the train. "St. Michael's School" adorns the shirt of one boy who jumps up and grabs a handrail near the ceiling as soon as the doors slide shut. He starts to swing, then hangs for a moment and jumps down. Girls stand nearby in beige salwars and long pink kurta tops embroidered with yellow rising suns and "Salman Girls School." Two of them standing next to me discuss points and registration procedures. We approach Kirti Nagar, surrounded by high-rise apartment blocks and billboards: a medical clinic with a sign that says, "Where care is culture"; a café with a sign that declares, "The future is female."

At Rajiv Chowk station, the overpass between the two Blue Line platforms is covered in reddish-brown *paan* stains despite the two-hundred-rupee fine for spitting. But you don't see anyone actually spit, just hurrying along to the other side. On the other side of the overpass, waiting for a train to Noida, a family of three is sitting against a wall on a busy platform, eating *rotis* (bread) and *sabzi* (cooked vegetables) from a tiffin container, a scene so common on any railway platform, yet an anomaly in a Metro station. People move *through* the Metro; they don't linger to perform ordinary activities, partly because of the short waiting times between trains and because of the restrictions on what can and cannot be done in stations. Even idleness is regulated by the few-minute intervals of departing and arriving trains.

At Yamuna Bank station on the east side of the river, the Blue Line breaks into two directions, toward Vaishali and Noida. The stations on this line are identical with rounded metal corrugated rooftops. The Vaishali part of the line follows Vikas Marg, a busy commercial road that typifies the city's aspirational culture. As you approach Laxmi Nagar station, bright billboards run parallel for "Toppers Institute" and an array of chartered-accountant prep schools. *"Agar aap ABCD jaanate hain tho ENGLISH bol sukate hain"* ("If you know ABCD then you can speak English") reads one sign written in Devanagari and Roman script. At Laxmi Nagar station, alleyways are packed with textbook shops, tutoring centers, and cyber cafés abutting the Metro station exit. Groups of girls in jeans stand chatting, clutching notebooks. Boys on scooters trundle through the lanes. A young boy—too young—sits casually with his feet partly up in a cycle rickshaw. He watches the students and all the activity; he seems to be waiting and not waiting for a next passenger to descend from the station.

At five-thirty in the evening, the area is bustling. Packs of teenagers

Figure 9. Vaishali station, Blue Line, 2012. At the end of the line, motorbikes coming from points near and far in Uttar Pradesh fill up the Metro parking lot. A billboard advertises new apartment complexes on one side of the tracks; on the other are complexes that have already been built.

stream out of the numerous institutes adjacent to the Metro station. Some board buses, others climb the stairs to the elevated Metro line. The students and institutes were here long before the Metro came, but things have densified and intensified since then. The Metro fits right in and speeds things up. Buses, scooters, cycle rickshaws, and jeeps cluster around the station. The people in the vicinity seem agreed on the fact that yes, of course, the Metro is great.

At Nirman Vihar, a ramp leads to the East Center mall. Inside, it's nearly empty. The mall connects to a small esplanade of ice cream shops and a Fun Cinemas, which I'm told is packed on the weekends. Snack sellers sit or stand with their carts near the station exit. One of them, Chaan Babu, tells me that he must be twenty-one years old. He stops his cart in four places during the day, including two nearby schools, another shopping area, and here at the Metro station. Sometimes he takes the Metro to Anand Vihar, "to go here and there," he says with a sheepish smile. He lives nearby and so doesn't need to take the Metro every day. He likes the Metro because you can travel comfortably, and you don't get stuck in traffic.

Toward Vaishali, mid-rise apartment blocks surround the station in what has become an instant bedroom community, with the Sahibabad industrial area on one side of the Metro line and Bisleri and Dabur plants on the other. Haldirams, Spensers, Nirulas, Globus, Big Life, restaurants, hotels, hospitals, coaching centers, multiplexes, malls, and banks are scattered down the line, with promises of fast food, fast fashion, better health, more cash, and more smarts.

At Vaishali station, the end of the line, Mahima has ridden her motorbike with one of her nephews from Vasundhara enclave, about ten kilometers away. She is on her way to Karol Bagh to visit her son, who is convalescing at the Ganga Ram hospital. For her, the Metro is about speed, but as she gestures toward the hundreds and hundreds of motorbikes in the lot, she says taking the Metro is not just about avoiding traffic but also saving on petrol.

DELHI-6

The image of the Delhi Metro as a liberating space has become part of Indian popular culture, even cinematic shorthand for the development of characters. In the 2009 movie *Delhi-6*, directed by Rakeysh Omprakash Mehra, Bittu Sharma, played by Sonam Kapoor, is a young woman who lives with her family in a *haveli*. The "6" in the title refers to the postal code of Old Delhi where they live. Bittu is trying to forge her own identity, a personal journey that is partly shown through her trips on the Metro. While her father, played by Om Puri, wants to get her married, she dreams of a different life where she goes from being "a nobody to a somebody."

The Metro is a new social space that intersects with her everyday life. She descends into a station and is briefly shown with other women applying makeup in a Metro station bathroom. A public bathroom where women feel comfortable to linger becomes film-worthy in a city where women have few if any options for using clean toilets when they're in public. The Metro bathroom in the movie is a little glamorous compared to the ones you actually find in stations, but the concept is the same: a reliable space to use the toilet, and in Bittu's case, change clothes. As Bittu moves away from her family home and neighborhood and makes forays into the city, she sheds her salwar kameez for a pierced belly button, revealing sleeveless top, and harem pants. She lets down her hair, pulls it back with a bandanna, and paints her lips red. We then see her at a photographer's studio creating a portfolio of sassy poses to send to the judges of the television show *Indian Idol*. In the process, she constitutes herself anew.[24]

Several scenes are framed by her going into and out of Metro stations. And in one instant, a TV news broadcast on a hanging screen on a crowded Metro platform indicates how the urban public registers an important plot point. Meanwhile, in the train, Bittu looks out the window, and we witness her aloneness in this in-between space, but then see her sense of anticipation and defiance as she glides up an escalator into Connaught Place. Delhi, old and new, connected by high-speed rail. But what kind of change will this mean for a girl rooted to family and place? The Metro allows her to get away and feel anonymous in the city, while it also shuttles her back to her family and community. This narrative of liberation does not threaten her place in her family, and so, in good filmy fashion, she does not change too much.

Delhi-6 offers a conventional story of gendered liberation. The more experimental Hindi movie *Dev.D*, directed by Anurag Kashyap, came out at the same time and offered a much edgier portrayal of the city. Abhay Deol's title character does not always know where he is going or what he aspires to. Seeing him on the Metro symbolizes the possibility of adventure, unpredictability, and even danger, matching the aimless wandering of his own troubled soul.

BUS RAPID TRANSIT

Chugging up Delhi's first Bus Rapid Transit (BRT) corridor one late afternoon, my auto rickshaw driver and I get into the inevitable discussion of how fast we are moving, how fast we used to move, who is moving faster, and what has to be done for all of us to move faster. He is not convinced about the efficacy of the corridor; he is still stuck in traffic.

In the dead of night, the corridor resembles a giant, empty bowling alley. Bus stop islands mark a spatial separation between types of vehicles. The six-kilometer stretch of road that the BRT occupies between Ambedkar Nagar and Moolchand on Josip Broz Tito Marg in south Delhi stands alone as prototype and social experiment. During the day and into the evening cars jam-pack the side lanes, buses travel down the middle lanes, and motorcycles and scooters clog the outer bicycle lanes. This trespass is the first indication that something is not right, that the space is not being used as it should be. Or that this new transit corridor is being absorbed by the city rather than transforming it.

When Delhi's first BRT corridor opened in 2008 it was seen as a victory of urban planners over the will of the powerful car constituency in south Delhi. The car-driving classes had the English-language media on their side, ridiculing and criticizing every aspect of the proposed corridor. The planners, meanwhile, came equipped with data and designs to show how it would work and who it would benefit. When polled, 85 percent of commuters on the corridor said they were happy with the system and that it should be continued.[25] Despite the fact that BRT systems have become celebrated globally, Delhi's experiment with having one was never seen by the car-driving public and elite media outlets in this way. Instead the short stretch of BRT in south Delhi was an opening salvo in class conflict. The bus-riding public who benefited from the dedicated bus lanes were not organized, at least not to the extent of the outraged car drivers. Members of the car-driving class, organized under the NGO Nyaya Bhoomi, brought a court case against the city, demanding that the BRT be scrapped. They lost the case in 2012, but even the Delhi High Court's judgment, which called public transport "a bitter but necessary medicine" for the long-term health of the city, was telling in its narrative spin.[26] The car drivers had their own narrative: They were the city's wealth creators and so needed to get around the city quickly. Their mobility would benefit everyone else's in a kind of trickle-down manner.

The data on the BRT showed that it is not that vehicles were slowed down, but rather that buses could be speeded up. This visual and experiential discrepancy affected how you saw the corridor. One early evening, I chat with Sneha, sitting next to me on a bus going down the corridor; she sells life insurance, and says the BRT has been great for her since she can go "point to point," something she can't do on the more expensive Metro. For car drivers, who complain to me off the road, the BRT is a sore spot, not managed well, a complete disaster. The new landscape that the BRT corridor makes has its own visual ideology, one that is interpreted differently depending on one's place in the transport hierarchy.

The Metro has had only a tangential relationship to the city's bus fleet. It operates above and beyond the road. The BRT has no relation to the Metro, no connecting stops or platforms with the extensive transport system just meters above it. The two systems are compared to one another rather than coexisting as part of an integrated network. The Metro is a success story; it marks Delhi as a global city and conveys prestige through its technology and the way in which it was planned and now operates. The Metro also fits neatly into the existing class dynamic of the city. Other than increased traffic around some stations, the Metro does not slow down car drivers. The upper classes like having a metro in their city, even if they don't use it; and if it takes others off the road, all the better. The BRT was always cast differently. It's not just that it redistributed the space of one six-kilometer stretch; it's that buses visibly moved faster than cars, and that they, packed with dozens of passengers, were given the right of way.

THE BICYCLE FIXER

Ram Shankar's cycle parts shop is lodged on the face of a colorfully painted wall, the façade of a concrete building. The wall has deep inlets and within those inlets are tubes, wrenches, chains, nuts and bolts. Ram Shankar sits in front of his shop bantering with a friend. At first, I think of asking to take their photograph and moving along; the scene is a kind of tableau as it seems to offer a complete picture and a fitting contrast to the high-tech Metro in their midst. But then I start talking to them, and they invite me to sit on one of the plastic chairs in front of the shop. The Okhla station is in our faraway front view.

Ram Shankar is fifty-five years old, with a dark, weathered face and a white, closely cropped beard. He does not see the Metro as a gift to the city but rather as transportation for *bade aadmi* (big men) and specifically for *sarkari log* (government people). The Metro, in his analysis, was built by the government precisely for government workers. He explains in Hindi, "The Metro is really very good for the government employees as now they have to reach office in time; if they are late for two-three days, they will lose their job." But he distinguishes between reaching office in time and doing work. "They don't do much work in the office," he says of bureaucrats, "but their jobs are secure if they reach on time."[27]

The government job is also a kind of gift. He continues, "The *bade aadmi* will have his son or daughter take a government job so they can give favors to their own private companies. This is how they loot the masses." Here the gift is given among people who already have power and it has in fact been constructed to increase their power. The Metro is a facilitator in this larger schema, even if some *chhota aadmi* (little people) ride the Metro too.[28]

As we continue to chat, a water truck pulls up and people gather to fill plastic jugs. It is hard not to be struck by the two different forms of infrastructure and the politics of speed they enact: a politics of fast transport and slow water.

"There was water shortage under Sheila's reign," starts Ram Shankar, "as there was more corruption.[29] You didn't see water trucks much. A few people would stand for three hours in lines to take water and sell it for profit. You can't get food or salary, but you can get water. Now the water trucks come two to four times a week, which is at least fifty percent more often than before."

We watch the water trucks and the people surrounding them with their jugs. The Metro trains approach on the line above us and then become hidden as they enter the station; every few minutes a train emerges out of the other end of the station. Our own time pass sitting in front of the shop is suspended between the two activities.

The Metro, unlike water trucks, offers no durable good. It gives an energy and potentiality, a forward motion for many; but it can also emphasize a kind of stagnation.

Still, groups of local women gather to sit and chat under trees on the

Okhla station premises. Once a month, they take the Metro two stops away to the Kalkaji Mandir—it is such a short distance that it's cheaper and not that much slower to take the bus or even walk, but riding the Metro to the temple has become part of the experience. At Kalkaji Mandir station, the Metro premises lead into the temple, making the experience complete. Once you exit the station, you simply follow a path around to the temple, and soon you are walking barefoot on wet stone.

PART II Expanding

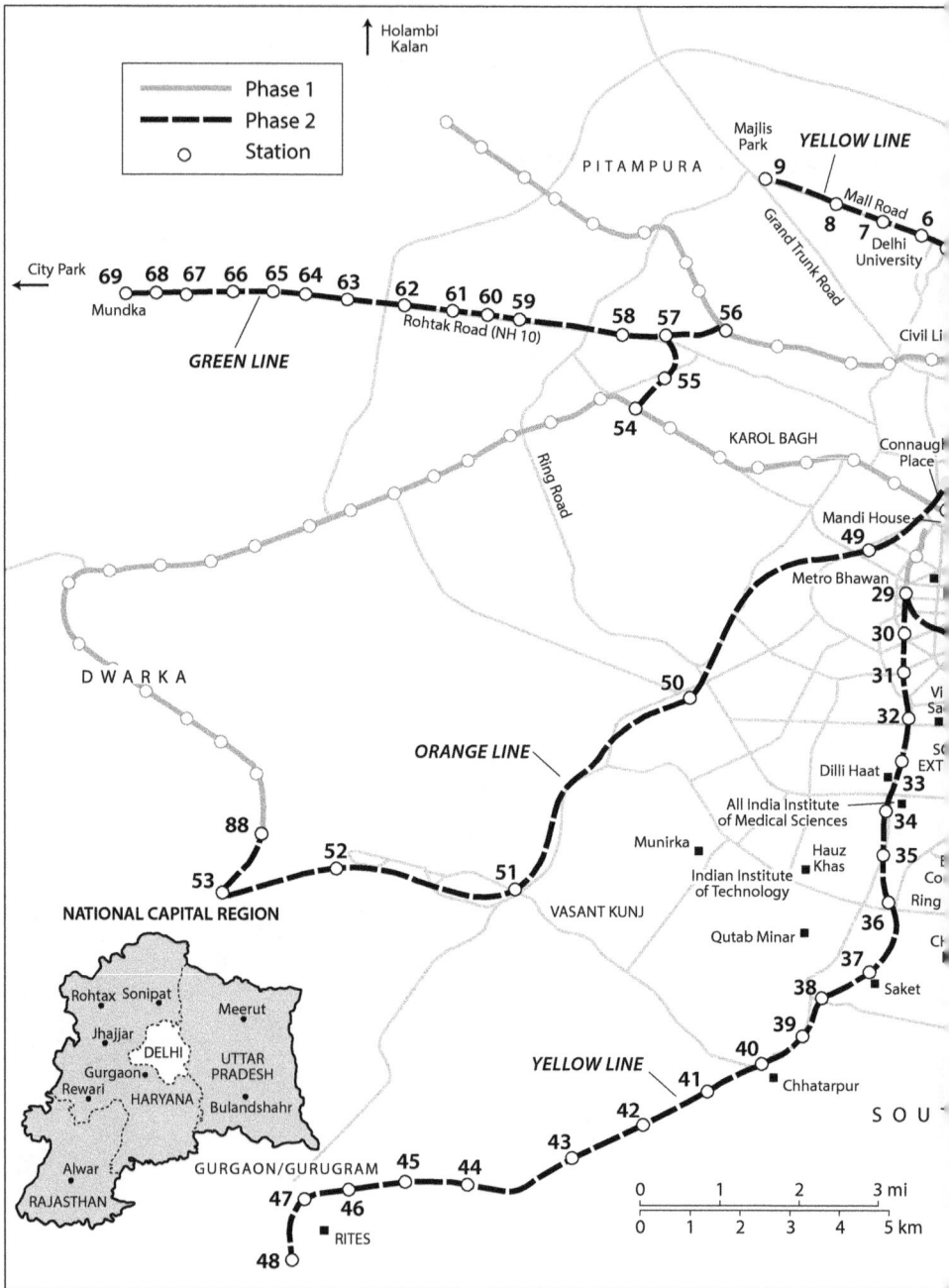

Holambi
Kalan

Phase 1
Phase 2
○ Station

PITAMPURA

Majlis
Park

YELLOW LINE

9

Mall Road

8

7

6

Delhi
University

Grand Trunk Road

City Park

69 68 67 66 65 64 63   62 61 60 59

Mundka   Rohtak Road (NH 10)   58 57 56

GREEN LINE   55

54   Civil Li

KAROL BAGH   Connaugh
                                Place

Ring Road   Mandi House

                                49

                                Metro Bhawan

                                29

                                30

                                31

                                32 Vi
                                    Sa

50   SO
                                EXT

ORANGE LINE   Dilli Haat 33

DWARKA   All India Institute   34
                                of Medical Sciences

88   Munirka   Hauz   35
                                           Khas

53   52   Indian Institute
        51   of Technology   Ring

NATIONAL CAPITAL REGION   VASANT KUNJ   36

                                Qutab Minar   37

Rohtax Sonipat   38 Saket
                                                 39
Jhajjar   Meerut
                                        40
    DELHI   41
Gurgaon UTTAR   Chhatarpur
Rewari   PRADESH   YELLOW LINE
        HARYANA Bulandshahr   42

                                43   SOU

Alwar   45 44
RAJASTHAN GURGAON/GURUGRAM

        47   0   1   2   3 mi
        46
48   0   1   2   3   4   5 km
    RITES

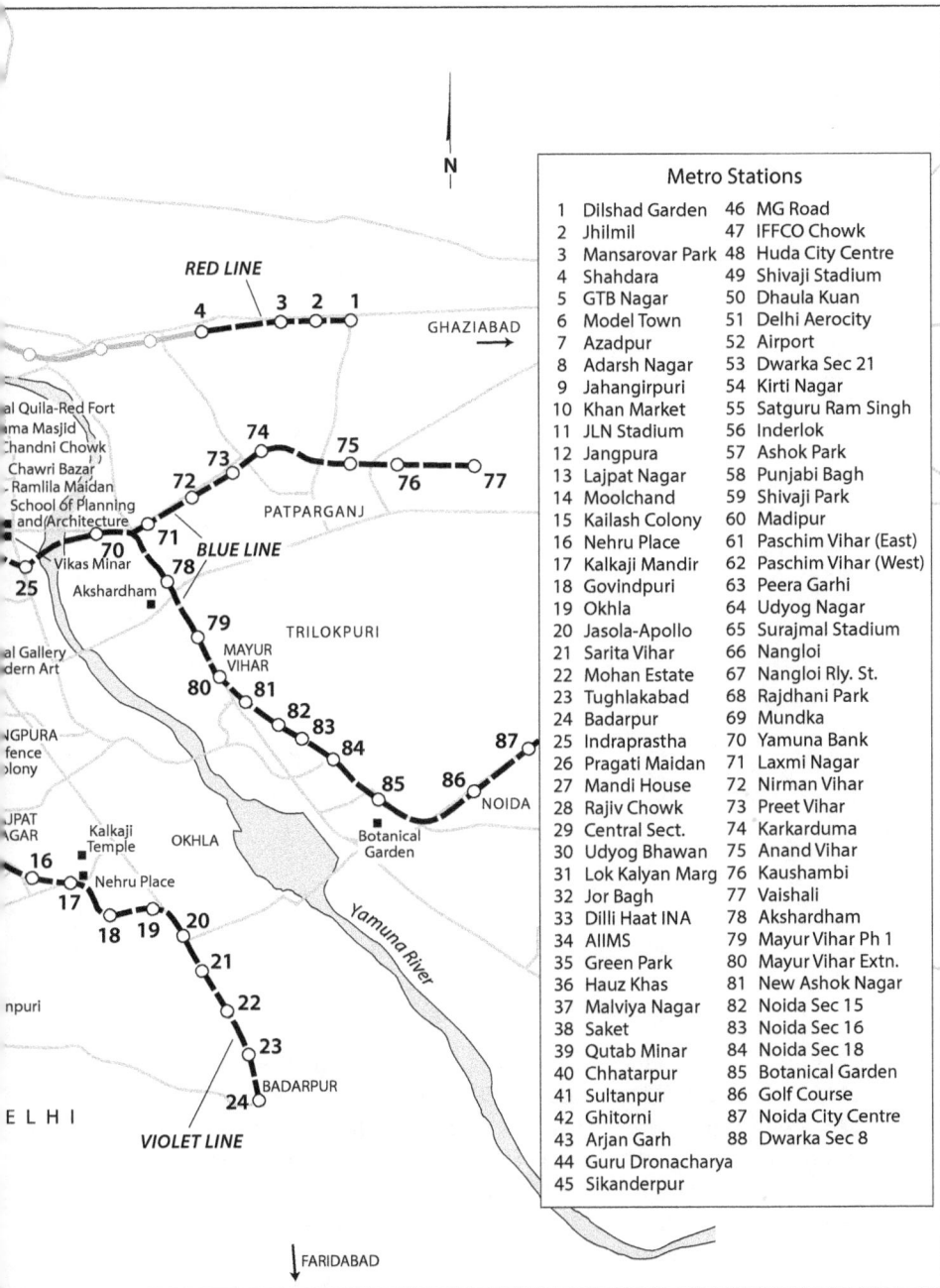

N

RED LINE

4   3 2 1

GHAZIABAD →

al Quila-Red Fort
ama Masjid
Chandni Chowk
Chawri Bazar
- Ramlila Maidan
School of Planning
and Architecture

74

73   75

72   76   77

PATPARGANJ

70
71   **BLUE LINE**
Vikas Minar
78
25   Akshardham

79

TRILOKPURI

MAYUR
VIHAR
80   81

82
83
84   87

85   86
NOIDA

al Gallery
dern Art

NGPURA
fence
olony

Botanical
Garden

JPAT
AGAR
16   Kalkaji
Temple   OKHLA
17   Nehru Place

18 19   20

21

22

23

npuri

24 BADARPUR

E L H I
VIOLET LINE

Yamuna River

↓ FARIDABAD

	Metro Stations		
1	Dilshad Garden	46	MG Road
2	Jhilmil	47	IFFCO Chowk
3	Mansarovar Park	48	Huda City Centre
4	Shahdara	49	Shivaji Stadium
5	GTB Nagar	50	Dhaula Kuan
6	Model Town	51	Delhi Aerocity
7	Azadpur	52	Airport
8	Adarsh Nagar	53	Dwarka Sec 21
9	Jahangirpuri	54	Kirti Nagar
10	Khan Market	55	Satguru Ram Singh
11	JLN Stadium	56	Inderlok
12	Jangpura	57	Ashok Park
13	Lajpat Nagar	58	Punjabi Bagh
14	Moolchand	59	Shivaji Park
15	Kailash Colony	60	Madipur
16	Nehru Place	61	Paschim Vihar (East)
17	Kalkaji Mandir	62	Paschim Vihar (West)
18	Govindpuri	63	Peera Garhi
19	Okhla	64	Udyog Nagar
20	Jasola-Apollo	65	Surajmal Stadium
21	Sarita Vihar	66	Nangloi
22	Mohan Estate	67	Nangloi Rly. St.
23	Tughlakabad	68	Rajdhani Park
24	Badarpur	69	Mundka
25	Indraprastha	70	Yamuna Bank
26	Pragati Maidan	71	Laxmi Nagar
27	Mandi House	72	Nirman Vihar
28	Rajiv Chowk	73	Preet Vihar
29	Central Sect.	74	Karkarduma
30	Udyog Bhawan	75	Anand Vihar
31	Lok Kalyan Marg	76	Kaushambi
32	Jor Bagh	77	Vaishali
33	Dilli Haat INA	78	Akshardham
34	AIIMS	79	Mayur Vihar Ph 1
35	Green Park	80	Mayur Vihar Extn.
36	Hauz Khas	81	New Ashok Nagar
37	Malviya Nagar	82	Noida Sec 15
38	Saket	83	Noida Sec 16
39	Qutab Minar	84	Noida Sec 18
40	Chhatarpur	85	Botanical Garden
41	Sultanpur	86	Golf Course
42	Ghitorni	87	Noida City Centre
43	Arjan Garh	88	Dwarka Sec 8
44	Guru Dronacharya		
45	Sikanderpur		

Map 2. (overleaf) Phase II of the Delhi Metro started to open in 2008 and was completed in 2011. It extended two lines, the Yellow and Blue, and added three new lines: Green, Violet, and Orange. The Metro widened its sphere of influence with this phase as accessibility to different parts of the city and interchangeability at new hubs increased. The Orange Line added another psychic dimension to the system since it is a dedicated express line to the Indira Gandhi International Airport. The Orange Line was also the first line to be built privately, by Reliance Infrastructure, and underwent multiple delays and construction issues. The DMRC ended up taking back the line from Reliance in 2013.

The road from Vishwavidyalaya station is sloped down, and the cycle rickshaws move quickly over the asphalt. It is a bumpy, crater-filled road. It is better to walk the distance. The strip that is Chhatra Marg, the main drag of Delhi University, is narrow enough that you can watch both sides of the road and see what is going on. Along the edge of the gutter there is sidewalk, but after so many monsoons, even the light ones that Delhi gets, the cement shifts to such a degree that if you don't look down the whole time you might just fall into a small ditch at worst or trip over an exposed metal rod at best. It is better to walk on the road and be part of its movement. You're better off to stick with the bicycles and fruit sellers wheeling their carts. The road is moving; you are moving with it. When you do this, cycle rickshaw drivers will slow down beside you and try to convince you that getting a ride would be better and faster. You think about it and gauge your distance, your thirst, the strength of your legs, and, most of the time, you keep walking. Despite the Metro and all of Delhi's cars and buses, even the new lime green ones and red, air-conditioned ones that glide where they used to chug, despite all of that, the city is a pedestrian city. The majority of people still walk.

From the road, as you walk, you notice things or come upon things in a different way than if you were being cycled by someone or driven by someone or driving or cycling yourself. You may come in contact with a cow, for instance. I hesitate to write this because of the clichés about cows on Indian streets. It's not that you see so many in Delhi, you don't. Cows tend to be in the upper and lower reaches of the city, where the urban and peri-urban are still being worked out. But even in Delhi, there is sometimes a cow sitting or standing on the side of the road, and sometimes a cow will move into the middle of the road and get in the way of traffic. A cow in the road is a bit like an iceberg, immovable, irrelevant, until.

It is rare to see a fallen cow, a stricken cow, as I saw one day, witnessed really, while walking down Chhatra Marg. It was at the Kirori Mal College turn, which at that time meant that I was almost home. On this day, it meant something else. A cow was sitting down, legs folded beneath it, in the middle of the road. She was perfectly still except for her twitching ears. Her coat was a creamy caramel color, a canvas for a single trickle of bright red blood sliding down her side, from which orifice it was hard to make out. The cow's stillness suggested an internal injury to me. And then just ahead there were these three boys packed on a scooter; they were stopped, and their three heads were turned back toward the cow in the middle of the road.

THE GANGWAY

The space between the coaches, the "gangway" in Metro parlance, is a porous space; there is no actual divider, only a narrowing with a lower ceiling than the rest of the train and accordion-like walls that enable the coach to twist and turn as needed. The space between the ladies' coach and general (or mixed) coaches is no different; there's no other demarcation. It is often a friendly space, especially when men and women on either side are traveling together. Other times men look into the women's coach, but they don't leer and mostly don't stare.

At rush hour, the coaches are jam-packed, and men form an almost natural line between the ladies' and general coaches that they mostly don't overstep. The line is straight and fixed, as if the men are pushing up against an imaginary divider. Since there is no physical divider, they press their hands on the roof and sides of the coach, lest they fall in.

The women's side can get crowded too, and then this space is like a standoff between the sexes. And yet this in-between space is not a stable place that may be defined once and for all. It is not static; it is always in flux and always changing in meaning. It does not stand for anything; it does not say anything. One minute it says one thing, the next another. Then it empties out and says nothing at all. A space waiting to be filled.

A common scene: The Metro doors open and men flood into the ladies' coach and then make their way across the porous border to the general coach. Women tolerate this infringement even though it is technically not allowed. If a Metro worker is there she or he will tell the men they can't go through the women's coach entrance, but they won't physically stop them. If a CISF guard is there, he or she will physically block their entrance. But even this protocol may change as Metro rules themselves are enforced or not enforced depending on the station and time of day.

A common sightline from the women's coach into the general coach: men packed in like sardines. More often, however, couples or friends of opposite sexes chat in the gangway that connects the two coaches. The men there always look forward into the ladies' coach, which is usually the first coach of the train. The men leave their bags on the women's side, and sometimes their children or spouses or girlfriends too, and they'll lean in sometimes to say something.

When the train is not crowded, and you are able to look down the length of it, there is usually nothing in particular to see, except for the slight sway from side to side as it snakes through the underground tunnels or on the elevated tracks.

At twelve-thirty in the afternoon on the Blue Line passing Karol Bagh, two young women are reviewing their medical textbooks. A young man who seems to be with them is reading from another textbook. Another man is playing a game on his phone. A woman with green spectacles is charging her cell phone in one of the outlets inside the coach. Some women are chatting nearby on the metal benches of the ladies' coach.

A couple is talking softly in the gangway, their faces close together. The textbook-reading guy changes places with the canoodling couple, so he can talk to the two other medical students; they are all friends and soon are in conversation about their upcoming exam; words like "blood trans-fusion," "oxytocin," "pre-natal" pass between them. At times like these, the space between the coaches resembles other middle-class spaces like cafés or even malls. The space between the coaches is an ethnographic space, a space of culture and sociality. It is a moving space that changes as people step in and out of trains. It is a collection of scenes and interactions.

The documentary film *Please Mind the Gap* follows transgender person Anshuman Chauhan as they negotiate the in-between space of the general and women's coaches of the Delhi Metro. At first you think the short film is about their in-between-ness being mapped onto the Metro's. They board the ladies' coach and look around self-consciously before moving

Figure 10. The gangway between the ladies' and general coaches, 2018. Who sits and who stands, when, where, and how becomes another way to think about transit etiquette and the politics of ease.

into the general coach. They cross the fluid space between the coaches, one that they embody. This fluidity is then contrasted with the security checks with one line for women and one for men, and the ways that bodies are handled differently in those spaces. The film seems to showcase a personal negotiation of gender identity on the one hand, and an attempt to queer the public space of the Delhi Metro on the other. Maybe the in-between spaces are more fluid than we think. Maybe all of the spaces in the Metro are. As for Chauhan, they say that they prefer to sit in the space between the coaches, resting their back on the accordion folds.[1]

SPONTANEOUS URBANISM

The Metro's first project manager, Elattuvalapil Sreedharan, who served from 1995–2012, is known affectionately and practically as the "Metro Man" throughout India. He has a hallowed place in the Delhi Metro Rail Corporation and in the nation, even many years after his retirement. This image was tarnished somewhat when Sreedharan joined the Bharatiya Janata Party in 2021 and ran for a seat in the Kerala state assembly the same year, only to lose to the Congress Party candidate. The eighty-eight-year-old technocrat became a partisan figure, even if only briefly. Nevertheless, Sreedharan is credited not only for getting the Metro built on time and within budget but also for having instilled a disciplined work culture and ethic at the DMRC. As one Delhi-based transport consultant who worked on evaluating Delhi's Metro for the Japanese told me in 2009, "Without Sreedharan, nothing would happen; if he went, all would stop. He asks the DMRC board of directors to do something, and they jump."

Sreedharan has been bestowed with numerous national and international awards and became known for his management strategies; he now consults on other metro projects in cities across India and is especially involved in the building of the Cochin metro in his home state of Kerala.[2]

Sreedharan is an engineer, and it was his management style and vision of seeing the Metro as an engineering project that became the system's hallmark and highest priority. In Sreedharan's time, the DMRC became such a privileged state entity—as I was repeatedly told by those who worked both within and alongside the organization—that it was able to do what it needed to get the system built. The DMRC did not have to cooperate with other urban agencies because it had the backing of the central government, more funding than any other urban project, and a project manager who was revered and listened to by everyone.

Nonetheless, once the Metro's first three lines (Red, Yellow, and Blue) were operational, urban planners and commuters began to critique the Metro, especially the user interface between the stations and the rest of the city. What was supposed to happen when you got down from the Metro and stepped across the threshold from the smooth train and gleaming station to the uneven city terrain? The Metro had been imagined and built as a stand-alone project, yet for any urban mass transit system to work, it had to enable commuters to connect to other forms of transport, such as buses, vans, jeeps, cycle rickshaws, auto-rickshaws, or taxis in order to get to their final destinations, to achieve "last mile connectivity." Hence, issues beyond safety and engineering—planning, design, architecture—came to the fore. These were also issues that required communication across and cooperation among several urban agencies.

In 2013, I met with the chief architect at the DMRC, Papiya Sarkar, to talk about the issue of the interface between the Metro and the city and Delhi's urbanism more generally. The Metro had already impacted the city; it was part of the urban landscape, yet it was still evolving.

At the time, Sarkar was managing the architecture of sixty stations in the Metro's third building phase. She also oversaw all of the DMRC architects, each of whom managed dozens of stations at a time, and dealt with the private, contracted architecture firms, both Indian-owned local ones and foreign design and engineering consultancies such as the French Systra.[3] But she was more than a manager. When I met with Sarkar and two members of her team in their office near the Patel Chowk station in central Delhi, it was clear that they labored over the meaning and ideas of architecture and urban image on a station-by-station basis. These issues were especially important for the aboveground, elevated stations, which affect the city skyline and interact with other traffic forms. We discussed, for instance, how a Metro line relates to a corresponding flyover and the environmental and aesthetic fallout of such competing structures. She and her team were also aware that they had an ancillary position at the

DMRC—although when I met Sarkar two years later, in 2015, she told me that architecture had gained stature in the organization, and I also noticed that her office had been moved to the primary DMRC headquarters, Metro Bhawan, on Barakhamba Road.

"Delhi's Walled City, the medieval city, was for walking," Sarkar explained, "Lutyens' Delhi is for the car." Her neat contrast was an old one, referring to the dense network of lanes of Old Delhi, with its sometimes shoulder-to-shoulder pedestrian traffic, versus the wide avenues and boulevards of the colonial capital built in 1911, a part of town that continues to be the roaming and residential ground for the city's political and bureaucratic elites.

"Lutyens' Delhi," Sarkar continued, "is exogenous, an imported plan, as opposed to indigenous," referring to Old Delhi. Two urban forms are also indicative of two contrasting styles of rule and the imperative to create historical continuity (Old Delhi) or disjuncture (New Delhi) in an urban idiom. Sarkar's historical schema recapitulates colonial-era hierarchies imprinted on the urban landscape, while it also opens up an aspirational narrative for the contemporary city.[4]

"Is the Delhi Metro exogenous or indigenous?" I asked tentatively. A pause followed by silence as her team members glance toward the floor. A moment later, Ankit, one of the younger team members, looked up and said, "It is spontaneous," and everyone nodded in agreement, and perhaps with some relief.

I found something telling in that moment, perhaps in the very spontaneity of the remark itself. "Spontaneous" suggests that something happens quickly or all of a sudden, which was of course not the case with the Delhi Metro; it had been considered since 1969, even if construction didn't begin until the late 1990s. It is hard to think of any major infrastructure, let alone megaproject, that could be spontaneous; it goes against the kind of planning that is required by an infrastructural project, including the various forms of excavation, removal, and retrieval necessary before the building can even begin. On reflection, I took Ankit's word to suggest that the Metro was somehow organic, a need emerging from local realities. Those realities included the city's traffic congestion and pollution but also the way the city had changed after the liberalization of the economy. There were more places to go to and less time to get to them.

Metro technology and expertise may be global, but the need or desire for a Metro was also a reflection of the city's own globalizing, he seemed to be saying. The city had come to a point where it demanded a state-of-the art, globally recognized form of mass transit, one to take its people to the kind of office and other jobs created by economic liberalization. To extend Ankit's remark, global technology and expertise became incorporated into the urban landscape and reproduced many times over as metro systems are now being built and are already running in numerous other Indian cities. That spread might also be cast as "spontaneous," which suggests something that is inevitable, a response to local needs and not external pressures. It may have precedents from elsewhere, but it has evolved locally; it is not imposed.

NEHRU PLACE

At Nehru Place station, I get down from the platform and come across a man and a woman; they are gray-haired but not old.

"Does the Violet Line go to Mandi House?" they ask me.

"Yes, it does, it's the last stop."

"But the map downstairs does not show this, it shows the terminus as being Central Secretariat."

"This train definitely goes to Mandi House; I've taken it there myself."

They laugh, and the man says, "So the line goes where it says it doesn't go yet."

"Yes, the maps are not able to keep up," I say, with great authority.

The Metro operates at two levels on the landscape: It is both history and fortune-telling.

RUPALI

For Rupali, the worst day to ride in the ladies' coach is on Karva Chauth, the festival when Hindu women fast for their husbands' longevity and a day that has also become an occasion for dressing up and partying. Rupali says, "Their hands are covered in henna, and their *dupattas* are flying everywhere as they try to negotiate the crowds and where to hold on."

One woman that day asked her in Hindi, "So, where are you traveling to?" This question could be taken as code for, "When will you be vacating your seat?"

"Green Park," Rupali said, but then relented with, "You want to sit?"

"Definitely!" the woman cried and took the seat with a sense of triumph.

The ladies' coach does not always represent female solidarity so much as accommodation and at times conflict. Another way to look at it is that the ladies' coach is not merely a container for women; rather, it allows them to enact their own urban practice.

Rupali rides the Metro each day from north Delhi to her job as a teacher in south Delhi. She also likes to read stories about Metro happenings in the *Times of India*. For her the Metro is not just something she rides but is a total social experience that encompasses how she sees and interprets the city: the running of the trains and the running commentary about the trains. There was the time, for instance, when a girl was sitting with her boyfriend in the ladies' coach. As the coach got more crowded with each stop, women started to ask the boyfriend to leave the coach and give them the seat. His girlfriend was defiant, however, and put her hand on his shoulder, not letting him get up. The girlfriend told the women to go to another coach to get a seat; she defended her boyfriend's right to sit there. Then the Metro police arrived on the scene, and the boyfriend got up right away.

And then there is the young couple Rupali notices every morning walking to her own Metro station. She's never talked to them, but by watching them each morning, she speculates that they are newlyweds living in a joint family, and that the few minutes' walk to the station each morning is their alone time. It's in their gestures and the way they look at each other, she tells me.

A recurring theme in Rupali's stories: that women don't always act as one might expect them to on the Metro. "I think people think Metro is for 'relax'; it's my space and if I adjust for someone else, it takes away my privacy."

"So, in the bus there's more of a sense of community and the Metro is more anonymous?" I ask.

"Yes, but not so anonymous; the same people ride the Metro every day. Women who were in my coach yesterday, I see them the next day and the next but with no smile, nothing; you are there, I am here, fine. Very few women begin to talk to each other. Colleagues will talk to each other. Everybody is busy with their own things, but people are reading more, especially girls are reading books, newspapers, and ones from that day only, not old papers.

"One day I asked a lady who was riding from Noida with me at what time her morning paper arrives. In my flat it comes at seven thirty, so it comes after I've left, and so I read the newspaper in the evening. This lady told me she requested the newspaper-wala to deliver her paper at six, so she waits at the gate of her complex and takes the paper and then goes into the Metro. She tells me that she is a schoolteacher in Dwarka and likes to get an update of what's happening since she has to post something new on the memo board at her school where she teaches. I see her quite regularly now."

Women in the ladies' coach, in Rupali's view, are not so much sisterly as territorially inclined, never willing to give up a seat, even to another woman who is much older or visibly pregnant. And it's true that the real value of the ladies' coach, beyond the certainty that no one will touch you inappropriately, is the ability to get a seat. The ladies' coach is not just a safe space for women but is also a numbers game. You can almost always get a seat more easily in the ladies' coach than in a general coach. And when the ladies' coach is filled up, women traveling together will expand the seating space by sometimes sitting on each other's laps. For longer commutes, getting a seat is key, some might say sport. Once procured a seat will likely never be given up.

Then there are also people who should take a seat but don't. Rupali explains, "One time I was very surprised, there was one lady, and she works in somebody's house, pretty well dressed, but we could tell what kind of job she has."

"If she was well dressed, how could you tell?"

"The way she was talking and the way she was talking to her friend, her language, her Hindi diction. Certain words she was using to make fun of the lady she was working for. Not crude but making fun of every member in the family. She was like, 'When she gets up, she says this this

Figure 11. Jangpura station platform, Violet Line, 2016. Pink hanging signboards and floor decals direct women where to stand to enter the ladies' coach.

this and then her daughter gets up and she has all these tantrums: I want this, I want that.' But this girl she stood all the way from Rajiv Chowk to Gurgaon; she did not sit and there were one or two empty seats, and I indicated to her, 'That seat is empty,' and she kind of looked around and had a funny expression on her face that said, 'No, I'm fine like this, this is my space, not there.' They feel like they just don't belong; the Metro doesn't belong to them; it's not their right."

Rupali rides the Metro each day to Saket, where she works as a teacher. She had been living in north Delhi previously, but then moved to east Delhi, so she could afford to live in a nicer housing society. She found one just a few minutes' walk from the Mayur Vihar station. She prefers only to commute by Metro although she sees the system as having a decidedly upper-class air.

Sometimes she'll describe the "disconnect" she feels as compared to when she used to commute by car: "You're not on the road, so you don't *see* anything." Rupali prefers the Metro to the road, even if this memory is nostalgic for a kind of street that may never have existed. Maybe her nostalgia is about the interface between the road and everyday life. Maybe the Metro is at a remove, even though it creates a new kind of social space in the city, with new forms of camaraderie. Maybe she doesn't remember the feeling of being stuck.[5]

And then she says this about the road: "We are able to see what people are doing, what they're selling, what crowd is there, shops and all that. Metro's a total disconnect."

Still, Rupali says that she likes the patch from Mandi House to her flat near Mayur Vihar-I station, going over the Yamuna with the Akshardham temple complex in the background. "You don't even need to visit Akshardham," she tells me, "since you have seen it from the Metro."

Rupali compares the social divisions on the Metro to the ones in her housing society in east Delhi. "It's very divided in terms of communities, lots of Banias, Aggrawals, few Brahmins, two Muslim families; but no one mixes up with anyone. Lots of Bengalis, but they do their own functions and all that. A little South Indian community; they all stick together. Another big divide: whether you're an owner or not. 'You don't own it? Oh, I see.' My neighbor, educated, balanced, works for the BBC, but then asks me, 'Why do you have such a big place if you are single?' You don't need a proper kitchen; you must not eat or shop for groceries. You're basically no one."

Sometimes Rupali longs to be in Mussoorie, the hill station where she grew up and might retire to one day. But then she says, "When I think about leaving Delhi, my heart shrinks."

CHIEF MINISTER

"Our experience was this: Give it to the experts, let them do it, let there not be interference, and this is what I think we developed," the late Sheila Dikshit (1938–2019) told me in 2015 about the role of the Delhi government in the Metro's construction. Dikshit, who served three consecutive terms as chief minister of Delhi from 1998 to 2013, was the politician most associated with the Metro being built. I had contacted one of her secretaries to ask if I could meet with her, and after a few weeks of back and forth by phone, I was given a date and time to come to her house in Nizamuddin East, one of the more elegant colonies in the city. To reach her red-brick house, I got down from an auto rickshaw and followed the boundary wall of the gardens around Humayun's Tomb. After passing through the security stall in front of her house, I went up a flight of stairs where she greeted me inside, dressed in a light-colored sari and white cardigan, with her gray hair pulled back into her signature bun.

"I've been to the Paris Métro, I've seen the London Metro," Dikshit told me, once we were seated on a sofa in the large sitting room at the front of the house. Delhi's Metro was comparable to these iconic systems, in her view, if not more modern. "It's clean and you don't find people misbehaving. It's just the ambience of it all." The Metro was about transport—"quick transport, clean transport, good transport, reliable transport"—but it has also contributed toward a "cultural change." Like many in Delhi's power elite, Dikshit found this to be a welcome aspect of all the technology. The Metro would make Delhi better.

Dikshit had lost the chance for a fourth term as chief minister when in 2013 she and the Congress Party were defeated by the Aam Aadmi ("Common Man's") Party leader, Arvind Kejriwal. This was a stinging defeat for her, one fueled by the Anna Hazare anticorruption movement that emphasized a more grounded understanding of "the people."

When I visited her in February 2015, it happened to be during the aftermath of her party's most recent electoral defeat in the Delhi elections. She was not cheerful that day, and I couldn't help thinking it must have been a reminder of her personal loss two years earlier. Yet I could also see her resolve as we started to talk about her role in the making of the Metro. She impressed upon me that the Delhi government did not benefit from the Metro. The physical facilities the Metro required—land, power, enough water—all that was *given* by the Delhi government. What her office did was provide the services required to run an efficient system.

"The Metro project had been going on for at least a decade before I came into office," she began. "Implementation came when Congress came. As a local government we did not go into the nitty-gritty of the Metro's construction, you know, where they're getting what and whatever, but if power had to be supplied, we had to ensure they got a dedicated power. When the Metro started running, Delhi's power situation was much better than it had been, but it was not absolutely reliable. Power would be inconsistent, so that had to be ensured; we helped with that. Whatever may happen, you can't have a power breakdown in a Metro train."

We were on our second cup of chai by now, and I had been dipping into a plate of cookies on the low coffee table between us. There was a constant sideshow being managed by her aides, of others wanting to meet her, of people coming in and out, but this didn't seem to break her concentration.

"Then, there were some residential areas, for instance, on Pusa Road, where the residences were coming in the way of the Metro. There were lots of people, tens of families, all of whom were naturally worried about where they would go; they had to be given an alternative, and that was provided by us. People who lived there went into DDA (Delhi Development Authority) flats which were lying empty; they were shifted there. In east Delhi, there were a whole lot of *jhuggi jhopris*, sort of semi-structures (squatter colonies).[6] The people living there had to be relocated, so we did that, we organized that, and shifted them so they were as near as possible. They agreed to leave because they knew the Metro was coming. That was not the case with the *sabzi mandi* (vegetable market) shops; that is still not sorted out."

Now she stopped and went into another room to take one of the many phone calls that had been coming in. I sat in the white-walled sitting room and imagined her circling it when no one was around. She had told me she did her daily walk here, inside.

"We had a lot of glitches, also," she said when she returned a good ten minutes later. "But please remember one thing: In a congested city like Delhi, lots of things were done beforehand. The Metro people worked very efficiently; everything was bang on time. What is worrying me now is the maintenance of stations; it's not up to what we would like it to be as citizens of this city."

Dikshit never let anyone forget that she was not just a politician but a Delhi citizen herself. She often recounted how she rode a bicycle as a girl growing up in Delhi and took buses as a college student. The message was about transport and how the city had dramatically changed from when she was a child, but it was also about her own liberal upbringing and what it meant to be an upper-middle-class woman still in touch with everyday urban life. In interviews and her 2018 memoir, she describes how her husband proposed to her on one of those buses.[7]

"Transport in a city like Delhi is very critical," she said. "It's primary. If you look at Delhi today you see the traffic jams; this is in spite of the fact that you have got a public transport system. Now, can you imagine Delhi without this public transport system? Impossible, you wouldn't be able to move! Metro is one of the essential requirements of any metropolitan city. Delhi has a density of population that is about the highest in the country. Then you have people coming in from Noida, from Gurgaon, from as far away as Meerut. Delhi is a growing, ever-moving city, which is always requiring something new, something innovative, something to meet the challenges. Transport is a great challenge."

Then she added, "We used to go to college in the fifties and sixties, chugging along in a DTC (Delhi Transport Corporation) bus and that was good enough. Today that can't be done. Vishwavidyalaya is absolutely jam-packed."

When Dikshit took office, dealing with the city's traffic jams was one of her priorities. She oversaw the building of flyovers all across the city, which helped car traffic flow but also permanently bifurcated and dwarfed surrounding neighborhoods. She also supported the move to switch from diesel fuel to compressed natural gas, which for some years improved the city's pollution levels.[8] She was for the Metro, but also, for a time, the more controversial Bus Rapid Transit corridor. Later she would claim to have changed the face of the city in her three terms as chief minister. She had also become the face of the city.

Dikshit saw herself as the city's promoter but also protector when it came to the Metro. "There were difficulties in coordination with other agencies, urban development, DDA, Delhi government, and ultimately the Committee," she said. "But I must say that Delhi's Metro is an example for everywhere. Compare ours to Bangalore, Calcutta; those systems didn't go past a point. It's only in Delhi that it went on and on and on. You see the Metro practically covering the whole of Delhi; then it went to Noida, then to Gurgaon. At first, I was a little skeptical, you're spreading it all over, it's *Delhi's* Metro. You're spreading it, it's very convenient, but don't do it at the cost of Delhi, financially and otherwise."

Transport was one of the many areas where there were "no full stops," a favorite expression of Dikshit's to emphasize how the city's growth means that its problems and challenges will never end, only evolve, and thus always require new solutions.

"There are people who may not be able to afford the Metro," she admitted, "but ninety percent of the people are able to afford it. These kinds of public transports do bring equalization. I travel in my car as an individual, but if I travel in a public transport then I meet all kinds of people, rub shoulders with everybody. There are no distinctions whether you are earning this or that. Now if a man going to office in the Metro is the same as the laborer going in the Metro, it's a great equalizer; it's one of its great contributions. Metro is a social binder, a public good. Have you heard of any incident which is unpleasant as far as the Metro is concerned? So, it must be just fine. There is speed, there is cleanliness, there is time."

CITY OF MALLS

On the way to Rithala, a large mall comes into view from the train; its faded colors stand out in the otherwise brownish landscape. Once outside the station, at the end of the line, cycle rickshaw drivers ferry people between the Metro and the mall. They ride up to the entrance of the vast parking lot of the mall but are not allowed entry beyond this point, where a few security guards are assembled. The cycle rickshaw, with its squeaky metal parts, and the driver in his dirty clothes, are antithetical to the space of the mall, where heavy-set women in salwar kameez, and young boys and girls in jeans, come to stroll. The shops are ice cold. And there might be more shop assistants than customers.

The mall is adjacent to an "Adventureland" amusement park, and at first it is hard to tell where the mall ends and the park begins. A narrow pedestrian bridge crosses a small fake lake. Outdoor food stalls sell popcorn and "authentic" *chaat*, street food. Mechanical rides rise up toward the horizon. On the mall side, amid one of the concrete concourses, there's an island of short green grass, a lawn not more than three feet by five feet, demarcated by a raised concrete curb. A gardener, the *mali*, sits crouched there, rubbing dirt between his aged fingers as he tends to the sprouts.

I walk the length of the parking lot to the outer entrance, past the security guards to the waiting cycle rickshaw drivers. From here there's a direct view to the Metro, a concrete edifice extending across the skyline. Between the mall and the Metro lies a large construction site. A cycle rickshaw-wala tells me, with a mixture of awe and disdain, that the half-made structure in front of us is to be a five-star hotel. Some of these hotels as well as IT parks are owned and being built by the DMRC itself, which has to diversify in order to maintain its own fiscal sustainability.

Meanwhile, this new India, the spaces of consumption of both goods and experience, are for the moneyed classes, professionals, and aspirers. It is true that Metro stations have created desirable routes for cycle rickshaws, and that drivers sometimes earn a few rupees more per kilometer than they are used to as they ply back and forth between Metro and mall. As it turns out, they too are part of *Delhi's Master Plan for 2021*, page 149 of the "Reader Friendly" version; it points out that unlike other forms of transport, they are nonpolluting. But ultimately the place of cycle rickshaw drivers is only being reinscribed on the new urban landscape as they encircle more spaces to which they are not allowed entry.

VIOLET LINE

Outside Mandi House station, Monika and Sushmita, two Kathak dancers in their early twenties, explain how they travel by Metro for their rehearsals on nearby Baghwan Das Road. They're from the northwest of the city. Besides the time-saving and sun-protecting aspects of the Metro, they tell me, they also just like riding it.

"We're dancers so we like to watch people. We observe them. But if we're alone, then phone, long live the phone!"

"If we're going to a new place we look at the map and the app. We love Mandi House; we like to sit here; it's a place for artists."

"This city is good but there is a lot of competition in every field. This city never stops; everybody is always working. Even physically if you're not working, mentally you're working. Dreams are always going. In Delhi, yes, you can achieve your dreams. We can visualize it can happen. It will take time, but it's possible."

Farther south on the Violet Line at Lajpat Nagar, the central market is flanked by Metro construction, squeezed really. Two yellow-helmeted construction workers bob their heads over the light blue Metro construction wall to bargain with a market seller. They move their hands toward a hanger and haggle, just like everyone else. Behind them tall orange cranes reach toward the sky, moving mounds of dust and gravel that will one day make this an interchange station with the Pink Line.

From Lajpat Nagar station, the Violet Line is all aboveground and makes a wide arc. You start being able to see the ISKCON and Baha'i Lotus Temples, red and white respectively against an expansive green park. It's like you're on a monorail, slowly panning the city at a close distance. Then you wrap around to Nehru Place station, filled with shops and a food court, mirroring the hustle and bustle of the electronics market across the street, where you go to get your cracked phone screen repaired, buy printer cartridges, laptop cords, and pairs of socks. Between the station and the market is a movie multiplex showing the latest Hindi feature films. People getting on and off at Nehru Place station are smartly dressed in slacks and shirts, men and women. At the station, you can get a Starbucks coffee, a French croissant, an American donut.

Toward Okhla, the view becomes more industrial. One can peer down into people's homes or across to people's rooftops. Kites bob in the sky. There is a stop for Apollo Hospital, which aims to look like a hotel. The hospital surroundings are bleak, empty stretches of brown landscape, but there is an attractive, manicured garden right next to it. From the Metro, the Apollo looks less like an oasis and more like a mirage.

At Sarita Vihar station, large enterprises line either side of Mathura Road. The main lane adjacent to the road is reserved for car showrooms: Toyota, Maruti Suzuki, and then an elegant glass cube of a building for Aston Martin on the one side and Rolls Royce on the other. In one view, you're able to see the city's hierarchy of transport from the cycles and buses on the road to the Metro to the cars in these showroom windows.

On the way to Tughlakabad, an imposing, dramatic sight: the Badarpur Thermal Power Station with its two gigantic candy-striped exhausts. The structure takes over the landscape the rest of the way.

At Badarpur, the station exits onto a major road where several buses are lined up. The station is hemmed in by the two-tier roadway to one side and a parking lot full of motorbikes on the other. Helmets are being sold outside the station, along with ice cream and *gol gappas*. A man is allowing his toddler to piss into the parking lot. There's a small covered area with a sign reading "free saplings" for people to take and plant elsewhere. One young man sifts through them, trying to find one in good condition.

I meet Madhu, who travels to Badarpur on the Violet Line each weekend to visit her parents, something she's been doing since her wedding day. She lives with her husband, their baby, and her in-laws in Karol Bagh, while her parents live in Faridabad, a half hour from the end of the Violet Line. Faridabad is a much better place than Delhi, Madhu tells me, since there is less traffic and less commotion.

Madhu doesn't only visit her parents by Metro, she travels all over the city on it to see clients, since she works as a freelance physical therapist and also does contract work with the Indian government as a doping tester for athletes. It's on the Metro where she learns about the latest fashions: "You're not going to see this on the bus, you're going to see it on the Metro, that a blue kurta is going to be with a yellow pajama. The rings, the solitaires, the haircuts, nail art." But it's also where she makes the following reflection:

"Indians are taking on Western culture. We are not into Indian culture anymore. Changing culture is there; life is so rushy. We're adapting to a more Western culture which is more comfortable for us; standard of living we're learning from them. It's helping us. In a sari, you can't run in the Metro."

There's a kind of lament as Madhu explains the dichotomy she sees through what people wear in the ladies' coach of the Metro. Yes, Western clothing styles may help women move more quickly through the space of the Metro system, but this is a transactional, practical modernity in her view.

"The first time I took the Metro, I thought, oh god, it's a/c, it's running so fast, it's so convenient. Now I know every route I have to go; I'm independent on it. The ladies' coach is not too rushy. I get a seat; it's easy for me to be there."

But there is a drawback: The Metro is making people more impatient. They assume everything in their lives should appear in a five-minute framework, just like an approaching train, says Madhu. "The Metro makes people more rushed even though it saves them time. People fall on the station stairs, flip-flip-flip-flip." So, there is a consequence to all this rushing around, a potential collapse, or just falling flat.

One time, while on "doping duty" in Gurgaon, Madhu tells me how she only "got free" close to midnight. "I was in too much of a rush. Gurgaon is not safe. From a safety point of view, at night nothing is safe actually." That night she was dropped at the Guru Dronacharya station on the Yellow Line and reached Rajiv Chowk just as the last metro on the Blue Line was leaving. There were a few young men as well as three or four policemen at the station. "One guy approaches me and asks, Where do you want to go? I told him, Karol Bagh. He asks, Can you share an auto with me? He keeps waiting to see if I'll say yes." She finally tells him her husband is picking her up. She stays in the station to wait for him.

"That guy was still waiting, and when my husband arrives, he asks again if he can share the car with us. Part of me wanted to give him a ride, that's human nature. But driving in the night in the city with a stranger; it's not an option. Metro is safe, but when you get down, it's not at all safe."

METAL AND PLASTIC

In an auto rickshaw stopped at a red light, a bicycle wheel bumps into us from one side. A motorcycle driver is looking from the other side, through his shaded plastic protector. You don't know if he's ogling you or just looking, like you are at him.

APPROPRIATE ARCHITECTURE

One morning I take the Yellow Line to Chhatarpur station, which is south of south Delhi but comes before Gurgaon. The city peters out by the time you get to Chhatarpur, as the built environment recedes into the foliage. That's not to say there is no built environment here; there is, just of a different kind. A reddish-orange statue of the monkey-god Hanuman towers above the expansive Chhatarpur temple complex. Less visible are the many "farmhouses" in the surrounding area, large and small estates where some of the richest Delhiites live. These homes may include acres of gardens, walking paths, swimming pools, multiple-car garages, on-site sub-housing for armies of cooks, cleaners, housekeepers, nannies, gardeners, guards, and more. The structures can be low and unassuming from the road, but when you get behind their gates, you find private villa-like oases that soak up the fertile lands of the urban periphery. The Delhi Development Authority gives special dispensations and permits for building on these "agricultural lands," ones that allow owners to develop "farmlands" into country homes.

I descend from the elevated station and get into an auto rickshaw to travel the fifteen minutes to Vasant Kunj, an upper-middle-class colony northwest of Chhatarpur. I am to meet Preeti Bahadur, an architect whose firm built one of the early Metro stations when the DMRC made a point to hire local, Indian architects. The tendering process for station design changed in 2009, however, after a construction beam meant to support the elevated Metro track came crashing down in Zamrudpur in south Delhi. It was a catastrophic accident; seven construction workers and an engineer were killed; fifteen others were injured. It was not the first Metro construction accident, but it certainly was one of the worst and most dramatic in terms of how the pillar collapsed. Metro project manager E. Sreedharan resigned because of the incident, citing his moral responsibility, although he was reinstated within days of the accident by then Delhi chief minister Sheila Dikshit. Most significantly, the DMRC publicly attributed the accident to a design deficiency. The portion of the viaduct had been designed and constructed by the Mumbai firm Gammon India, which went on to be blacklisted by the DMRC for two years. Soon after, the Japanese International Cooperation Agency, which is the development institution that evaluates the Delhi Metro project and administers the multi-billion-dollar loan from Japan to India, inserted a clause stating that international consultants had to be engaged in the engineering of viaducts and the architecture of stations.[9]

Yet Indian-owned architecture firms are still central to the process of designing Metro stations, because once the foreign architects leave, it is the job of locally owned architecture firms to complete the design detail, that is to say, to make the designs fit with DMRC specifications. Bahadur's

firm is involved in this process. When, in 2013, I asked DMRC chief architect Papiya Sarkar about the post-2009 change in the tender process, she
explained, "The problem is the expats are here for a year, then plans are
left with local Indian firms who don't feel the plans are theirs."[10]

When I reach Bahadur's office, she leads me through the residence-like
building, where young women and men sit in front of computers and work
over large tables across several connected rooms. Bahadur, in a stylish salwar kameez, is both warm and professional, and we eventually come to sit
at her desk.

"Indian contractors quote low," she starts, "they can't do all the fancy
stuff," but foreign architects make the designs "too complex" and "use the
wrong materials" for the Indian climate, such as perforated metal.

"The foreigners do the floors very well and are good at the passenger
flow figures," she concedes. Beyond that, their designs, in her view, are "a
disaster" in terms of how their design requirements would be serviced.
Bahadur's use of pointed vocabulary such as "Indian" and "foreigners" creates a binary based on national origin that seemed to go against the transnational ethos of the Metro's construction, and yet she was talking from
her experience of the daily work of design.

She pulls up the designs on her desktop computer of one French architect's vision for a Metro station in Mumbai that she's currently working
on. These were station designs the French firm had given her, where the
roofs were in the shape of a diamond, a peacock, and a temple. It was hard
not to miss the symbolism in these intricate, material representations
of "Indian culture." The shapes had a museum-like quality to them, at a
remove from their usual contexts and put into the infrastructural space
of the Metro. Before I can react, Bahadur, with a mix of satisfaction and
frustration, says, "They all got scrapped. Too elaborate." And then: "When
a foreigner comes to India, they see cows and bulls and want to represent
this in their idea of India. We are trying to make our stations more urban,
with the use of more glass, for instance. The French designers want to use
concrete *jaalis* [lattice work], but the DMRC just nixes it, since pigeons
will come and crap all over it again and again. You must see what works
for Indian realities. You should see the way they visualize India."

Bahadur's critique of the Orientalizing tendencies of the European
architect in India was not just about the symbols being created but also

the materials being used. In her reading, the French designs were of the past, and she wanted to design for the future. She saw a station not as a monument in space but rather a living place through time. "A station should be functional," she explains. "The focus should be on issues of maintenance, being leakproof, how to clean the glass."

She then shows me a station design full of glass panels and says, "Who will clean them? They were scrapped." And then the jagged, crisscrossed metal of one Spanish-designed station that was straightened or scrapped.

"They are good architects," Bahadur insists, "but not appropriate for India."

Bahadur's own vision is one that embraces the local through a global idiom of urban sustainability. Her idea is that as global as the Delhi Metro may be, it must still rely on local materials and sensibilities, on an architecture that is in tune with not only the atmosphere and climate of the city, but one knowledgeable about the resources that would go into maintaining the station and system in the years to come.

Her vision of a sustainable, urban India is also an industrial, mass-produced one, with its reliance on materials such as glass and steel. The fact that the foreign architect plans did not in the end get implemented is only a partial victory, if one at all, since the work left to Bahadur and her firm is not visionary but, as she puts it, "tedious." She could correct the foreigner's plans but she could not envision them anew.

I come to see that Bahadur's idea of "the urban" is grounded in the desire for sustainability and knowledge of local context. The issue is not her nationality nor the Europeans', but rather the longer-term, more entrenched understanding of a place and its people. The idea of what is "easier to clean" or maintain is really a recognition of not only the climate but also the kinds of labor necessary to keep up different materials and how they are used, of reproducibility and cost-effectiveness. The regularity and inevitability of the crapping birds propels Bahadur's own vision of an environmental awareness based on material conditions and requirements. On the one hand, Bahadur sees many more restraints in her Metro work as compared to her firm's other projects. On the other hand, she believes the Delhi Metro contributes to a larger cause, one that will take time. She applauds the Delhi Metro project manager E. Sreedharan's ability and vision to get the Metro up and running.

"Now," she concedes, "is the time to build a network," and then, somewhat to my surprise, adds, "We can always redo the stations later."

CHAWRI BAZAR

The Metro's undergroundness does the most service as you cross Old Delhi, the sixteenth-century Mughal heart of the city. On the Yellow Line, I get off at Chawri Bazar, which was originally the deepest station. The DMRC calls this station the "time machine" to emphasize the contrast of the high-tech boring machine used to dig so deep into the earth with the centuries-old structures aboveground. It's a long way up on multiple escalators.

I emerge from the engineering marvel and the clean lines of the station into a thick landscape of vendors, vehicles, and crumbling façades, where electrical cords hang from above and wires are strewn across the sky, where linen and suits hang from people's homes, and cycle rickshaw wheels clash with scooters, pedestrians, and each other. The station funnels people into the bazaar, where people walk every which way. Others enter the station to go somewhere else entirely. Two different styles of order meet each other as people come out of the station and into the market. I look for a cycle rickshaw but then decide to walk.

I meet Amit, who commutes to Chawri Bazar from Green Park each day. He works in a hardware shop that has been there since 1938. The shop is on the same traffic circle where the Metro exits are located. "Inquiry counter *ho gaya*," he tells me, referring to the fact that people coming in and out of the station continuously stop to ask him for directions. "There is so much traffic, then there are jams," he adds. Yes, with this much traffic, there are jams. We look at the swirling cars, cycle rickshaws, carts, and bicycles going around Chawri Bazar, each with a distinctive honk. Then, as an afterthought, Amit says, "With the Metro, the commute has become easy for all of us."

A few shops down, Vinod and Lokesh sit at their electronics shop. They are older and stoic compared to Amit. Their shop has been in the same spot for forty years. It is a skinny sliver in the wall. Lokesh sits in a large

Figure 12. Chawri Bazar station entrance, Yellow Line, 2009. The Metro connects, as do the clumped, spooled, and crisscrossing wires pictured here.

crevice with his legs propped up on the counter. Vinod sits on a stool on the sidewalk. They share these thoughts with me: With the Metro, time is saved. In a jam, peace is received.

Crossing the narrow lanes, I soak up this hectic and huddled urbanism. These old parts of cities, no matter the city, fit the definitions of "the urban" so well. They have the requisite density of people and commercial establishments, where everyone seems dependent on everyone else, and it all seems to be going so well. These areas also have the design elements of cities that have been thought out over long stretches of time. From the redstone Jama Masjid, devotees see the Red Fort, and from the Red Fort they look down on Chandni Chowk, and that was exactly the sixteenth-century point, a triangular compact between religion, politics, and commerce.

Now there are two Metro lines that cross the length of Old Delhi, the Yellow and the Violet, the latter of which is known as the "Heritage Line." The station interiors on this portion play up the old city façades. They are all underground stations, framed above by a wide stainless-steel band across an elongated triangle, popping up like spikes in the old city. At Lal Quila (Red Fort) station, the entrance juts out of the road to make a sharp entry point. Across the road, at the commercial center of the old city, Chandni Chowk abuts a small temple laced with ringing crimson bells. You exit the station and you are in it: uneven steps, the stench of garbage; two men at war over a car door snagged on a motorbike handle. In the shadow of the station, the smell of alcohol rises like vapor from two men sound asleep. The glass panels of the Metro station reflect the red sandstone of the older buildings and the dense, looping traffic. Workers and rickshaw drivers sit chatting on steel benches that form part of the station façade.

On a different day, I take the Metro to Chawri Bazar with a group of visiting poets from China. We walk in the lanes and then come to Red Fort. The best known of these poets, someone who brought literary salvation to the masses in the years after Tiananmen Square, is intrigued by the old city, but tells me he expected it to be cleaner and "more developed." I come to see he has a particular vision and perhaps experience of what "city" means. In the old city, where I feel particularly "in it," the urban and all it can and has meant, he seems to see the city as a future goal or destination. I decide that there's no point in defending the Indian city.

AJAY AND GITA

Ajay and Gita are hiding out at a Love Commandos safe house for inter-caste couples on the run. Ajay is a compact and energetic twenty-five-year-old, clean-shaven and earnest. Gita, who is twenty-one, seems shy at first with a slight, sweet voice, but this comportment changes once she, too, begins animatedly to describe their predicament. Theirs was a "caste problem," Ajay explains. They come from the same district in Haryana, but he is from a lower caste, she from a higher one. The way he describes it, his voice low and intent, Gita is a Jat, a dominant caste in the Punjabi subcaste schema, while he comes from a lower caste that works with wood, *lakadee ka kaam*. Gita chimes in using the English word, "carpenter."

These words and designations are meant to create a distance between them, but they seem to have the opposite effect. They seem to be part of their intimacy, of their acceptance of each other. Ajay and Gita met at a government polytechnic college in Haryana. They were classmates, "sitting on the same bench," studying for a diploma in electronics and communications. They were friends and then their friendship became love—*pyaar hua*. Theirs is a story of love, aspiration, and a pivotal moment on the Delhi Metro.

Ajay says, "I don't know exactly when our friendship got converted to love and went to a higher level. There was no scope for any physical relationship. It was a matter of the heart. Our families do not understand that love is something that happens in the heart, they think it is only physical love." Gita jumps ahead, "First we tried so hard to get our families to accept us. 'Just accept us, accept us,' we said, 'Let us get married in a good way.'"

Ajay's plan had been to wait two years before getting married to Gita, so he could secure a good job. "But her people," Ajay explains, "once they came to know about us, they had another idea." This other idea was to get her married to another boy.

Ajay continues, "They wanted to push her out of the house. They found someone else for her in a matter of ten days—not even. In that many days they found a boy whose background they did not even know, and whether he is good or bad, they were ready to send her away with him." Ajay emphasizes the "ten days," again and again. Now he is indignant. In love's computations, time equals familiarity: This other boy equals ten days, while Ajay and Gita equal four years.

"He was someone my father met, but I did not meet him," explains Gita about the boy her family wants her to marry. "You see, he had a government job and some land." Was this boy also a Jat, like Gita? Ajay interjects, "Yes, same caste, meaning a mentality that he has land, money, that he's rich, even if he has committed four murders or some other crimes. That's the mentality."

Where caste was a problem in relation to Ajay marrying Gita, it was now a "mentality" that enabled Gita's parents to foist this other boy on their daughter. What is essentially a financial deficit in Ajay's profile becomes understood as a "caste mentality."

Gita says, "My parents did my engagement with this other boy and printed marriage cards, without asking me, for the same day as my older sister was to get married. They trashed the old cards and just printed both our names together on new cards."

Now it is Gita's turn to be indignant. Her future seems to hinge on the phrasing of a wedding card, and it is the manner in which her parents quite literally wrest control over her life's narrative. It is at this point that Ajay obtains information on the internet ("*net pe*") about the Love Commandos. He gets in touch with them and describes his and Gita's predicament of one, being locked up by their families; two, having their cell phones taken away; and three, being threatened physically.

Days before the wedding, Gita goes with her mother to get fitted for her wedding clothes at a market in Bahadurgarh where they are supposed to meet her aunt.

"Once there," she explains, "I took my mother's phone and pretended to call my aunt." She then gets out of her mother's sight on the pretense of looking for her aunt. Following Ajay's instructions, she makes her way to the Mundka station, the last stop on the Green Line. An array of jeeps, vans, and buses wait outside the station, ferrying passengers to and from the Haryana border. Gita meets Ajay at Mundka as planned, and they buy tokens and get on the train. Ajay is familiar with the Metro, but it is Gita's first time, though she is too worried about being followed to notice it much. She speaks to her father on the mobile, saying she cannot find her mother and so she is coming home, when she is actually on the Metro with Ajay, going away and not coming home.

"We first go to Inderlok," Ajay explains, "and then change lines and go to Rajiv Chowk." He pauses for a bit, and then admits, "It didn't leave us with a good feeling to have left our families in this way. But their mentality is a little different. Here we have made a new family, found new brothers and sisters."

Thinking about the future, Ajay says that now he has to get back on his feet. This means getting a job. He had received a diploma in junior engineering from the polytechnic. He also wants to try again to convince the families to relent, even though Gita's family has in the meantime filed a kidnapping case against him. On a more somber note, he adds, "If they don't accept us, we will start our life separate from them."

RING ROAD

As a child, as I held hands tightly with a parent or uncle, I never knew how we'd get across the fast-moving lines of honking traffic on the Ring Road, and then before I knew it we were getting across and not getting hit and arriving on the other side. This was before there was a traffic light between the two parts of the market, which came later, and before there was a pedestrian underpass, which came later still, and made the crossing easy and not treacherous at all.

In 2016 half of Ring Road as it passes through South Ex is a construction site. Metro construction is hacking its way down Ring Road and through the Part I and II markets. Even the massive storefronts have been diminished, covered in dust. "Sale" signs droop down. Not only is parking nearly impossible, there is almost nowhere to walk. It is a full-scale turnover. Cars are at a crawl. SUVs stalk the lanes. They have shiny metal surfaces, smart trims, leather seats. Their passengers sit high.

On the Ring Road the traffic stream has been cinched to one side of the road and rerouted into and out of the colony on the Part II side. I walk across the high footover-bridge they have made for the construction site, so people can still cross back and forth between the two parts of the market. The underground pedestrian subway has long been closed, since that is where the Metro will come up. On this high, temporary footbridge, one has a bird's-eye view of the construction site. Huge yellow tractors move rocks and lift mounds of dirt. Layers of brick, concrete, and earth are exposed on the sides of the large trough where the station will be. To look down below on either side, the construction site is an ordered underbelly to the congested thoroughfare. Below are only shades of brown, from the cream-colored concrete planks to beige mounds of dirt. You don't actually hear any construction, only the traffic whizzing and honking below. A worker sits on metal rods neatly clumped in rows, adding some symmetry and order to the great unearthing. There are squares upon squares and rectangles upon rectangles, some higher, some lower. Other workers squat amid piles of pipes, poles, and rods that have been mechanically arranged, deposited by machines and levers, soon to be installed and hoisted up. Stacked thin like bamboo, I can sense their weight in the straightness and seeming fixity on the ground, until more machines will come and move them around.

Figure 13. South Extension, Part II market Metro construction site, 2016. What looks like a split screen is actually a single frame and seamless reality.

Mega-construction disrupts cities, destruction before construction, but this site at South Ex is also a strange kind of oasis, at least from this angle above. The combination of the height and direct sun exposure is almost dizzying; I cross Ring Road as if on a high wire. I'm not sure if they should let people walk above and across like this. Still, the Ring Road, a place which never stops, has been forced to pause. Its depths have been plummeted and revealed. Once it is covered up and is all surface again we will forget it, and happily so, because then we will be going up and down escalators and marveling at the Metro once more. But for the moment, I walk above this pause, where there is an ongoing consideration of angles and dirt and depths and lengths.

GRIEVANCE AND GOVERNANCE

When I interviewed former Delhi chief minister Sheila Dikshit in 2015, she told me that if I really wanted to know how the Metro got built, meaning how various departments *didn't* sabotage the whole project, I should talk to P.K. Tripathi, who had been her right-hand man when she was chief minister.

When I go to meet Tripathi a month later, he is in a new post. He is the head of the Public Grievances Commission. Before we get to talking about the Metro, I am curious to ask him about his current post, one that I notice comes with a very large office. Anyone can come to this office to file a grievance, he tells me. We are in a constellation of buildings near the ITO junction on the west bank of the Yamuna River; much of the city's governance happens here.

The complaint can be against the Delhi state government, the police, the municipality, he goes on. The commission is not a court of law but rather an advisory board. Lawyers are not allowed; you have to come on your own. Lawyers charge fees, he says, and this can be costly.

This is a kind of people's platform then, though not a people's court. You cannot be in a dispute with anyone else, say, for instance, if your neighbor is making an illegal construction. That is for the civil courts. However, if you believe the municipal authorities are allowing illegal construction, you can come here and make a complaint against the municipality. There is a clarity to the office's purpose, what can and cannot be registered, that makes me think it must be very efficient.

Tripathi goes through a mental list of typical complaints: water delivery problems through pipes or tankers, polluted water, electricity problems, faulty building construction, illegal construction, encroachment on government land, poor condition of roads, parking conditions, missing manholes, caste certificates not getting issued on time. Then there are complaints against the police. We only take up the serious ones, he says, someone has been detained, someone has been beaten. First, we send a copy of the complaint to the department in question.

I come to see the commission as a kind of clearinghouse for complaints. "Whatever is doable, we take up," Tripathi says. "We do not want to step into *the place* of the government. There is a difference between advising and directing."

I sense the commission is more like the city's water pipes, with irregular flows, than the city's Metro system. Tripathi gives me such an example. One time, people living in Gautam Nagar came to make a complaint. Gautam Nagar is a low-income colony in south Delhi, sandwiched between high-income areas such as South Extension, Gulmohar Park, and Neeti Bagh. It's a seven-minute ride or fifteen-minute walk to the nearest Metro station at Green Park. Gautam Nagar residents made the following complaint: *Hamaare drain jo hain, theek nahin banae hain* (The drains in our area have not been built properly). It was a complaint that in essence said: We are not getting clean water; we are being flooded with dirty water. To fix the problem, many departments would have to become involved, and none of those departments were talking to each other. Nobody was coordinating.

Tripathi's first involvement with the Metro also had to do with water. At the time, in 2001–2, he was the head of the Delhi Jal (Water) Board. By this time, he said, the "ethos" was that all city agencies were to be working in the service of the Metro. "We were like service providers," he explained. "It's not that we were separate agencies so that we could throw our weight around." Everybody was coordinating.

"The message from the chief minister was clear: Metro has to come, so you must be positive, and you must find a solution. Sreedharan was a great engineer and a great administrator, there's no doubt about it, but the type of support he needed and got from the Delhi government was phenomenal. The whole administration was told that you don't have to quarrel with him; right or wrong, you have to ensure that the Metro work is not stopped or delayed."

Within this framework, there was an explicit agreement that agencies had to have meetings, not only arrange them, but show up at them and engage positively. Tripathi continues, "There was no question of 'no, no, no,' I don't have the time or I can't give this priority. This was to be the topmost priority. You have to prioritize it." If land was to be acquired, you acquired land; if pipes were to be moved, you moved the pipes. Whatever the Metro wanted was to be given, otherwise how would the Metro come to be? There was an understanding that engineering was one thing, and the Metro people were very good at that, but they couldn't be expected to acquire and move all that had to be acquired and moved. It was these potential delays that would have stopped the project at each and every turn. Tripathi says, "Our one-point mandate was that Metro has to come. So, all departments were given a very clear direction. There was a will."

Most of the coordination had to happen with the Delhi government, not the central government. This coordination included land acquisition (except for the lands controlled by the Delhi Development Authority, which works under the central government), water, sewer lines, traffic diversion, and power. "Some agencies did create some problems," Tripathi says, "they levied some taxes, but by and large, the Metro construction did not stop.

"This way of governing has not seeped into other areas, but for the Metro, it does continue. Metro brought a new system of maintenance. They will clean the tires of their construction trucks before sending them back on the road. Many good practices not seen before in Delhi were brought in. They brought in their own people to guide traffic, etc."

The Metro both relied on the city's infrastructures and had to alter them in order to establish a new infrastructure. If the water supply was disrupted due to Metro construction, for instance, tankers had to be brought in to deliver water to the affected locality.

"The biggest problem with Metro was, you lay the pipe," Tripathi explains, "they were able to do it, but then you have to restore the road, and that was often a problem because once you dig or make a tunnel then the whole area subsides. So, the road will also subside when the soil gets loosened. There were sometimes debates. The Metro was not best at everything, they were not experts in water, so sometimes when they laid a pipe, there were problems. For example, they would not do the finishing and then there might be a leakage. Everybody will blame Jal Board. The Metro had become so holy, which was necessary for it to get built, but they would blame you, what are you doing wrong? But we didn't blame the Metro, because that was internal. We wanted to ensure that everything goes on." And so, everybody was coordinating.

MORNING COMMUTE

It is one of those mornings where there's a backlog of men in the ladies' coach, and the women already sitting there keep telling the men to move ahead because this is the place for ladies. One man going past says, 'It's okay," but with a look that says, "What's the big deal?"

I'm standing next to Rita, who has a tight ponytail and is dressed in a black kurta top and straight black trousers. She practices commercial law, and this is her daily commute from Kailash Colony and she's going just one more stop to Jawaharlal Nehru Stadium station. Enough people get off with her so that some seats become free. I sit in one of them and start talking in Hindi to a young woman sitting next to me. She's in a simple churidar pajama set with a dupatta draped around her front. Her name is Neelam; she's twenty-years old and has taken a bus from Faridabad to Badarpur station. She's now on her way to Central Secretariat. Neelam works as a domestic servant for a family in Badarpur and is headed to AIIMS (All India Institute of Medical Sciences) to buy some medicine. The medicine is for her, not her employer, she tells me. I wonder if it's cheaper at AIIMS and so that's why she's traveling all the way to get it there, or if it's a prescription or specialized medicine that she can only get there. Without more of a rapport, I don't feel comfortable asking too much about her medicines or her health. She tells me that on the Metro, "Time waste *nahin hota hai*" (you don't waste time). This is something.

Then I'm sitting next to Smruti, who is forty-five years old and is going to Chandni Chowk to shop for salwar kameez suits. Before the Metro was there, she would take an auto or a "personal conveyance," which I take to mean a car but she also could mean a scooter or some other kind of two-wheeler. She thinks the Metro is very good. I also sense she's eager to get back to her phone.

On the other side of me, a woman's music is so loud it's seeping through her earbuds. A classic iPhone rings. One woman talks loudly to her phone about a five-thousand-rupee payment that has to be made. A kid sips from a red-striped water bottle in one hand and clutches a child-size umbrella in the other.

Renuka has gotten on at the end of the Violet Line in Badarpur. She is going to Vishwavidyalaya station, which means she'll have to change to the Yellow Line at Central Secretariat. She is studying for her bachelor's in communications at Hans Raj College, which is part of Delhi University. Renuka is not the typical B.Comm. student; she is thirty-three years old and has a child on her lap. She used to go to the university by car. I wonder what she will do with her child when she has to go to class or meet her professors, but I don't ask her this.

On the other side of Renuka is nineteen-year-old Naina. She also got on at Badarpur and is also a student, but she is going to Shahdara station. She'll have to change twice, first at Central Secretariat for the Yellow Line, and then at Kashmere Gate for the Red Line. She is studying Chemistry Honors at Shamil College. The Metro is convenient, Naina tells me, but when it's late, it's difficult.

As we approach Central Secretariat station, the PA system reminds us that luggage check-in is available at Shivaji Stadium and New Delhi Railway stations on the Orange Airport Express Line. In the shuffle of people getting on and off at this interchange station, I find myself sitting next to Urvashi. She is twenty-six and has come from Faridabad. She would have had to have taken another conveyance to get to Badarpur station, a bus, auto rickshaw, or car, most likely. She is going to Noida City Centre where she works in marketing at Ericsson. This means changing at Rajiv Chowk for the Blue Line.

"We can reach anywhere on time, the most important thing," Urvashi says to me. She is originally from Uttar Pradesh, though the "real" U.P., she tells me, not the part that Noida occupies. She did her B.Tech degree from Bareilly. I know this is a highly regarded engineering school and nod to her in recognition. When later at home I look up Ericsson, I see that it is located in Noida on Knowledge Boulevard. I also see that the Swedish communications giant has 24,495 employees in "South East Asia, Oceania and India," and that as of December 31, 2016, its overall "gender breakdown" of employees worldwide is 23 percent female and 77 percent male.[11] This happens to be about the same gender breakdown of the Delhi Metro ridership (25 percent female, 75 percent male).

Amudha is traveling in a general coach to get to the Blue Line interchange, though she is leaving work. She has already cooked for the day at a home in south Delhi. Her own home is in a Tamilian enclave in the working-class neighborhood of Trilokpuri in east Delhi. Residents near Trilokpuri are currently refusing to move, be displaced, halting the Metro construction from connecting two stations whose ends are hovering above the locality, she tells me. But Amudha is not one of those whose dwelling is imperiled. It would shatter her life to have to move, she says, a life completely built up around her network of friends and family. And then there are the repairs she's done to her house over the last few decades, the markets she goes to, the feeling of home and familiarity she has. When I ask her what *shahar*, city, means to her, she says, "My home, my commute." As the Blue Line expanded and extended, Amudha still took the bus to work every day; only recently has she started riding the Metro, and now she doesn't like to take the bus. She tells me in Hindi, "Before I'd been so afraid of the Metro; I avoided it. It was also expensive. For one thousand rupees a month, I could ride the bus unlimited."

Now she's used to the Metro and the time it saves her, and she only wants to take the Metro. She gets on whichever coach she can get a seat and then sits comfortably. It turns out it wasn't her work commute that accustomed her to the Metro but rather when she started taking the Blue Line to visit her newly married daughter living in Dwarka. It was the first time they were living apart, and she missed her terribly. "A commute of the heart," she says.

ORANGE LINE

On the Orange Line, the train goes for five, ten, fifteen minutes without a stop. A line with just six stops, a line with an endpoint and purpose. Streets and lanes obsolete, a blur of green. We are flying by and aiming to fly. Then we slip underground.

A man wearing long shorts with a butterfly tattoo on his calf and a baby boy in his lap, across from me, as we sit quartet style. Next to them a kind of still life: a plastic bag full of bananas, a package of Lays chips, a container of yellow dal with spoon. We're not commuting, we're going.

THE PLAY ABOUT THE METRO

The construction of the Yellow Line to Gurgaon is the backdrop of a love story in Neel Chaudhuri's play, *Still and Still Moving*. The play shows how Metro coaches are public spaces and yet also intimate ones. These spaces reflect what is going on outside, but they also produce their own form of compressed sociality. By the end of the play it dawns on the two main characters that they are now living in a new city as the great geographical distance between them has dissolved because of the Metro. It is also the point in the play when the couple breaks up. I saw the play in Delhi in 2015 and met with the playwright soon thereafter.

Chaudhuri is in his mid-thirties and lived in Bangalore and Mumbai before he came to Delhi to study at the National School of Drama (NSD). "It's rare for an urban-educated, predominantly English-speaking kid to get into NSD," he told me one Saturday morning as we sat in his theater company's rehearsal space in the south Delhi locality of Hauz Khas. "There's an assumption maybe that these kids can afford to go somewhere else. They have this kind of government dictate."

"To support the languages, you mean?"[12]

"Yes, exactly."

The play is about the relationship between a college student and an older man, each living at opposite ends of the Yellow Line, which is still under construction in the course of the play. The two men never ride the Metro together, but the journey to reach one another across the city informs and infuses their time together.

The Yellow Line extends from north Delhi all the way south to Gurgaon in the neighboring state of Haryana. The play takes two recognizable endpoints of the National Capital Region that have come to define the northern and southern poles of the city—Vishwavidyalaya station at Delhi University and the handful of stations that line the IT hub of Gurgaon, ending at Huda City Centre station. The student's traversal of this Metro line becomes part of the psychic space of the play, which concerns the two men's romance, as well as the relationship between the older man and his teenage son.

"Most of the scenes of the Metro are designed around images I've actually observed," Chaudhuri said. "I've tried to evoke the sense that I've had while watching this or seeing that. I was remembering a time when we were in college and we had a friend who lived in Gurgaon and sometimes on the weekend we would go to her place, and it would really feel like we were going to another state, which we were, and it would take us two and a half hours to get there. I was thinking about the idea of distance and bridging distance and what it means to live across cities and to love across cities. And how that might have the danger of being overstated but also the danger of being taken for granted. How much people kind of invest in crossing space to be with each other."

The absence of women in the play also says something about the city, a city where women are ubiquitous, but don't always have the same place or ease of movement. How do people inhabit space? The space they travel in, the space they occupy? Although the play's protagonists have no scenes on the Metro, the comings and goings of the college student are signified by the Metro and punctuated by scenes of male sociality on the train. On the stage, the Metro is inferred through lighting and the movement of anonymous riders, holding onto poles or seated beside one another.

"People have been puzzled by the play," Chaudhuri said. "They don't see the link between the Metro and the play, and they are not sure about the sequence of events." It's true that the play questions linear narrative by interspersing the main narrative (the relationship between the lovers and the one between the father and son) with the continuous movement of the Metro up and down the city, as well as the more frenetic movements of people in and out of stations. Chaudhuri seems to be asking how the city is like a story, or perhaps, more accurately, how the city *is* story.

There's a scene toward the end of the play of two laborers locked in a kind of embrace. "This is something I actually saw in the train," Chaudhuri recounted. "I was far off from them, and there was this beautiful embrace; they were curled around one of the Metro poles. I felt like it was a vision in a dream, it was so beautiful. To me it was just two guys with their shirts half off and kind of holding each other. There were a couple of people looking at them uncomfortably and then I don't know what it was, my curiosity was out of control, so I got up and I went and sat closer to them. And then I could hear that they were having a conversation about work, one of them was cursing, saying, 'he's an asshole' and 'he didn't give me the right order and how the fuck am I supposed to know.' And all the while they are in this tight embrace, and then I thought, are they lovers, are they drunk, are they just really tired?

"I think that that possibility that it could be any or all of those things is what really kind of appealed to me. And that the Metro allowed them to be completely anonymous. So, there they were, they weren't self-conscious at all. There was no sense that we're in a space with other people, people are looking, people are watching, none of that. They held their own and then they got off the train.

"Delhi is a homosocial culture, one of the contradictions and conundrums of this city. Men are extremely comfortable with one another in close physical proximity and yet can be extremely homophobic. Both times I've produced the play the assistant director has been a woman and has asked, do we put a woman in there [in what is supposed to be a general car]? I felt like I didn't necessarily need to have a fidelity to what the Metro actually looks like, I really wanted to focus on how men are on the trains, and the various situations they can get into, situations of aggression, situations of surrender, accidental situations.

"There is the scene where the guy receives bad news and kind of collapses. It wasn't quite so dramatic, but that happened to me. I was sitting next to a guy on a train, and he had just received a call that his father had passed away, and he just kind of broke down, and there was just me and this other guy and we didn't know what happened and then he eventually half told us. And I thought, how cruel to be in this space, to be among strangers and to get this kind of news. At the same time, I was so grateful to this other gentleman who was there, and the idea of the comfort and familiarity of a stranger who addresses only the moment; he's not addressing you or your past or your relationship with your father, he's addressing you in that moment. All these senses of the Metro, how people come together, for me, became a useful way to punctuate a story that's effectively about the distance that's created between two individuals and how they negotiate that distance."

ASPIRATIONAL PLANNING

At the Unified Traffic and Transportation Infrastructure (Planning and Engineering) Centre (UTTIPEC) office in Vikas Minar, I share Chinese takeout lunch with Nirav, Alia, and team leader, architect, and urban designer Romi Roy. We're talking about transit-oriented development, or TOD, which aims to plan cities around pedestrians, creating mixed-use spaces, rather than planning them around private vehicular traffic.

Roy, a Delhi School of Planning and Architecture graduate, came back to work in India after the Mumbai terrorist attacks in November 2008. The event changed her perspective and made her connect with her country again. She had been working for a private firm in Shanghai, and before that was living in Austin, studying architecture at the University of Texas. What excites her the most about being back in India is bringing all of the heads of agencies together through UTTIPEC, which falls under the Delhi Development Authority. As former Delhi lieutenant-governor Tejinder Khanna had told me, "In Delhi there are fifty different types of road users, and no single body where all agencies are concerned." Khanna not only started UTTIPEC, he was also instrumental in getting E. Sreedharan on board to manage the Metro.

Roy thinks the Metro is good for the city but believes heart and soul in transit-oriented development, or TOD, where pedestrians are the privileged users of space. For her it's about putting pedestrians over car users. Roy has little patience for anti-Metro activists. She admires people who work with government and who engage, not people who just "go to conferences or make critiques." At first, I'm baffled by her stance, since I can see that half of her job is fighting within and among government agencies, where she has no problem lodging critiques. But then I see that her point is the engagement and the working within. At the same time this "working within" also means changing certain things about how government agencies work. The government needs to attract and hire young, talented people, for instance. Her UTTIPEC team seems to embody this ideal. Although when Roy sends me to meet her division head down the hall, I sit in his office for some time and watch as several subordinates bring him this and that. He was clearly more of a *sarkari*, a government bureaucrat, sitting in front of a pile of files on his desk. His office had a completely different feel from Roy's team's open-plan office, where maps were being unfurled and computer diagrams generated amid animated group discussions.

In my office visits to UTTIPEC, I listened in on discussions and "participated" to the extent of giving my nonspecialist views on the urban plans under discussion. Everything was on the table—from bike lanes to skywalks, recessed boundary walls to new pedestrian-centered, mixed-use communities. Boundary walls that came to the edge of the road were a continual point of critique. These ubiquitous walls blocked the view of buildings and shops from the street and were the favored site for men to urinate. The idea was to open up the interface among shops, residences, and vendors with foot pathways, to create more visibility, more transparency.

Alia, a recent graduate of Delhi's School for Planning and Architecture and one of the UTTIPEC team members, tells me how they translate policies into actual urban spaces:

"We are visioning it," she says, "and then we let out projects to developers."

"How do you vision a project?" I ask.

"We first analyze problems in the city as a whole, such as housing and mixed-use development. Then we need to show some pilot case." The test case, in this instance, was the Karkarduma station on the Blue Line to Vaishali, just one stop before the major Anand Vihar bus terminal, which connects to cities and towns across the neighboring and most populous Indian state of Uttar Pradesh. The main idea for the station was to keep pedestrians suspended in midair walkways, allowing them to get down precisely at the crossing they need to.

When I visit the station, it is operational but in the midst of major construction. The design she has shown me is decidedly futuristic. The keys to this vision, Alia explains, are mobility and safe accessibility. The team is very concerned about women's safety and the rights of pedestrians. At the same time, "women" are always characterized as middle-class, office-going women or students.

Alia uses her own neighborhood as an example of how privileging pedestrians might work. It turns out she lives in one of Delhi's many unauthorized colonies, Jamia Nagar, south of where we are. She describes it as "a mixed-use space" where "you can walk to get everything you need, including medical attention; cars have to be left outside the colony." Alia's father bought her a car so she could get to work, but she says she will be ready to ditch it, along with the stressful traffic jams of the city, as soon as the Metro stop being constructed near her home is operational.

In the promotional designs of Karkarduma station that she shows me, I see that it is a middle-class rendering of a young, smartphone-centric population—people who might relate to the walking lifestyle of those living in a European city rather than to the poorer people on bicycles and on foot they (the representative figures in the designs) would see in front of them every day. And yet the goal at UTTIPEC is "How can we go beyond a car-

Figure 14. Green Line, 2018. The Metro makes a visual impact on the city, while the mostly elevated trains offer a multitude of new vistas onto the city.

oriented city?"—a tag that engages with issues of social status in the city (privileging private-vehicle owners), even if these issues are being framed as being about the environment and good health rather than social equality. On the one hand, this approach recalls Amita Baviskar's idea of "bourgeois environmentalism"—how upper-class concerns around aesthetics, leisure, safety, etc., shape urban spaces through state discipline; and on the other, transit-oriented development seeks to curtail the dominance of cars in the city and the space they take up, on the road and when they are parked, in the service of public forms of transportation and especially to make Delhi more safe for pedestrians.[13]

Yet TOD still serves a neoliberal agenda, where walking is cast as liberating, and the street has new value in the form of property development for high-end services—even as Alia's model is her own unauthorized neighborhood or harkens back (across town, more accurately) to the often maligned, densely populated old city. Vernacular and historical urban forms are repurposed for contemporary aspirational planning. A planning that privileges the language and ideas of upward mobility rather than social equality, and yet aspires to achieve both.

RENU AND SHIV

Renu and Shiv got married under duress. I meet them in the same Love Commandos safe house where I had met Ajay and Gita. Shiv explains how the couple managed to be together when they knew their parents didn't approve of their relationship.

"We began to talk and meet often. We went all over Delhi by Metro—Old Fort, Red Fort, movies, and lots of times at New Delhi Railway Station." It was during this period, where "friendship *ho gaee*," the friendship happened, and then, Shiv says, "I slowly realized she is the perfect girl to get married to."

We are in a flat up the stairs from a busy market area. Secluded in a large room with mattresses lined on the floor, three couples chat softly as they sit or recline on small pillows. Invisible to the world and especially to their families, they are intensely visible to each other. At first the couples keep talking over each other and their stories get intertwined, when in real life they were not, at least not until they reached the safe house. The young women sit braiding each other's hair, the young men massage each other's heads.

"I am from the lower schedule caste, *chamar*," Shiv says carefully, "Here, actually, the whole country has a problem with my caste." There is a problem with Renu's profile too. She is a higher caste than Shiv, but is originally from Bihar, which as Shiv remarks is seen as "a poor and backward state."

Shiv says, "We heard relatives asking things behind our backs. Where is the girl from? What does her father do? They asked and I told them she is from Bihar. They said, 'Our son won't marry someone from there, we have a problem with that.' My problem is that I am going to marry someone who I want to live with."

Theirs was a relationship that began at home, Renu explains. Her family had rented a room out to him at their place in Gurgaon. Shiv used to come over and talk, mostly to Renu's mother. Her mother liked him, his good manners, and the fact that he was educated. Renu had noticed him too. She had not been looking for a boyfriend but became familiar with him during his visits to talk to her mother.

Shiv believes his parents should be the ones to select a girl for him, that it is their right because they have "taken care of us all our lives." But once Renu makes her feelings known to him, he quickly falls for her.

The problem with telling the family was that the question of marriage was immediately put on the table. Shiv was not ready to get married. He is still studying and does not have a job. He not only cannot support Renu, but he is being supported by his family and is living with his aunt.

The breach in trust with the couple and their families occurs at this juncture: The families are hurt and upset by the not knowing, and everyone has a hard time getting over this fact. It is not that they do not try, they do, and like Renu, Shiv does not give up on trying to convince his parents. "My father was so mad," Shiv says, "He wanted to hear the news from me directly, not through my aunts. He came to see me and beat me up. He stopped giving me money and told me to move back home."

"Our own planning failed," Shiv continues, "I had to go home, stop my studies, and work in a call center to support myself while we kept trying to convince both sides." This retreat into the family becomes the first step toward their social disconnection.

Both Shiv and Renu tell their parents that they cannot marry anyone else. After a lot of convincing, Renu's family agrees to meet with Shiv. Of course, they already know him and have met him many times before, but this is the first time since the revelation of his relationship with their daughter. Shiv admits he was afraid at the prospect of meeting with them. "Parents can kill children over this in Haryana," he says.

Renu interjects, "My papa is good; they only talked."

Shiv continues, "I told them, 'I'm from a lower caste, and that can't be changed. But please tell me what I can do? Do I need to earn 15,000 or 50,000 or 70,000 rupees? Do I need to get a government job to come take your daughter's hand?' But all her father said was that I should have taken his permission before starting to go out."

Renu's mother softens and admits that Shiv is a sincere and "good boy" from a "good family." But she still does not agree to them marrying due to caste and the pressures from family and society.

"My mother suggested to my father to let me marry Renu," Shiv explains, "then my uncle came and said that the family will disown us if they let me marry her. Growing up we always heard about our family, that elders know better, that they will match you to the right family, a good home with good values, and that relatives will be the backbone of your life, that they will secure your future, like social security. If you marry by choice, we were told, you will be all alone. I said to my parents, 'Okay, I will not marry Renu if you can give me on stamp paper that the girl I marry will make us all happy.'"

Shiv's father eventually tells the couple to do what they want, but it is clear that his words act as more of a dismissal than a show of support. The couple is back to square one, and each is becoming more isolated. Shiv struggles with his call center job because he has to walk four miles to get there each day. Renu's parents threaten her, make her stop working, and take away her phone, restricting her physical and social mobility at once. Shiv now feels compelled to have an exit strategy. He is afraid that Renu's parents could send her to Bihar, where she would be out of his reach. He is also resigned to society's "false standards" where, he says, "respect is given only to anyone who is financially well off."

By this time, he has also been reading posts on the Love Commandos website and chats with one of their volunteers online. Moving forward means getting married. A lawyer friend of Shiv's advises him not to go in for a court marriage because in Haryana, word can get around, "people talk and relatives have resources." These "resources," several couples in the room pipe up to explain, are nothing less than *goondas* (thugs) dispatched by the family.

When more of Shiv's relatives show up at the house to pressure his parents, Shiv abandons his plan to wait for his next paycheck from the call center and leaves the house. He travels ticketless on a train the ninety kilometers to Gurgaon. He then contacts one of Renu's girlfriends to relay a message to Renu. The girlfriend arranges for the two to meet.

"I left the house with no phone, no money, and no idea that by 5 p.m. that day I would be married," says Renu.

"We don't have our school certificates or documents," Shiv says, "since they are with our parents at home. We want to study, to go back to work, to eventually live with my parents."

LAYERS AND SEDIMENT

At an art exhibit in central Delhi, a video features staged shots of two Buddha statues suspended on the Yamuna River. A Metro train moves across the landscape in the distance but is also connected to the river, skimming its surface perhaps or connecting what lies around it.

The Metro is a new layer of the city, a sediment of it, albeit one mostly aboveground, a mediator between land and sky, framed by its own wires and cables. The Metro is the shiny thing, but it also blends into the landscape. The Metro moves across, like the river. The statues, like stations, anchor it.[14]

All the while, new, organic positionings are emerging. A metallic organism, yes, but one that brings unity to the picture. A kind of tying up and laying out. An invitation to the simultaneous.

GREEN LINE

Days before Delhi's state election of February 2015, on the way out to Mundka, Bharatiya Janata Party posters beseech passengers to *"chalo chalein Modi ke saath"* ("Come along with Modi"). Returning to central Delhi, ads from the Aam Aadmi Party promise the institution of a mobile phone safety button and CCTV cameras covering the entire city. Women sleep and chat under the posters.[15]

The crowd in the ladies' coach changes along the route: Women wear more synthetic fabrics, the designs on saris become bigger, the gems on jeans shinier, there are more downcast looks and fewer confident bodies. These details are hard to assess, hard to document, but when all else in the Metro is constant, they are also hard to miss. The view outside is miles and miles of three-story concrete buildings, stacked one against another, chipped and crumbling.

Outside the station, flies buzz everywhere. A lone path leads into the neighborhood next to the station, lined with a beauty salon, a mobile phone shop, and a trickle of people coming to and fro along a narrow open sewer. The station itself is more clunky then sleek; it hangs over the road. It feels both planned and arbitrary, as people circle around the station, fitting their lives to this new intersection of metal and road.

By mid-2018, the Green Line extends to City Park station. Arvind Kejriwal of the Aam Aadmi Party is the Delhi chief minister. Prime Minister Narendra Modi inaugurates the 11.2-kilometer Mundka–Bahadurgarh corridor remotely from his office through a video-conference call; he stands waving a green DMRC flag, with an Indian flag in the background, as the first coach stands at the platform. This low-tech flagging off seems incongruous with the might of the Metro, but it does the trick. City Park is the station serving Bahadurgarh, which is just over the state line in Haryana, along National Highway 10. The line travels due west from the center of Delhi and as you travel on it, it can seem barren in places, developing in others.

Anoop, in his mid-forties, stocky, with a round face and mostly gray hair, routinely changes to the Green Line at Inderlok station in west Delhi: "There's an interchange and the train gets flooded with Jats muscling their way in. I'm a small built man; it's intimidating." Here, the space of the Metro becomes a concentration of the street above; it is not seen as a neutral or anonymous space but one filled with the tensions and anxieties of the world outside it.

Meanwhile, on the ladies' coach Garima, twenty-one, and Mohini, twenty-five, tell me they are studying to become teachers at the TN College of Competition in Punjabi Bagh. We're speaking in Hindi, and Garima, in black-rimmed glasses, black leggings, and a mid-length yellow kurta top, is the more talkative of the two. She says that the Green Line is better than the Red Line, "it's cleaner." Mohini offers that the "outside environment" is not good whereas the Metro is comfortable, even if you're alone on it. Mohini, in jeans and a long-sleeve gray kurta, has a long loose ponytail that reaches her hips; the last five inches of the ponytail have been dyed an orangey blond. Garima adds that since the Green Line got extended, "This area has become famous."

We approach Udyog Nagar station, where there is a large informal settlement to our left, semi-structures with corrugated metal rooftops, most accented by Videocon satellite disks. It's the same when we get to Maharaja Surujmal station: many trees as well as housing made more "formal" by its proximity to the Metro line.

A woman in a bright red pencil skirt, white button-down shirt, and black pumps who has been sitting in the ladies' coach with us, gets off at Nangloi Railway station. She stands out sartorially on the Green Line, and yet no one seems to notice her.

The female public announcement voice comes on in English: "Use smart cards to make your travel cheaper and more convenient." The same message is followed by a male voice in Hindi. This Hindi-English ambience extends to some of the advertisements in the ladies' coach. One ad for Oriental Insurance has a Hindi ad on one side of the coach and an English one on the other, both reading: "Are you planning to go abroad? For your stress-free trip buy our Overseas Mediclaim Policy."

At Mundka station, I meet Divya, who is a twelfth-class student in a gray pleated skirt, white shirt with Bal Bharati School insignia, and tie. She travels between Mundka and Bus Stand stations. When I ask her what she plans to do after completing school, she gives me a surprised look and says, "College, of course!" We've taken the escalator down to the station exit by this point, and she stops to wait on the steps for her brother. She can't find him and asks to use my phone to call him. They find each other, and she goes off.

Back on the train, at Ghevra station three girls get on; they all have smartphones. One goes to plug in her phone in one of the outlets in the ladies' coach.

A flat white sky, one with no discernible clouds, no variation, just a soft whiteness covers us like an umbrella. It's not a sky you look up to, it's one you feel under.

At Tikri Kalan station, a Hindustan Petroleum factory comes into view, as do advertisements for Pankaj's rusk cookies, Achievers Study Point, and Bikaner Sweets. There is a vast apartment complex coming up, half-built, as well as Prince Public School in the foreground. There are no people.

At Tikri Border, showrooms for Maruti Suzuki, Hyundai, Tata Motors, and Toyota line the station exits. A woman in the ladies' coach is munching on a green apple. There's a Minute Maid mango juice box on the floor under the bench of seats. Unusual on the Metro.

Figure 15. Mundka station, Green Line, 2018. This lane has become the thoroughfare between the Metro station and Mundka village. Vehicular traffic in the background travels on National Highway 10 to and from the Haryana state border.

At Modern Industrial Estate station, which is sponsored by PDM University, two small girls in bright dresses too large for them race around the platform. I watch them through the window of the ladies' coach and can see looks of fear and amazement on their faces.

Many people get off at Bus Stand station. It's completely built up here, with ramshackle buildings all around. A group of men below the elevated Metro line are sitting in a circle under a large tree, on beige, plastic chairs. I can't tell if they are just talking or playing some kind of game. As the train begins to move, a heavy-set woman in her kitchen talking on a mobile comes into my line of sight, and she quickly becomes framed by a large red-brick building that is her building, with an advertisement for "chicken 'n grill" on the façade.

The crisp female PA voice comes on again: "Customers are reminded not to board the coach for ladies. Doing so is a punishable offense." As if on cue, a man gets on and sits in the ladies' coach; we women all exchange glances, small smiles. Usually when this happens someone will tell the guy that it's the ladies' coach, and he'll get up and move on to a general coach. But this time nothing happens until he notices the glances and then eventually gets up and leaves. In this case the separation between the coaches has no physical parameters, just head and eye movements.

CYCLE RICKSHAW-WALA

As he moves inches above the asphalt, subject to the city, the cycle rickshaw-wala must maneuver like no other. The clanking metal vehicle, with canopy and vinyl seat, travels at three times walking speed, a pace for keeping eyes on the street.

In Delhi, cycle rickshaws still operate under the Tonga Act, the one for horse and carriage, not motor vehicle. But only a fraction are licensed anyway. The rest ply illegally, informally, at our mercy. When rickshaws replaced tongas in the 1950s, they soon became the lifeblood of newly formed refugee colonies, letting residents live, work, and get their children to school, once again. The cycle rickshaw, despite its feudal aura, has always been a product of a changing urban modernity, even a form of urban security.

Capital-city politicians say they'll soon be gone, laying the blame for the city's congestion notably at their feet. High-society drivers see them only as a nuisance, with their irregular shape and sudden movements, with their slowness, and sometimes too quickness, with their vulnerable human cargo, looking as witnesses.

They will be replaced, they all say, by the e-rickshaw, as so-and-so city has done, with a gleam in their eyes, and a firmness in their sitting thighs. At Metro stations around town, e-rickshaws wait in a queue to fill up with passengers. At even more stations, lines of cycle rickshaws offer point-to-point passage for a streaming line of commuters.

It is unclear whether the politicians have read *Delhi Master Plan 2021*, which states near the end, as an aside and besides, that cycle rickshaws have their place as the only nonpolluting mode of transit. Maybe they wrote it, maybe they believe it, maybe they want to incinerate every word. But then the master plan also illuminates a hierarchy of vehicles—the truck, the car, the bus, the three- and two-wheeler. It's not just about pace, but also who takes up the most space. The Delhi Metro, it should be said, stands apart in this rendering, a product of the state with its own lane, so to speak.

The cycle rickshaw is in fact the yin to the shiny Delhi Metro's yang. Since the Metro's multi-lakh crore, construction-destruction arrival, catching a "rick" has become more essential than ever. Like the tonga before it, it covers what's known in transport talk as "last mile connectivity." That on which the system depends in the end. In this case, the rickshaw is that unplanned, waiting in the shadows, liminal form. To count on that thing that ultimately remains uncountable.

The cycle rickshaw-wala is the male underclass, undercaste migrant to the city, most often from Bihar or Uttar Pradesh, but also Jharkhand and Orissa. He makes two hundred rupees a day when the day goes right, five hundred when the stars are aligned, and nothing when the rick gets impounded for not paying the fine. The rickshaw is his home base, his urban place, even if he rarely owns it. On the margins but also there for all to see.

The cycle rickshaw-wala develops essential relationships in the city. For those who transport goods, merchants can be their protectors, intervening with traffic police and municipal ward officers. Those are the ones who take the bribes, a fixed weekly or *hafta*, with a simple equation involving payment for no violence and vehicle salvation. All the while, he ferries schoolchildren, workers, housewives, singletons, couples, groups; people's shopping, televisions, plants, parcels, tables, chairs, mirrors, fixtures, the occasional sheet of glass, and the once-in-a-while rant.

He may seem like a bicyclist at times, with toned calves and strong arms, but with each push of his pedal, he inhales all vehicular emissions in his midst. The pollution of others. He does not, it turns out, have lungs of steel. He has the shortest life of them all.

Commuters can be polite, even proper; though many are not. Here the dance of social class and caste is played out again and again, out in the open, under sun, rain, and cloud. Who will touch whom, with which hands, in what amounts, and in which manner? Will money be thrown? Will words be yelled out? Or will everything be silent and transactional, no shouts? Who in the end is a nuisance to whom? And who can't live without the other?

The cycle rickshaw-wala negotiates the urban terrain in his own way. If you are polite and worthy, he will go gently over the line of potholes leading you home like a trail of crumbs. If you are not, he will still treat you well enough, since what choice does he have?

The cycle rickshaw-wala is of the outside. No one really knows where he sleeps at night, even if he naps in his rick after lunch, legs hanging over one side, covered in a blanket in winter. We know he sends money to his village, that he sees his wife maybe once a year, that he might have a child he has yet to meet. But what ultimately do we know of his insides, his inside? If he is smart, he'll never tell.

Cycle rickshaws lay bare a relationship of movement, of time and distance but also, essentially, of weight. They are as light as feathers compared to trucks and four-wheelers, though it's they who physically bear the weight of urban progress and consumption. Cars gain speed and dominance around the cycle rickshaw-wala, as his loads—human and non—get heavier behind him, and as he pushes the weight forward.

METRO MOB

On September 28, 2014, three African students riding the Metro were chased after and attacked by a Metro crowd turned mob. The three males—two from Gabon, one from Burkina Faso—were taking the Metro back to their home in Noida when they got into an altercation with three other Metro passengers. The dispute moved from the train to the platform when one of the African students was pushed out of the train when it stopped at a station. The students were then pursued all the way to a Delhi police kiosk in the busy Rajiv Chowk station at the city's center, Connaught Place. They were then alternately heckled at and jeered at by the mob and beaten with metal rods. Locally, the shock was initially about the fact that something so untoward, so chaotic, and so undisciplined could happen on the Metro. Then, once videos of the event were uploaded on YouTube, stories in the national and international press focused on the racial aspect of the story.[16] The students were not only black but also foreign nationals studying at one of the country's new private universities. There was first a rumor that the students had been harassing a female passenger when three Indian males intervened and started beating them up. This narrative was celebrated minutes after the event when the mob started chanting *Vande Maataram*, the national song with colonial-era nationalist overtones. This singing underlined the xenophobic nature of the attack.

The story from the perspective of the African students emerged only after the incident. They said three Indian passengers were taking photos of them while laughing, and when they protested, a scuffle ensued. At Rajiv Chowk station, one of the African students was pushed out of the train, and the others followed, thrashing all three of them on the platform, where a Delhi policeman also happened to be. The policeman took the six to the police kiosk within the station, and it was during this period that people began to relentlessly pursue and attack the three African students. On this point the story told by the African students, which appeared on the online news website, Firstpost, is supported by the videos taken of the event, which went viral and led to the story being picked up internationally.[17] One of the students, Yohan, who studies at Amity University in Noida, described what happened:

"They were daring us to come outside. As the policemen who had rescued and brought us to the enclosure left the spot, the cop who was deployed in the kiosk also stepped out after some time and told the mob gathered outside something in Hindi, which we could not understand. We bolted the booth from inside to save our lives, but the frenzied mob smashed the glass façade and entered the police booth. They started hitting us with sticks and rods. Some of them were throwing furniture on us."[18]

In the video, the African students are in the police kiosk, with clear panes of glass all around. Their panic inside the booth is visible from the outside as they scramble and climb through the windows of the kiosk to the roof in an attempt to escape the mob violence. Then one of them gets on top of the roof; he is a tall man, he could almost look imposing were it not for the fact that he is hunched over, looking down at the mob jeering at him. Then, men from the mob climb up after two of the students, striking them with long metal objects. Police at turns look concerned and bored but act only to separate the mob from the African students at the end of the video, which lasts a painfully long five minutes. On the sidelines of the video footage, blurred and shaky, stands a Yes Bank ATM, with a poster reading, "Invest in a Prospering India. Say Yes to Growth." It is not right side up for most of the video but becomes strikingly legible by the end.

There is something disturbingly light and almost festive about the look and sound of the crowd turned mob. At the edges of the crowd, people, nearly all of them men, are holding their phones high, capturing it all and perhaps trying to negotiate the line between participant and observer. Where one stands in this crowd can distinguish one's role as an accomplice as opposed to a witness, especially for those buffering their own involvement by holding up their phones.

The African students were eventually saved from the mob and taken to the hospital by several policemen who cordoned off the area near the Delhi Police kiosk. On the one hand, this could be seen as an isolated event, and it is certainly not what usually happens on the Delhi Metro. On the other hand, it was a story that everyone could believe, especially in light of other racist episodes targeting Africans in Delhi.[19] Racial slights and insults among Indians and between national and ethnic groups are not uncommon in the capital city. In this case, the Metro could be read as a microcosm of urban society, with all of its diversity and its prejudices. It could also reveal the underside of the new civility that has come to be expected and even celebrated on the Metro. The aspect of the story that seemed to turn it into a national and then international news story was not that it was a racially motivated attack in a cosmopolitan city, but rather that it happened on the Delhi Metro, which has been cast as a liberal, disciplined space. Rather than be seen as regressive, Delhi's Metro crowds have more often symbolized a new social order, and the Metro itself a kind of governance. If the Metro is meant to be the city's new social engine and social leveler, it came as a shock to see it as the site of an unruly mob.

THE TECHNO-COSMOPOLITAN

Ashok Verma stands out from the crowd of shoppers coming up the pedestrian subway at the South Extension Part II market. The DMRC architect is dressed in a tucked-in, well-pressed, short-sleeved shirt and trousers, wears black-rimmed glasses, and is carrying a large black briefcase. I spot him right away. He is middle-aged and mild-mannered, with spiky buzzed hair and a closely cropped moustache. We make our way to a Café Coffee Day to talk.

Verma had come to the DMRC from another government agency, the Central Public Works Department, or CPWD, which is quite literally in charge of the brick-and-mortar aspect of nation-building: government institutions, paramilitary structures, border security posts, and military campuses. The DMRC recruits most of its in-house architects from the CPWD.

Once we had ordered our coffees and sat down, Verma described the two agencies as having opposite work cultures. At the DMRC, everything was "time-bound," "targeted," and "money was not an issue," he said. "When I was at CPWD I was a different person. Nine-thirty was starting time; people reached at ten, ten-thirty; even then I was an early comer. At DMRC everyone is there at nine a.m. You could say the system and environment changed me."

Verma's responsibilities largely consisted of "the management of architectural planning." He gave consultancies to different firms to design the stations, even if responsibility for those designs remained "in-house." He usually worked on dozens of stations at a time, and described his work as follows:

"A consultant brings a scheme related to the bulk and size of a station; we check their calculations, the number of gates, the number of ticketing units, the placement of operational areas. We have to restrict. *Any fantasy has to be killed.* By the departmental officers in effect. Then we forward the scheme to different departments and convey inputs back. Our mandate is to run trains."

I was somewhat surprised by Verma's description of his own job as having to restrict and kill "fantasies." When I probed him, he spoke of design elements that he saw as being more decorative than functional. Verma almost seemed to take pride in the fact that his office had the power to kill fantasies. The role of the architect—as someone in touch with the life of a place—gets eclipsed by technical management. In Verma's description, the DMRC's bottom line is about the management of numbers and not

Metro station aesthetics, what architect Rahul Mehrotra calls "statistical architecture," whereby cities are managed statistically rather than built creatively.[20]

From Verma's perspective, I saw that even if he thought the Metro was a marvel, it was also just a job, another assignment in yet another government agency. Verma was foremost a manager of architecture who oversaw dozens of stations. For him the "big picture" was not the city but the Metro system itself. His task was to get stations to meet their specifications in a timely manner.

And yet, as I was to discover, Verma also had his own brand of cosmopolitanism, one that enabled him to build intercity expertise within his role as a technocrat. In 1999 Verma went to Tokyo for a two-month architecture course given by the Japan International Cooperation Agency, which works with the funders of the Delhi Metro. When Verma went to Tokyo, the Delhi Metro was already being constructed, but only a small part of the Red Line to Shahdara had been finished, and when Verma had visited the site at that time, he had thought it would just be a small line "like in Calcutta" and "possibly mismanaged like that one had been." Although he would go on to design and manage Metro stations, at that point he could not envision such an infrastructure in India. He also had never ridden a metro before. He recalled arriving at the hostel in Tokyo: "I put my luggage down and went out; my first curiosity was to go to see the underground metro. But there was no window system for tokens, and I had no local currency, so I just came back."

He laughed and continued, "Later, we went as a group with our local hosts who knew how to use the vending machines to get the tickets. After fifteen days we became trained in the system and started acting like locals."

Verma was both involved in a transfer of expertise between Tokyo and Delhi and has an embodied experience of metro travel. So, he gains technical skills and sophistication but also a feel for things. Tokyo's metro becomes such a material example, and for Verma, personal experience, of something to be emulated, heightened by the fact, no doubt, that the Delhi Metro is funded in large part by a Japanese loan.[21]

Once Verma was back in Delhi, he recognized that the Delhi Metro had the same rolling stock as Tokyo's system, which gave him more confidence in the system being built in his country. His recognition both makes him less skeptical of the project and makes him more willing to practice and take part in the work norms of the DMRC. He described his reaction to first riding the Delhi Metro:

"When I first started riding the Metro here, I felt good. It was at an international level." And then he said, "In Tokyo all the streets are clean, along with the Metro. Here only the Metro itself is clean." The recognition of Delhi being at an "international level" (what he saw in Tokyo) is followed by what the city lacks: clean streets. Verma seems to see Delhi with new eyes but in two different registers: what it has matched and what it lacks.

Verma then connects this aspirational value to the actual commuting experience when he reflects, "In this part of the world, when you ride a hot, crowded bus it affects your productivity, your self-respect. In the Metro, you go *aram se*, comfortably." He describes his own preferred position in the Metro as being "at the junction," the space between the coaches: "I just close my eyes and feel very relaxed that no one will push me."[22]

THE POLITICS OF SPEED

At a meeting to save Delhi's first Bus Rapid Transit, or BRT, corridor, a few dozen architects, law students, and activists sit across an array of sofas and chairs. The scene seems strange to me at first. Everyone knew the battle against the city's first BRT corridor was waged by the car-driving, upper-middle classes of south Delhi. When the Aam Aadmi Party (Common Man's Party) won the chief ministership of Delhi in 2015, they soon announced the BRT would be scrapped. It is March 2015, and the BRT is set to be demolished, taken down, uninstalled. The south Delhi car constituency is relieved but also gleeful, in the "I-told-you-so" kind of way. Meanwhile, bus riders are not surprised something is being taken away from them; it had been too good to be true.

The day after the announcement to scrap the corridor, I see a posting on an urban listserv about a meeting to "save the BRT." I show up at the appointed hour at a private ground-floor residence in the Hauz Khas area of south Delhi, just west of the actual corridor.

As I enter, one of the meeting organizers, Aashish, recognizes me and addresses me as "ma'am," which was the norm when I taught him in a master's program at the Indian Institute of Technology in Chennai more than five years before. It is a coincidence to see him here and a nice surprise. The room soon fills up. Aashish starts the meeting by holding up a dirty air filter, pointing to the large black circle of exhaust fumes formed, he tells us, over six days of Delhi pollution. "Mothers," he says, "are effectively smoking." The air we breathe from vehicular exhaust has become a notable equalizer in the city. It is also a problem and condition that will be passed down to younger generations, whether on the roads or in wombs.[23]

Karthik, a doctoral student at MIT, thinks of the Save the BRT movement as class conflict, and says that the meeting is meant to figure out how to organize the bus riders who are benefiting from the corridor. People share ideas about getting on buses and talking to riders, getting them to volunteer, but also recording their experiences. There can't be any "Metro bashing," he adds. And we shouldn't enter the design debate either, which was about where the bus stop islands should go or should have gone. The BRT didn't fail because of faulty design, but because the infrastructure was not managed properly; it was doomed to fail. Even the Central Road Research Institute brought out reports criticizing BRT. "But they like to make roads for private vehicles," someone says, "they value mobility rather than accessibility." This movement, by contrast, was to focus on the users of the corridor (who benefited most by it), the redistribution of road space (social equity), and air pollution (health and safety for all).

Ruchi makes a presentation to the group; she had worked with architect Sandeep Gandhi to design the BRT. She speaks with passion and precision about transportation. For her and the design team, the BRT is about democracy on the roads, modal share, and road design based on numbers served. Cyclists alone, she says, equal the same number as car users but take up a fifth of the space. The issue is about space, but it is also about technology and the politics of speed. Whose mode of conveyance gets privileged? Who gets to take up more space and move faster through the city? BRT is revolutionary because it essentially gives the bus rider the right of way. Ruchi reminds the group that the then Delhi chief minister Sheila Dikshit supported BRT initially and was very much behind it, but that "she didn't get the project" and turned tables in the election year.

When the meeting ends, I leave and walk toward the main road, looking for an auto rickshaw. It is eight-thirty at night and the colony is still busy, guys on motorcycles stopping to get *paan* or cigarettes, people walking by, also looking for autos or just going somewhere within the colony. I still can't find an auto by the time I reach the busy Aurobindo Marg, a multilane thoroughfare that would be intimidating to cross. I wait as auto after auto passes me by, most already filled with passengers. The few that slow down and stop don't want to take me to where I want to go. I walk back toward the colony; a guy passes me and makes kissing noises. He is more annoying than threatening but makes me aware of the growing darkness of the night. The nearest Metro station is a good walk away and the wrong line for me anyway. Out on the road, in the dark, I feel like I am floating in a sea of car headlights and men, all men, I realize, passing me by. Soon I get picked up by two people from the meeting who see me from their car. Ruchi is driving and offers to drop me home. We, along with Nilesh, who was also at the meeting, talk about the difficulty of the campaign. The problem is with the public outreach, Ruchi says, which the Metro has in spades from all the English-language media. "If the Metro has some new signage, there's an article about it in the *Times of India*," she adds with sarcasm. The Metro remains the city's darling, whereas even the police were against the BRT. They just want traffic to move, they don't want jams of any kind, and they certainly were not issuing *challans* (tickets) to any car owners for being in the wrong lane. As for the meeting, Nilesh points to the inherent problem of group interests and social action: "Probably half the people at the meeting drive cars and do so in the bus lane of the BRT."

The Bus Rapid Transit corridor was dismantled by the Delhi government in 2016, after having been deemed a failure.

PART III Visible

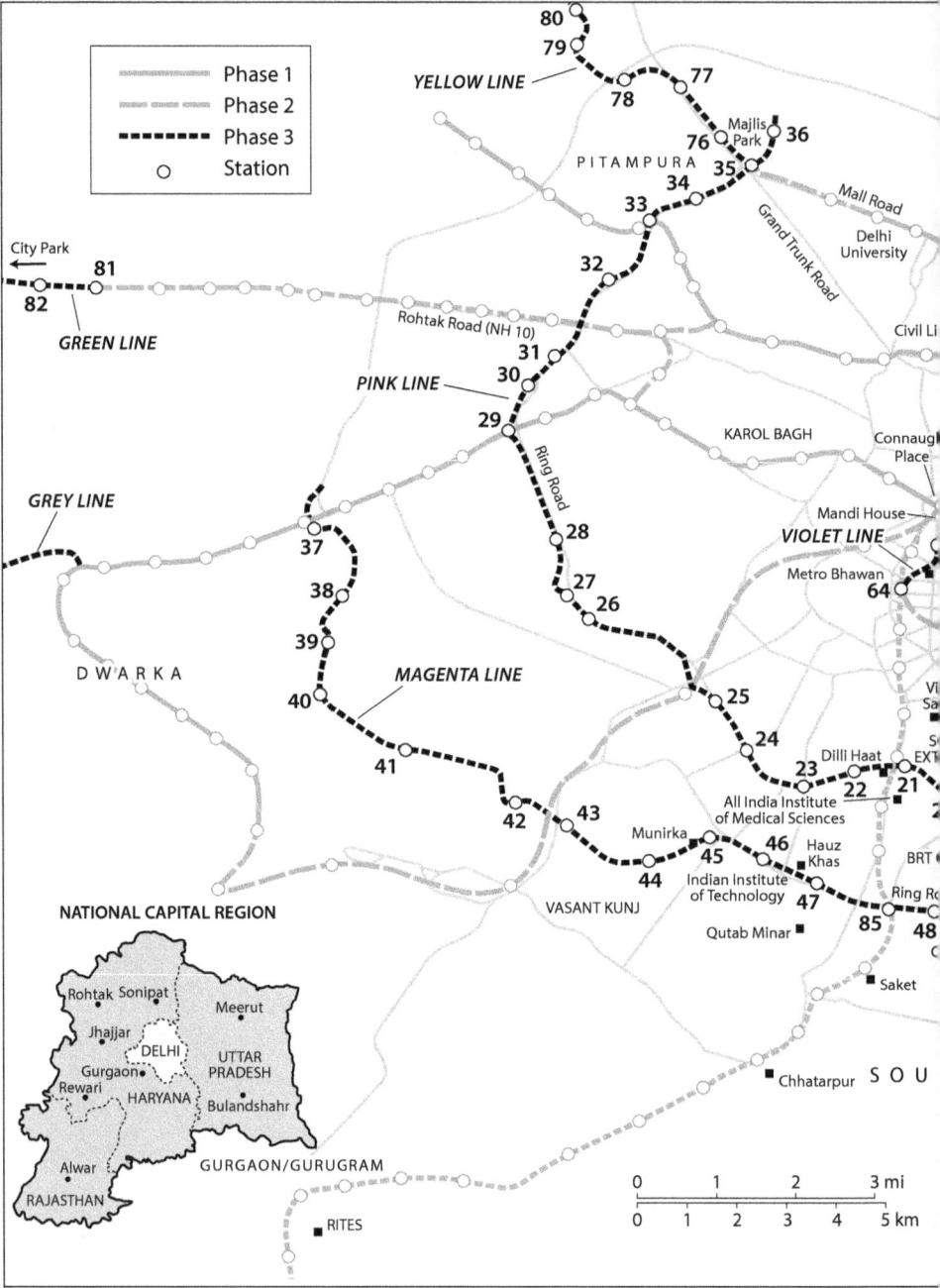

Phase 1
Phase 2
Phase 3
○ Station

YELLOW LINE

80
79
78
77
PITAMPURA
Majlis
Park
76   36
35
34
33
32
31
30
29

City Park
81
82
GREEN LINE

Rohtak Road (NH 10)

PINK LINE

Grand Trunk Road

Mall Road

Delhi
University

Civil Li

KAROL BAGH

Connaug
Place

Mandi House

VIOLET LINE

Metro Bhawan
64

GREY LINE

37

38

39

40

41

DWARKA

MAGENTA LINE

Ring Road

28

27
26

25

24
Dilli Haat
23
22   21
EXT

42   43

Munirka

46   Hauz
45   Khas
44   Indian Institute
      of Technology   47

All India Institute
of Medical Sciences

VASANT KUNJ

Qutab Minar

BRT

Ring R
85   48

Saket

NATIONAL CAPITAL REGION

Rohtak Sonipat
Meerut
Jhajjar
DELHI
UTTAR
PRADESH
Gurgaon
Rewari   HARYANA   Bulandshahr

Alwar
RAJASTHAN

GURGAON/GURUGRAM

Chhatarpur   S O U

0   1   2   3 mi
0   1   2   3   4   5 km

RITES

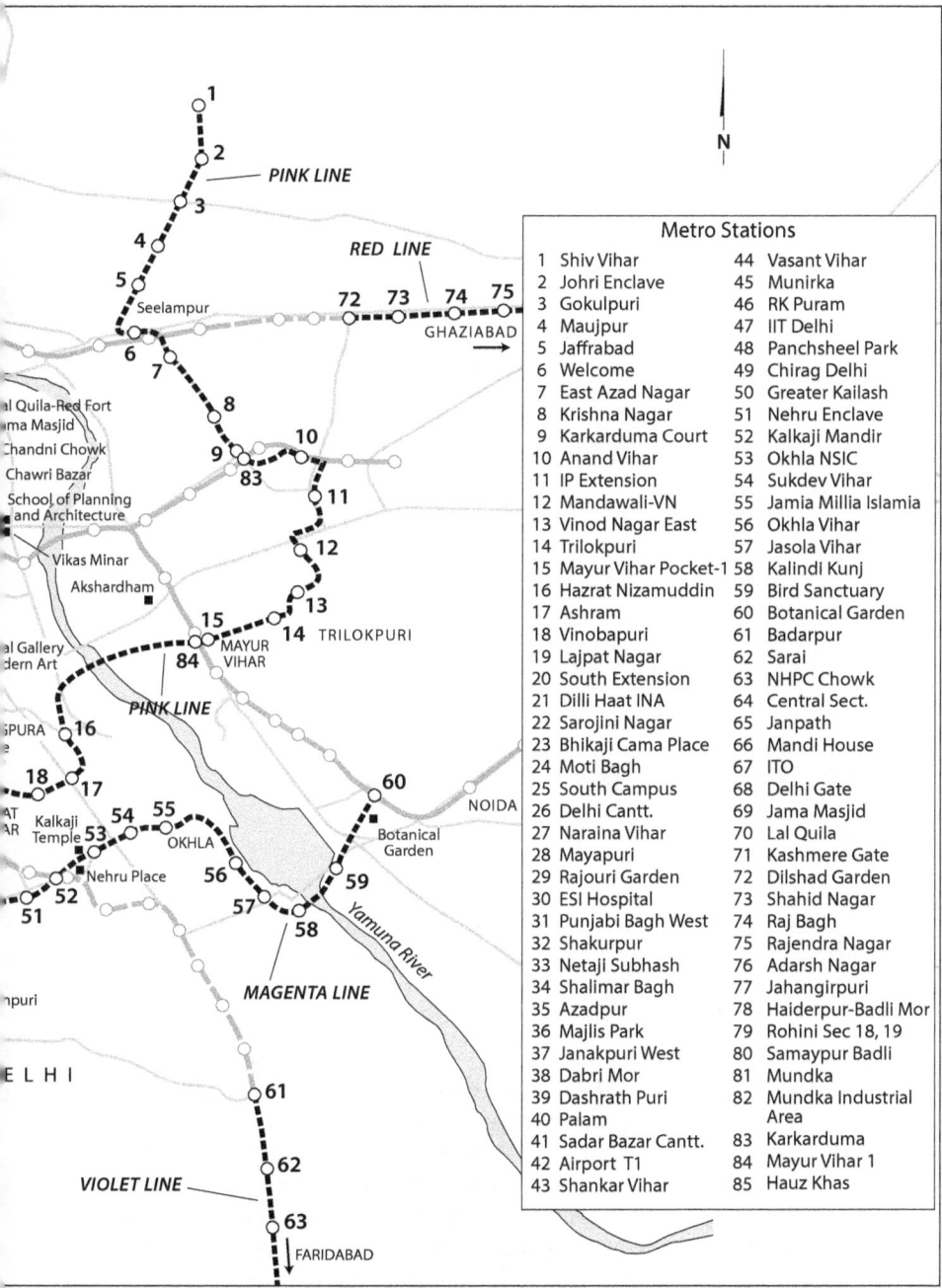

Metro Stations

PINK LINE
RED LINE
N

#	Station	#	Station
1	Shiv Vihar	44	Vasant Vihar
2	Johri Enclave	45	Munirka
3	Gokulpuri	46	RK Puram
4	Maujpur	47	IIT Delhi
5	Jaffrabad	48	Panchsheel Park
6	Welcome	49	Chirag Delhi
7	East Azad Nagar	50	Greater Kailash
8	Krishna Nagar	51	Nehru Enclave
9	Karkarduma Court	52	Kalkaji Mandir
10	Anand Vihar	53	Okhla NSIC
11	IP Extension	54	Sukdev Vihar
12	Mandawali-VN	55	Jamia Millia Islamia
13	Vinod Nagar East	56	Okhla Vihar
14	Trilokpuri	57	Jasola Vihar
15	Mayur Vihar Pocket-1	58	Kalindi Kunj
16	Hazrat Nizamuddin	59	Bird Sanctuary
17	Ashram	60	Botanical Garden
18	Vinobapuri	61	Badarpur
19	Lajpat Nagar	62	Sarai
20	South Extension	63	NHPC Chowk
21	Dilli Haat INA	64	Central Sect.
22	Sarojini Nagar	65	Janpath
23	Bhikaji Cama Place	66	Mandi House
24	Moti Bagh	67	ITO
25	South Campus	68	Delhi Gate
26	Delhi Cantt.	69	Jama Masjid
27	Naraina Vihar	70	Lal Quila
28	Mayapuri	71	Kashmere Gate
29	Rajouri Garden	72	Dilshad Garden
30	ESI Hospital	73	Shahid Nagar
31	Punjabi Bagh West	74	Raj Bagh
32	Shakurpur	75	Rajendra Nagar
33	Netaji Subhash	76	Adarsh Nagar
34	Shalimar Bagh	77	Jahangirpuri
35	Azadpur	78	Haiderpur-Badli Mor
36	Majlis Park	79	Rohini Sec 18, 19
37	Janakpuri West	80	Samaypur Badli
38	Dabri Mor	81	Mundka
39	Dashrath Puri	82	Mundka Industrial Area
40	Palam		
41	Sadar Bazar Cantt.	83	Karkarduma
42	Airport T1	84	Mayur Vihar 1
43	Shankar Vihar	85	Hauz Khas

Seelampur
GHAZIABAD →
al Quila-Red Fort
ma Masjid
Chandni Chowk
Chawri Bazar
School of Planning and Architecture
Vikas Minar
Akshardham
al Gallery dern Art
MAYUR VIHAR
TRILOKPURI
PINK LINE
PURA
NOIDA
Botanical Garden
Kalkaji Temple
OKHLA
Nehru Place
MAGENTA LINE
Yamuna River
npuri
E L H I
VIOLET LINE
FARIDABAD

Map 3. (overleaf) Phase III of the Delhi Metro opened between 2015 and 2020, adding the lengthy Pink and Magenta Lines, as well as a short patch of four Grey Line stations. This phase brought the number of stations to 285. Now the Metro not only bisected the city in multiple directions but moved out concentrically as well. New interchange hubs at Lajpat Nagar, Kalkaji Mandir, Hauz Khas, and Rajouri Garden took crowd pressure off existing hubs elsewhere in the system. There were new station design elements, more places for advertisements, and more flow. By 2021 driverless trains were introduced on some lines.

The All India Institute of Medical Sciences (AIIMS) station is located on a wide, busy road that streams with traffic, a typical congested south Delhi thoroughfare. On the several flights of stairs leading down from the Metro, a few families sit huddled. They are neither coming nor going but instead are part of the overflow from various lines around the hospital complex. Stairs lead up from the Metro platforms and end at the entrance to the hospital. On any given day an array of people sit or lie down on the raised concrete path just inside the gates of the hospital. Sometimes families cook on small stoves they have brought with them. Most people look worried, and many look unwell as they wait under the strong sun. Men sit cross-legged on the ground, cradling their toddlers, while women fan sick relatives.

At times, the Metro stations merely accentuate the two worlds of this city—one of movement, speed, luxury; another of stagnation, deprivation, lack. One thin woman in a plain red sari that falls at her hips rather than sways at them tells me she has come from far away and has taken the Metro to reach here. She is sick and waiting for *davaee*, medicine. The fact that the Metro was the last part of a long relay-style journey involving several forms of transport and several hours of travel has little meaning for her, except that the Metro brought her to the threshold of the hospital. Her experience of crossing the city, once she boarded the train at the northern end of the Yellow Line, was confined to her experience on the Metro. Now she stands and waits for the delivery of medicine and wonders when she will be able to go back down the steps of the station that is within eyesight.

Over the last two decades, the Metro has physically become part of the street, as concrete and metal have been built into, onto, over, and under the asphalt. Its hundreds of stations now intersect with the large roads and radials of the city. The system stands apart from the street—it is clean and quiet by comparison—but it also absorbs the street as stations come to reflect what is going on in their midst. People bring in the street to the

Figure 16. AIIMS station, Yellow Line, 2016. In a spillover space from the hospital aboveground, many people are waiting.

Metro, even if they're not throwing trash or spitting, as they do on the street. They bring their needs and desires, their forward momentum.

At AIIMS, the two worlds of the Metro and the street have a particular intersection; they bleed into each other, as the station itself becomes a kind of waiting room. People pace and huddle and get information from one another. The station feels like less of a passage through and more of an arrival. Both the Metro and AIIMS are revered state entities, the state's best results at producing the "world-class" in terms of health care and transit. Nevertheless, in the meeting of the Metro and the hospital, there is also palpable despair and lack and not-enough-ness.

STRIKE

In 2017 and then again in 2018, Delhi Metro workers, including train operators, station controllers, technicians, operations and maintenance staff, threatened a strike, demanding higher pay, greater safety standards, better working conditions, and the right to form a union. In 2017 the strike was averted when the Delhi Metro Staff Council and the DMRC reached an agreement that would implement the changes workers were asking for. A year later, workers said that the changes had not been implemented, so they threatened to strike again. The second strike was also averted, this time when the Delhi High Court intervened, saying the strike by Metro workers was illegal and not justified.

I sat down one day with Ravi, the general secretary of the Delhi Metro Staff Council, soon after the Delhi High Court order. I had been reading about the possible strike in the newspapers, and Ravi's name was mentioned in several of the articles. No one knew him in my immediate contacts, so I found him on Facebook and sent him a message. He responded, and we arranged to meet at a Café Coffee Day.

Ravi is thirty-one years old, young to be in his position. "I belong to Bihar," he tells me; "People from Bihar have leadership in their genes." He sports a close-cropped beard as well as a watch and two gold rings. He looks neat, contained, wearing jeans and a short-sleeved, checked, button-down shirt, but still recognizable from the colorful and ebullient Facebook profile photo I had seen of him and his wife on their wedding day.

Ravi has been a train operator for three years, and before that, a station controller for three years. In March 2013, he had taken a competitive exam to enter the DMRC. "We are the front line; we take care of issues in the train and stations. It is challenging, so everyone is attracted to this job. You have to take care of the three thousand people sitting behind you.

"Working with DMRC is a great experience. They are a proactive, customer-responsive, customer-centric work environment. They are always trying to solve problems. I love the DMRC, I belong to DMRC. I don't want to defame it. DMRC as an organization is not bad, as an institution, as an employer. I talk to many types of people at DMRC, from different sectors of India, different states, cultures, attitudes, ideas.

"The problem is some officers coming from Indian Railways, an old system. They do not let nonexecutive staff grow, in terms of pay, allowances, recognition, promotions. You work for fifteen-twenty years and are not promoted to executive staff, while a person coming from Indian Railways with six months' experience is made an executive. These are issues of promotion and pay."

On the one hand, Ravi derides the culture of the Indian Railways that has seeped into the DMRC; and on the other, he cites the labor protections that Indian Railway workers have because they are unionized. These are not contradictory points. Ravi's analysis of how and why there is a rift between workers and executives at the DMRC begins with the Indian Railways. Although nonexecutive staff can only enter the DMRC by taking a competitive exam (as Ravi did), "deputations" from Indian Railways and other agencies can happen at the executive level.

"DMRC has its own work culture; Indian Railways is destroying that culture. Indian Railways is improving with the recent and last minister, but their recruitment still favors near and dear ones rather than being competitive. You see this in the executive level of the DMRC, where there are examples of hiring near and dear in a hidden manner, even wives for positions."[1]

"There are good officers as well, but some want to keep their dominancy. Ego problem is there. Officers don't listen to their subordinate staff. You have to improve your system with feedback. We take feedback from customers and relay it to executive staff. If staff relays their own feedback to executives, then they will target that person.

"They transferred me, rotated me more. With a rotating shift, transferring workers becomes a way to harass them. If you have to report to Faridabad and the Metro is not even open in the morning when you have to leave, what do you do?"

Ravi cites the Trade Union Act of 1926, which gives the right of employees of any public sector employment to organize for collective bargaining. I pass him my notebook, and he jots down from memory the history of Indian labor laws supporting the case for forming a union of Metro workers:

1936—Payment of Wages Act

1965—Bonus Act

1923—Workman Compensation Act

1948—Factories Act

1947—Industrial Dispute Act

1952—Employees Provident Fund Act

1948—Employee State Insurance Act

1961—Maternity Benefit

1972—Payment Gratuity Act

"Indian Railways has a trade union membership in lakhs [a lakh equals a hundred thousand]. There are standards in providing for rest breaks. In DMRC, breaks are only for those working in Metro Bhawan. In 2015 we fought a lot for breaks for train operators. In Indian Railways, there are two people in the cab of the engine; they work for five to seven hours with a break. The junctions are very far apart. Metro train operators work for four to five hours at a time. Every two minutes they must take care of two to three thousand passengers. We got this after the Metro had been in operation for thirteen years. It takes almost three hours to go to the end of a Metro line and back. There is the issue of bathroom breaks, especially after consuming one-and-a-half liters of water. These are natural requirements; everyone needs a break, then they can work more efficiently. If not, it disturbs my biological system.

"DMRC is a baby organization; all major Public Sector Undertakings (PSUs) have trade unions. It's even worse at other metro systems in other cities in India. Chennai Metro, the perks only go to executive staff. It can become a tradition. This problem of executive and nonexecutive will arise in every metro. We may form a federation of metro staff across systems. The major issue lies in the wages; officers, executives, government bureaucrats decide, they sit on pay committee revision. There are no representatives from different organizations. Discriminatory policies get developed. The life of the working person, no one lasts very long. In other trade unions they work full-time, are free to function as an organization. Make us free, let us listen. This is a lifetime process. There must be balance; it will only happen when there's an organization parallel to the executive staff."

Our conversation circles back to the most recent strike threat. Ravi says, "The DMRC went to the high court saying the strike will disrupt service for twenty-five lakh people. The Court directed us not to strike. We are law abiding. We say to the Court: then instruct them to solve our issues. It is an unbearable situation; no one wants to strike. I have dedicated four years to the staff council. I delayed my marriage for this. DMRC discourages labor leadership; they use quasi-judicial charge sheets and in the majority of cases you are removed. There are also cases of false charges, framing, etc. This fear of termination should be removed. DMRC should open up. Terminating someone's job is like a capital punishment. If you lose your job you are not eligible to take a competitive exam (you're too old), and you're not experienced for the private sector. You will lose your life."

BUS

He's not at ease, this guy sitting next to me on the bus from Green Park. An IT professional from Chandigarh, he seems desperate to make a connection, first with the logo on his cap, then a brother in Sunnyvale, an education professor father, and finally the Google cafeteria. By the end, I'm worn out by his galloping English even though he is harmless and nice enough.

The ticket collector has a cooler presence. He stands on the side, clutching sharply folded notes, directing people where to sit, a sure smile on his face. He's twenty-five years old and makes 15,000 rupees a month. He knows he's doing well, and anyway someone has to serve the public. Those making 4–5,000 a month have it hard. And then, he goes, the Metro is just like the bus, but there's a/c inside.

INFRASTRUCTURE BY EXAMPLE

At Vikas Sadan in INA Market one afternoon I meet Balvinder Kumar, who headed the Delhi Development Authority (DDA) at the time. Despite its name, the DDA, which is the planning body for the city, falls under the purview of the central government's Ministry of Urban Development and is not to be confused with the New Delhi Municipal Council, which overseas city services ranging from fixing potholes to issuing birth certificates. The DDA is known for acquiring land and is also in charge of providing affordable housing on that land. It is the agency that manages, organizes, builds, and demolishes.[2]

Kumar was a mentor of Romi Roy's, who I had met when she was the head of Unified Traffic and Transportation Infrastructure (Planning and Engineering) Centre (UTTIPEC). Roy had told me that you have to work with government or you should not complain about things not working. I have this in mind as I go to see Kumar.

Vikas Sadan means "house of development" and is a massive government office, a complex that feels like a *mela* or fair when you enter on the ground floor. People are standing in lines, squatting in corners, pouring over papers. They come from all over the city with requests or complaints. Every single person in this ocean liner of a building has a story to tell. It is bureaucracy in action: the government and its people.

Once I announce myself at the information counter and my appointment with Kumar is confirmed, I am escorted by a subordinate up several floors and through a maze of tall metal cabinets standing at odd angles. I can't tell if the cabinets are storing documents or are themselves in storage. We come to a tiny office where a man sits behind a desk, sweating and shuffling papers, as six others sit around him with chits in their hands. For a moment I think this is Balvinder Kumar, but then the incongruity of his title and the size of the office hits me, and before I can speak I am led down an adjacent corridor and deposited in front of a solid wood-carved door. The door opens from the other side and a new subordinate takes me inside a huge office and reception space large enough to hold at least fifty people.

A few minutes later Kumar enters the office, and I explain that I have some questions about the Metro in relation to the city's urban plan.

"In the long run," he says, "the whole focus on planning will be around the Metro corridors. Like in Western countries, the main development areas are around the Metro corridors. We will adopt a similar kind of concept."

The "concept" he's talking about is transit-oriented development, or TOD, which is extremely popular in international urban planning circles.

"Implementing TOD policy, once it comes, will give the direction of development in coming times in Delhi. What we are saying is that intensive development should take place along the corridor, number one; second, all land use should be mixed—commercial, residential. If somebody is staying there (in a particular locality) then he should not have to travel much. Even if he has to travel, he should take the Metro rather than road and cars. So, I think with this TOD policy things will improve, and it will move in a direction which is needed in Delhi, keeping in view the present scenario where there are too many traffic jams, too much congestion, aggravated parking problems. We have to encourage people to take this Metro route, rather than using car, vehicular movement."

"What about people being pushed out of the city because of the high cost of living?" I ask.

"Beyond the Metro line there are villages and agricultural lands. The DDA will go for world-class infrastructure there. A rural network, twenty-four-hour electricity, green buildings, likewise. That whole area can be developed into a smart sub-city."

"Like Gurgaon?"

"Yes, like Gurgaon, you could say, but the better part of Gurgaon."

We begin to talk about the city's urban development more generally, but I can tell that he is bored. He gives me rote answers, noting how "big and massive" the city's problems are and all that has to be done to fix them. He keeps getting interrupted, first by one of his secretaries, then by phone calls. I can feel our time dwindling, and so on a whim I ask him about his public Facebook posts, which I had noticed were about the nature and practice of spirituality. His face immediately softens and breaks into an embarrassed smile. We start discussing the relationship between spirituality and materiality, and he explains that each day he gets requests for land to build religious places. "I deny all of those requests. We have too many of those places."

We move on to what underlies any kind of urban development: land acquisition. We discuss the "land pooling policy," which is the DDA's way of procuring land and quite literally "making more city." Kumar believes this policy is one of the key factors that will determine Delhi's future. With this process, people pool their agricultural lands and offer to sell them to the DDA. Kumar imagines this will occur for 20,000–24,000 hectares of land, which is now on the outskirts of the city, beyond any of the existing Metro lines. This "urbanizable" land, once procured, will become "mixed use," meaning residential, commercial, and institutional development. This is how Delhi has developed and grown since the time of partition and independence, as villages and agricultural lands circling the city were slowly encroached upon and then urbanized.[3]

"DDA affects every strata of society, since what we do determines the land use pattern of Delhi. We prepare the master plan, a document which tells us what kind of areas are to be developed, slum rehabilitation, height of buildings, what FAR (floor area ratio) is admissible for various land uses, etc. Huge challenges are in front of us; with more than 1,800 unauthorized colonies, forty percent of the population resides in unauthorized colonies and slum areas."

Kumar goes on to describe the "world-class infrastructure" that will be built on these far-off agricultural lands once they are incorporated into the city, creating "smart sub-cities."

"This is a required transformation in Delhi, where there are huge deficiencies in infrastructure. There will be twenty-four-hour electricity, green buildings, and other high-class infrastructure where women are safe and children are safe. A place where water will be used and reused as they do in Western countries. Sustainability is a must."

Our conversation edges back into the realm of bigness and hugeness. Finally, he relents, in Hindi, *"Yeh problems kabhi katham nahin hothi."* These problems never go away. Kumar adds that the Delhi Metro is the city's only successful example of urbanization. "There are some bridges here and there, but," he says, "we have yet to see a second example."

MAGENTA LINE

A long, fenced walkway connects the Violet Line to the Magenta Line at Kalkaji Mandir station. There's not much to look at; you couldn't quite consider it an urban stroll or a place of *flânerie*, but it does take you from one line to the next and that is something. The Magenta Line looks newer and has some small modifications. The seats are colored magenta in the ladies' coach, blue in the others. Sliding platform doors protect people from falling or jumping onto the tracks. These doors feature advertisements on the dividers between them: for a travel website, hair removal cream, shaving cream, acne gel.

An old, crumpled woman comes to sit next to me on the metal bench on the platform. She is wearing dirty pink sandals and a synthetic, printed

Figure 17. Botanical Garden station, Magenta and Blue Lines, 2018.

sari. It's not as common for me to meet someone in their seventies or eighties on the Metro; there are fewer people over seventy on the Metro as compared to other age groups. She is taking the Metro to Tilak Nagar to see her sister. She says going up and down in the Metro is tiring. And yet the lilt in her voice tells me that she's happy to be here underground, sitting and waiting for the next train.

At Botanical Garden, on the east side of the Yamuna River, I get down and walk to the garden. It's empty except for the guards and gardeners. The place is bifurcated twice over by two Metro lines. I ask one of the gardeners if he ever rides the Metro, and he proudly proclaims that he does. It is hot and humid, not the season to be walking around this place.

Back on the train, I enter a general coach and stand, clutching a pole. A woman with large, noticeable scars sits at the end of one of the rows of seats in a "designated for ladies" section. She has been burnt on her face and hands. She's traveling with a child, maybe her daughter. She is trying to use her cell phone to call someone and asks a man next to her for help. He seems to be helping her and dials a number on her phone before handing it back to her.

In the ladies' coach a young woman boards the train with a T-shirt that says "Femme Vibes" on it. On the platform when I exit at Greater Kailash, another young woman is wearing a T-shirt that says, "Trauma Queen." Someone else walks by with a bag that reads: "Let That Shit Go."

While the Metro circulates, there is an ongoing strike by auto-rickshaw drivers in the city. They are protesting taxi apps like Ola and Uber. The competition has been bad for them. I come across an off-duty driver not far from the Greater Kailash station. Raj Kumar has been an auto driver in Delhi for the last twenty years; he's from a village in Uttar Pradesh but lives with his family in Badarpur on the Violet Line. He has three kids, a girl and two boys. About the strike, he tells me, "We go for eight rupees, they go for six. We want our bread, and that our children learn to read and write well."

It starts to rain, and I get under the cover of a tree next to Raj Kumar's auto rickshaw.

"For us the Metro is good," he tells me, "you get small trips all the time. We don't wait at the station, we're not allowed, not all stations have auto stands. This is a bad thing. The Metro doesn't bother us; it's good for us. It's clean; we go on it too, as well as our wives and kids and sisters. The women go in ladies' coach. Fare is okay, it's normal. There's no trouble there."

Raj Kumar's biggest concern is that his three children are able to get good jobs one day. I ask him what would make a job good.

"Oh, I don't know, that's for them to figure out; they are reading and writing. I want them to know good people, be in good places, not dirty places. This is why I left the village."

"How would you compare Delhi to village life?"

"There's more and more traffic, not good for autos; we get stuck in traffic and the meter doesn't pay us extra for that. Some auto-walas charge the correct fare; others don't, but all are not bad. We rent our autos; that's what poor people do. We rent our homes. Everything is getting more expensive. Look at the price of dal, it's so expensive, we can't eat dal."

RADHIKA

Radhika works on the pagination team for a national newspaper, where she fine-tunes page layouts. Slim with black-rimmed glasses, she seems slight and quiet at first as we sit together at her workstation. She is from

Allahabad, in Uttar Pradesh (U.P.), where she'd been doing a diploma course in printing technology before coming to Delhi in 2001.

"I didn't have anyone here," she tells me. "I was first staying with relatives for the first month, and then I became a paying guest in Kirti Nagar. I used to take a direct bus from there to Ansal Bhawan in Connaught Place. In the bus you feel hot in summer; it's sometimes crowded, and at night, it's not safe. You get down from the bus and then take a cycle rickshaw for ten minutes; those ten minutes are not safe."

At first, I'm struck by how Radhika describes the duration of time in the cycle rickshaw as being unsafe, as the site of unsafe-ness. But then it makes sense, since calculating risk in the city is sometimes about the time something will take, for how long will you be exposed. And then she adds, "Life in Delhi is much faster than in Allahabad. People have lots of time there. Here no one wants to interact; they are busy with themselves; you feel isolated."

A few years after coming to Delhi, Radhika's sister joins her, and they start sharing a flat together in Pitampura, northwest of central Delhi. They take their first Metro ride on the Red Line from Shahdara. I expect to hear her talk about the trains or the speed, but instead Radhika lights up and says, "The first time I rode on the escalator, I felt so high!" She starts to laugh. "There are no facilities like that in Allahabad. It was a strange experience; I was scared, I thought I may fall down; it was going upwards very fast.

"Now I'm used to the Metro; I read the newspaper and all. Commuting is easier; you're not stuck in a jam or at a red light. People are educated on the Metro compared to the bus crowd. On the bus there are all kinds of people, so you can't feel safe. A woman was about to pick my wallet once. It was winter, and she wrapped her shawl around me and opened my purse. My friend saw this and pushed her away. People tend to behave on the Metro. Though, I got pinched once. I snatched the guy's collar and slapped him. He said, 'No, it's not me!' I said, 'What were you doing?' I saw him doing it. I took him to the Metro police. He was apologizing and denying it; he was scared. This was seven-eight years back, before there was the ladies' coach."

After marriage, Radhika moved to Indirapuram, back in U.P. but on the Delhi border. She says she still feels a part of the city, "Delhi is my home, I love the city." From Indirapuram she used to take a shared auto rickshaw to the Anand Vihar station on the Blue Line, but once the line was extended in 2010, she gets on at Vaishali station, which is in U.P. itself.

"Before, you had to take two autos, one from U.P., then at the border you'd have to change to a Delhi auto and stand in a long queue to get a booked auto. One time it was Rakhi and I couldn't get an auto back. I was stranded at Barakhamba Road, so I took the Metro to Dilshad Garden and then my husband picked me up. It took one and a half hours! Now with the Vaishali station, there is no need to change autos or cross borders."

When her newspaper office moves, Radhika takes the Metro to Patel Chowk station and walks the few minutes to the PTI Building on Parliament Street. She rides in the ladies' coach. Her husband does not take the Metro. He works for Barclays bank and takes an office cab to work.

"I'm comfortable traveling at night on the Metro if I'm getting picked up by my husband at the station. In the morning and evenings other cars are extremely crowded. In the women's car, even if you're pushed it's okay. I go into the general car if I'm with my husband, but if I'm carrying my daughter, I'll go in the ladies' coach since it's difficult to stand in a crowded compartment."

POSTURE

On the weekends there seem to be more people sitting on the floors of the Metro trains, especially at either end of the train and in the gangways between coaches. I see a father and little daughter one day. He's teaching her something, maybe the alphabet; he's sitting on the ground cross-legged, and she is on his lap. I see groups of friends, chatting; I see families. They've now put up a sign in each car, a pictogram featuring two people sitting in the gangway with a red line drawn across it. This sign is not meant to cancel out the space, only the activity. Sometimes a foreigner riding the Metro will say, Oh, *they* don't follow the rules here. Or locals will say, *they* are not behaving properly. *They* do not know better.

The rule tries to break the habit. But it is still something people do. This bodily posture, of sitting cross-legged on the floor is so familiar, so required of other spaces, waiting in a government office, waiting at the side of a protest march, waiting on a railway platform or on a long train journey. There is something about the Metro that triggers going into this bodily comportment, even if the trains are moving fast and the doors are opening and shutting every few minutes, even if there is a flow of people passing by. It is a posture of intimacy, to sit and talk with friends and loved ones. It is a posture of rest.

INTEGRATION

At the Metro Museum in Patel Chowk station, neat models of stations show footpaths, greenery, and cars, indicating a suburban life where you leave your car at the station and commute into town. There are no vendors, no pedestrians, no bus stands, no cycle-, e-, or auto rickshaws, no taxis. In short, the models look nothing like any of the Metro station environs in this city.

For transport researcher Geetam Tiwari, to evaluate the Metro you have to see it as part of the larger transport landscape, the length of trips people take and the sectors of the population who can afford to take motorized transit in the first place, whether personal or public.[4] Tiwari, along with Dinesh Mohan, wrote some of the more important economic critiques of the Metro when it was first proposed. They used data to show three key points: that the Metro doesn't serve a large-enough swath of the city's population to justify the cost; that the Metro doesn't cover enough acreage of the city; that the cost of the Metro and its future maintenance hoards capital investment to the exclusion of other forms of transport, namely buses. They argue that a more developed and robust bus system would cover the key short trips in the city and serve the majority of the population much more cheaply and effectively.

When I talk to Tiwari at her office at TRIPP in the Indian Institute of Technology in 2018, she is resigned to the Metro's existence but reminds me that only 5 percent or less of trips in the city are made by Metro. This percentage is cited by many other urban agencies, including the Delhi Metro Rail Corporation. Sixty percent of trips are made on buses and the remaining 35 percent are made by private cars, motorbikes, auto rick-shaws, and taxis. The Metro is fine for long trips, in Tiwari's view, but the vast majority of trips, including those getting to and from Metro stations, are short. The Metro can never be the answer in Delhi, or any Indian city. To solve citywide problems you can't ignore walking, bicycles, and especially bus trips.

To start, why doesn't Metro improve the walk paths around its stations? she asks. This is a larger institutional issue, a different jurisdiction, by which she means a different urban agency in charge, the municipal government, so there's no interest. The question of interest goes to the heart of what the "public" in public transport is supposed to mean. It is public lands that the Delhi Metro Rail Corporation was more or less given at subsidized rates by the central government; the public that is the numerical majority rather than the moneyed middle to upper classes.

"The Metro is seen only as a technology, not as a system," says Tiwari. This seems to be a different way of talking about its stand-aloneness, which has been an issue from the start. But now, as the Metro system nears twenty years in operation, Delhiites know the technology and have absorbed it.

These kinds of critiques of the Metro project came not only from transport researchers but also from the government's own consulting agency, RITES, formerly known as Rail India Technical and Economic Service. RITES had completed the major feasibility study for the Metro in 1995, which green-lighted the project. But as one RITES urban transport manager, Yuvraj, told me, once the Metro was made, "Integration is a big casualty in Metro. Ideally, in an urban transport system, comfort level should be the same as you move from one mode to another. There should be integrated ticketing. Even the DMRC's own feeder buses are not integrated." He calls those things that take up space and slow down traffic the "undisciplined" elements on the road, or "side friction."

"What would make things smoother?" I ask.

"The multiplicity of authorities is okay but you need an agency for coordination. People have to have ownership over their work to care about it."

For Yuvraj and his team, the answer is not more parking spots for cars. He's against them because there can never be enough; instead he is a proponent of "safe paths for bicycles." Imagine the space it would require to

Figure 18. Huda City Centre station, end of the Yellow Line in Gurgaon, 2018. The metal structure pictured here is lime green in color, making for a dramatic centerpiece to the station.

park ten thousand cars versus ten thousand bicycles, he tells me. The few dedicated bicycle lanes I've seen in the city get invaded by motorized two-wheelers and even auto rickshaws on occasion. I feel Yuvraj has entered a utopic realm.

But then I meet Akash, a private architect who has worked with UTTIPEC and other government entities. He has imagined just such a bicycle network for Delhi, the greenway project, which his firm started to develop in 1998. It was to be a massive cycling network along the city's drains, linking all of Delhi's many green spaces without ever having to cross a road.

"You would only have to enter the park in your neighborhood and then have access to the whole city. Nehru Park, Lodi Gardens would start coming to your doorstep," Akash says to me in his office in Vasant Kunj one morning. He imagines kids biking to school, but also people getting their daily exercise on their way to work, by walking or biking on the paths, rather than, as he put it, making exercise "an event" that requires driving to a park. It was a project that signified the connections among schools, markets, parks, and the city's history, in a garden setting, with no traffic. A project that, he says, would completely change how you live life in Delhi. The pilot project for greenways was passed four times by UTTIPEC, Akash tells me, but who's going to implement it?

Reflecting on the Metro, Akash says, "The minute you come out of the station, the minute the Metro stops and you're dealing with the road right next to the Metro station, you get a shock. From a five-star facility, you come onto a rundown, broken-down pavement. You can't even walk sometimes. Fine you have a Metro, but you need to start accessing the Metro in a better way."

THE PHOTO THAT WENT VIRAL

Four women are in the frame, from left to right: a young woman in a pink sweater and jeans sits looking down at the floor, a mother in a purple salwar kameez suit and gray cardigan sits next to her toddler, tending to him, another young woman in black jeans and a sweatshirt hunches over a blue backpack looking at her smartphone, and finally adjacent to the bank of seats, another woman sits cross-legged on the floor, wearing a salwar kameez suit and a pink shawl clutching a diaper bag. The woman sitting, who will come to be identified as "the nanny," is looking off into space, although she is also on the edge of the photo frame, so it is unclear if her gaze is fixed on something.

This ordinary scene photographed in the ladies' coach of the Delhi Metro was tweeted by a journalist who happened to be riding the train one day. The journalist's tweet stated, "Seen in Delhi metro: Mother and child take seats while the child's nanny sits on the floor on a fairly empty train. Caste/class discrimination really is space-agnostic." To sit on the floor is to recall caste distinctions between upper castes who sit on raised surfaces and those who sit on the ground. On the one hand, it makes no sense to think of the Metro as a comparable space to, let's say, many Delhi kitchens where domestic help will sit on the ground or low jute stools but never at a table, even to eat. Nonetheless, the journalist makes this kind of visual transference that resonates for many. Within hours the photo and caption generated thousands of likes, retweets, and comments. The comments ranged from those thanking the journalist for having exposed such persistent social hierarchies to those lambasting her for spewing trash and untruths that made India look bad.

The photo went viral when it crossed multiple social media platforms including Instagram and Facebook, and became the subject of numerous online news articles, opinion pieces, and blog posts. For a moment it seemed that all eyes were trained on these women and their seating arrangements. Shekhar Gupta, editor-in-chief of the online news portal *The Print*, wrote in praise of the journalist's tweet (who he calls "our reporter") and proclaimed that "class is the new caste."[5] Gupta's article describes the substandard treatment domestic servants receive from families, a treatment that is symbolically rendered in their spatial arrangements in homes and in public.

It's not always easy to tell how people are socially related on the Metro, and in this case, the journalist said that she asked the nanny why she was sitting on the floor. Not surprisingly, the nanny said it was her choice to do so. Another interpretation of the photo is that it is not employers who tell their domestic help to sit below them, but the employees themselves who feel more comfortable doing so.

The veracity of the photo—the social reality it actually depicts—depends on whose gaze is being privileged: the journalist who frames the shot and distributes it; the mother who employs the nanny; or the nanny herself, who seems to be looking at something beyond the photo's frame. The journalist's commentary on the photo was refuted by the mother, who turned out to be a doctor at the All India Institute of Medical Sciences (AIIMS), the country's premier medical research unit and government hospital known for serving the poor. The mother-doctor says, by way of an open letter on her brother's blog then reported in *Outlook Magazine*, that they were all sitting on the floor and she had just gotten up to appease her child and then ended up sitting on the empty seat to feed him. She goes on to detail the supportive relationship she has with her nanny and how well she treats her.[6]

Perhaps it doesn't matter if the AIIMS doctor and her nanny were exemplifying a hierarchy or not. The image struck a chord and came to represent a contrast: the open, liberal, and equalizing space of a

Metro train versus the long-standing hierarchical relationship between employer and servant, an embodied relationship that is ubiquitous in the city. The journalist's commentary was accepted as truthful in a general sense; everyone has seen such scenes on the Metro, in restaurants, or other public places, and many live these relations each day inside their homes, either as servant or employer. It is a register of ordinariness that people were ready to identify with and comment on but also distance themselves from.

What is distinctive about the viral photo is not the image of middle-class women sitting higher than a working-class woman, but rather that the scene is framed by the Metro coach. The Delhi Metro may be a top-down transnational production cementing elite interests, but inside the trains, the space of the coach is meant to be a social equalizer: there is only one kind of seat or space to stand or sit and one class of ticket. According to Metro rules, no one is allowed to sit on the floor of the train, but you see it happening, especially when the train is not crowded.

Not only in the photo itself, but in a larger sense, the Metro has become a framing device. It has become a space of social visibility. The ladies' coach in particular is a site that produces globalized, gendered, middle-class norms. The viral photo bruises liberal sensibilities and says that the Metro is a container for and a conduit of persistent hierarchies of caste and class.

In a different kind of response to the photo, a trade union organizer in Chennai made a policy plea for the government to recognize domestic workers legally. This legal recognition would ensure them contracts and minimum wages, but also place others in a better position to detect and prosecute cases of abuse and trafficking. In an article in *The Print*, she asks readers to consider calling for legislative change if they were so bothered by the class dynamics exposed in the photo, to engage beyond their "momentary interest." It is the lack of public recognition that makes these workers not only vulnerable but, she says, "mostly invisible."[7]

The Metro makes a private relationship public, as public transport is also a moving picture of social relationships, sometimes laid bare. In this case, where Metro and digital platforms intersect, there is a capacity of the Metro as public space to spark debate on issues that on the surface have nothing to do with transport. Yet two mobilities, two kinds of movement are for an instant juxtaposed and captured on film. And with it, the great anxiety that exists about who is moving up in the world and who is staying in place.

VOIDS AND SOLIDS

Voids are open areas, solids are built up. The relationship between voids and solids creates a city's geometry: a meeting of angles and spaces, points and lines. The city gets etched in, filled up.

BEAUTY SALON

At a beauty salon near Amar Colony on the Violet Line, Mrs. Khanna, who owns the salon, and Arun, Indrani, Vikram, and Revati, who work there, talk to me about their Metro experiences.

Mrs. Khanna is in her earlies sixties, and I come to see that the salon is her life and that she cares a lot about her staff, their safety, their well-being.

"When the Metro started running and I wanted to go on it, my husband said, no, you have to come with me in the car. Then in 2009, he passed away; then I had to ride the Metro. My daughter is married, my son goes to college. I don't want to depend on anyone," Mrs. Khanna explains.

"Metro is also to keep fit; there are lifts and escalators, but I prefer to take the steps. I do Ketu puja on Tuesdays; 108 times we have to repeat. I close my eyes and do like this," she says, as she taps her fingers with her thumb.

"It's what the Panditji told me, *man mein karte*, do it from the inside. I don't want others to be disturbed." I ask Mrs. Khanna how long it takes her to do the puja, which I come to understand is about liberation and retirement but also resolving property disputes. "Twenty minutes." What had become a ritual she performed in the car is now slotted in the timed intervals of her Metro travel.

The salon is divided into two small areas, one for "gents," the other for "ladies." The ceilings are low and there are no windows, just the soft glow of a greenish-yellow light. We sit and stand among haircutting implements, mirrors, and swivel chairs.

Arun, with a ready smile, is in his late thirties and usually cuts men's hair. "The Metro is direct, the bus stops at lights. I like it, I go to Dakshinpuri, Ambedkar Nagar. On days off, I use it to go to Kashmere Gate to meet my family. I usually get a seat."

"Thirty-eight rupees up-down, a little less with a Metro card," says Vikram. He has the orange-red hue of henna in his hair and a slightly more weathered appearance. He remarks, "You save time, and you go comfortably. In Metro, there's no pollution."

Arun explains, "Men don't talk on the Metro. It's fine. If you bump someone by mistake on the bus, you'll get into a fight. This doesn't happen on the Metro."

"We don't mind if ladies push into us; we don't like gents pushing us," says Indrani, with her wide, round face and a heavy, black-haired bun.

Revati, who seemed somber at first, appears revived by our conversation and offers, "I make friends on the Metro. First, I offer them a seat, then I see them again and again. All ages, young and old. Office-time it's 'hello-hi.' We chat."

"Young girls on the Metro don't give seats. They are just on their mobiles," Indrani says.

"First, I was scared, especially of the escalator, then I got used to it. You wait in the morning for three minutes or four minutes; in the afternoon, for five minutes, six minutes. It's perfect, I tell you. It should just never stop underground, that is scary," says Revati.

"At office-time, it's a big problem, it can take you an hour to get through the line and come to work."

Indrani reaches over to Revati and hugs her while making kissing noises. She then leans over in my direction and whispers about couples on the Metro. They are everywhere and she doesn't like seeing them. They should stay in the parks, not in a public place like the Metro.

Habiba has been quiet this whole time but comes to join the group photo they've asked me to take. While they assemble, she tells me that she doesn't take the Metro because she lives nearby.

I take the picture with my phone and show it to the group. They all remark on Indrani's fair skin, they seem cheered by it, as if she's won a prize.

SUICIDE

Each week people jump from Metro platforms onto the tracks. Citing 2015 figures, the Delhi Metro Rail Corporation stated that in total there had been eighty suicide attempts at Metro stations, with seventeen deaths. In 2019, *India Today* reported twenty-five suicide attempts in seventeen months. The DMRC emphasizes that most suicide attempts lead to the victim being maimed, not killed. They hope this fact will deter people.[8] But if anything, the problem seems to be getting worse.

A lot of Metro-related media coverage is devoted to the reporting of suicide attempts. The articles are always short and to the point, and generally come from the Press Trust of India news feed, which is then printed in a number of daily newspapers. There is no commentary or analysis in these articles, although sometimes you can glean some of the larger issues that might undergird these cases. For instance, on February 11, 2018, it was reported:

> A 50-year-old man was crushed today when he jumped in front of a speeding train at Janakpuri East station around 5:25 p.m. The incident occurred when a train bound for Noida City Centre was entering Platform 1. The deceased was identified as K—— S. A suicide note was recovered from his person. According to the note, he took the extreme step because of on-going health problems.

A few days earlier, the Press Trust of India reported a similar story with a different outcome:

> A 32-year-old man was witnessed trying to leap from Rohini West elevated station down to the road below. Constable PC D—— immediately rushed and stopped him from jumping. He later told the security personnel that he had had a 'tiff' with his wife, leading him to said action.

On March 26, 2015:

> An 18-year-old youth committed suicide by jumping in front of a Delhi Metro train at Nawada station around 1 p.m. The deceased was identified as M—— Q——, a resident of Uttar Pradesh's Bijnor district. He was living with his uncle in Uttam Nagar area of Delhi. 'He died on the spot,' said a police officer. Earlier police said the train was headed towards Noida from Dwarka but later corrected themselves and said it was going towards Vaishali. Police are yet to ascertain the reason behind the suicide.

Reported on March 20, 2015:

Central Industrial Security Force (CISF) Constable S. M—— noticed a woman sitting at the end of the platform at Tagore Garden metro station in an apparent distressed composure. The constable alerted a lady sub-inspector who rushed to the distressed woman's side and counselled her. The woman said her husband used to harass her. She was taken to the station control room where she was met by her mother. The woman refused to register a police complaint against her husband as was suggested by security personnel on the spot.

On January 4, 2018, *Outlook News* reported:

A 74-year-old man jumped before a moving train at a GTB Nagar station on the Yellow Line, when a train bound for Huda City Centre was entering Platform 1. The deceased has been identified as B D——, a resident of Adarsh Nagar area in the national capital. He was rushed to a nearby hospital but could not be saved. A suicide note was recovered from him. It said he was taking the extreme step because of family issues.

Suicide attempts show another side to the Metro's institutionality. The Metro is an institution but also a confluence of security forces, of slow and quick thinking, of actions taken and averted, of alert and dull states, of advice and counsel, self-help and societal intervention. Metro tracks become a recurrent site of trauma for all involved. The Metro certainly does not cause the suicide attempts, the system does not lead one to attempt suicide, but it makes attempts more visible. This public-ness and outside-ness strikes a contrast to the personal and familial dramas that sometimes play out in stations. It is precisely the Metro's efficiency that may be attracting some to attempt suicide at its stations.

Fareed, a suicide prevention counselor in Delhi, explains to me that in the past the most common methods of suicide were for people to take the insecticide TIC 20, the floor cleaner Fanal, or sleeping pills. Having counseled people and worked on a suicide hotline for over twenty-five years, Fareed speculates that the Metro may promise a more immediate and instantaneous death than poison or pills. He says the Metro is "accessible to everyone" and runs from early morning to late night. It offers a huge "window of opportunity" and is "suitably anonymous." The incidence of suicides on the Metro is certainly a new pattern, only because the Metro was not there before. Presumably people would have found other means or other places before the Metro.

Fareed describes three typical suicide patterns in Delhi:

One. There is the man, usually in his fifties or sixties, experiencing a midlife crisis. He could be a farmer who will never be able to repay his debts, or someone with a failing business, a dreadful marriage, or an affair that has come to light. Basically, a situation of deep shame. Someone who feels there is no way forward.

Two. Students, as a result of school-leaving exams. There is an NGO that comes up every June just for that. They have a hotline for about ten days. The callers tend to be seventeen- and eighteen-year-old boys, the demographic that receives the most academic pressure from their parents.

Three. Women soon after marriage or who are in an abusive marriage, or who have not been able to get married. Some kind of dead-end marriage situation.

At the same time, Fareed notices two major trends in Delhi families over the last fifteen years. First, divorce is no longer a stigma. Everyone has a divorce in the family now. Many kids in upper-middle-class schools like Vasant Vihar and Delhi Public School are children of divorced parents. And second, every family has an intercommunity marriage, whether crossing caste or religious lines. His point is that the fabric of society is changing so fast, many don't know how to keep up. He speaks of how important Valentine's Day has become for the fourteen-plus crowd, and how problematic it is if you don't have a girlfriend. By seventeen, you must have had some kind of sexual intimacy with someone.

For the Delhi Metro Rail Corporation, suicides are a technical problem; they interfere with the purpose and functioning of the trains. DMRC project manager Mangu Singh sees suicides as an issue of time and as a break in the system: "Suicide attempts on Metro tracks throw the entire system out of gear. This happens despite our really quick response to the emergency. Even in cases where the body gets entangled under the train, we manage to clear the tracks within a period of twenty minutes. But even these twenty minutes hurt the Metro system as trains on the corridor start bunching and there are consequent delays. We also pull out the affected train operator because the trauma is huge for him too."[9]

DMRC officials don't like to talk about the incidence of suicides at Metro stations. It is a technical inconvenience but also goes against the image of the Metro as liberating, efficient, and aspirational. When I ask DMRC officials about suicides, they talk of the coming of automatic screen doors, like those in the Singapore and Hong Kong metro systems, but then also say that the doors are not to prevent suicides but for the smoother functioning of the trains. And anyway, most stations will continue to have exposed tracks. While the DMRC cannot address the underlying causes, they have started to train staff and personnel to identify potential suicides and respond to them.[10]

Brinda, who works with the suicide prevention organization Sanjivini, thinks the DMRC needs to be part of an awareness campaign since the Metro is a "natural space" to address it. "The Metro is a great leveler for the working population aged eighteen to forty-five, the lower middle class to the upper middle class. This is also a highly stressed population. They are educated, they understand Hindi and English." A demographic, more than an individual profile.

Prathima, another suicide counselor, says the problem is that people want too much today. They want the smart lifestyles they see on television. They get disappointed.[11] It is not that people want to die, she tells me, it is that they need a source of "fresh air." The Metro becomes the destination for what I come to see as a kind of useless, futile mobility. The noise, the lights, the crowds. An ordered space with regular rhythms.

MULTIPLE CHOICE

In the DMRC Junior Engineer Recruitment Exam study book, the language of infrastructure spills out. No one talks like this on the trains, but we're encased by it—the forms, the materials, the pressure points:

A structure which offers negligible or zero resistance on bending at any point is known as

(a) beam   (b) girder
(c) arch   (d) cable or string

The shape which a cable takes (hanging freely) under a uniform distributed load per metre run will be

(a) parabola   (b) hyperbola
(c) straight line   (d) elliptical

The simplest geometrical form of a truss is

(a) triangle   (b) parallelogram
(c) trapezium   (d) rhombus

The magnetic meridian at a point can be fixed by

(a) bar magnets   (b) electro magnets
(c) magnetic compass   (d) None of these

Lime is mixed with brick earth to

(a) impart plasticity   (b) increase durability
(c) prevent shrinkage   (d) increase permeability

The temperature at which bricks are burnt varies from

(a) 400°–700° C   (b) 700°–1000° C
(c) 1000°–1200° C   (d) 1200°–1500° C

The seepage force in soil is proportional to

(a) exit gradient   (b) head of water at upstream
(c) head of water at downstream   (d) All of the above

In a gravel road, the building material used is

(a) cement   (b) lime
(c) clay   (d) surkhi

Generally, the premix carpet laid in India is of thickness

(a) 15 cm   (b) 10 cm
(c) 5–7.5 cm   (d) 2 cm

In a structure generally the members used as tension members are

(a) wires and cables   (b) rods and bars
(c) angle and tee section   (d) All of these

The failure of a column depends upon

(a) weight of column   (b) length of column
(c) slenderness ratio   (d) cross sectional area of column[12]

JAHNAVI

Jahnavi and I are sitting in her office canteen, drinking sweet Nescafé from small plastic cups. She is a chatty, twenty-something journalist who covers the visual arts. This beat puts her low down on the journalistic totem pole, she tells me. She has to fight to get her stories in the paper.

Jahnavi lives with her parents in Ghaziabad in U.P., not far from the Delhi border, but has also lived in more central parts of the city. "I am a real Dilliwala," she says. "I love Delhi. It's a city made by its people. There is no one prevalent culture, no dominant culture."

And then she says this: "The person I am today is because of the way I commuted." Until the Metro came, Jahnavi always traveled by Delhi Transit Corporation buses. "How I traveled, how people treated me, how I fought with conductors, how I fought with bus drivers. That has shaped me as a person, that has made me more aggressive.

"I remember those bus numbers since I waited for them for hours. I used to wait for the 588 and it wouldn't come, and the bus shelter was so dark and isolated. I was a trainee at the *Express* in those days. I was earning, but very little, I couldn't afford autos."

I ask her if she ever takes the bus now. "I wouldn't, I wouldn't. I remember all my incidents, incidents I can never forget, of eve-teasing [sexual harassment in public places], of people touching me, feeling me. I can never forget them, even now. Those memories are so vivid that sometimes I get up at night and feel someone's hands on me. They've left deep scars on me; they've changed me as a person."

As we talk, I sense that Jahnavi's personal history of transit is also her diagnosis of the city's ills. I get engrossed and note how her frustrations about transit mirror those she has about her fellow citizens' civilities and incivilities. There are both repeated themes and inconsistencies in her narrative. By the end, I feel I should offer her my own diagnosis but don't have one.

"Earlier you had to think which buses went where, but now with the Metro, I can go almost anywhere, even if the Metro doesn't go exactly there." I assume, correctly, that she rides in the ladies' coach. "I treasure those twenty-five minutes being separated from the men. Even if they're not doing anything, I just don't want them there. It's a very confined space."

Figure 19. Hazrat Nizamuddin station, Pink Line, 2019. This station is named after and is adjacent to one of the major railway hubs in the city, a short walk or rickshaw ride away.

Nevertheless, she sees new kinds of aggressions on the Metro. "Those who used to wait for a bus now behave so impatiently on the Metro, not being able to queue up, rushing to get a seat, pushing and knocking over whoever comes in one's way.

"The Metro has brought us all together. You're privy to others' conversations, seeing their messages on mobiles, even if you don't mean to. Today there was a woman listening to devotional music and singing it out loud! I see a lot of people doing their own thing. They're not bothered by how crowded it is, or if someone's being pushed. They're just so lost in themselves. I see that a lot.

"The Metro has exposed us, in a way. How we are indifferent to people. Like if there is a pregnant lady standing, we won't get up." She clarifies that men will get up for women, but women won't. "We all go through pregnancy or will go through it, but we just won't get up. There are just too many of us, clamoring for too little. It's disturbing what I see, how women behave with each other."

Jahnavi speculates how Indian women are different in reality as compared to how they are depicted in culture and mythology: "I've seen a different side of women in Delhi. One minute someone is limping, the next she is racing to get a seat. In the confined space you see the true faces of people. How people will go ahead of you even at the security when you've put your bag in before theirs. You will end up hurting me." And then, she adds, "Whoever hurts me, it's fine."

Jahnavi recounts a story of a woman in her thirties who approached her in the ladies' coach, saying she was being followed by a man: "'Why are you afraid?' I said to her. 'It's a public space, he can't do anything.' This was at 11 a.m., just imagine. Even in a public space, it can be scary. There was this bond between me and this woman that got formed right there. We exchanged numbers and used to speak on the phone. She was a gemologist.

"I thought these women's coaches would transform into a public space where you could find discussion and debate, but that hasn't happened. We avoid talking to strangers. They're very abstract, these spaces. Immediately after that incident [the 2012 bus rape/murder of Jyoti Singh Pandey], there were these NGOs that would come into the Metro. 'You should react,' they would say, 'you could come to India Gate for these protests'; but people just sat silently. Nobody asked questions or said anything.

"The Metro has made life easier and simpler for me. I don't have to depend on office cars. I can reach the places I need to reach for my work. I'm seeing someone in Gurgaon now, and I can be there in one and a half hours. You cross three states and you're there. Every time I step on the Metro, I bless Sreedharan for having done this. He is a hero. It's something unthinkable what he's done."

CAFÉ COFFEE DAY

Dr. Vandhya keeps checking her phone. She's been sitting next to me for some time at one of the two Café Coffee Days in Rajiv Chowk station beneath Connaught Place. It's cramped here and the air conditioning is not very strong. There's a drip coming down from the ceiling, occasionally hitting me on the shoulder. Two guys in their twenties are on the other side of me with chicken tikka sandwiches and cappuccinos on the table between them. Dr. Vandhya looks preoccupied but also a little sleepy. It's noisy. I wait, but then we start to chat, and she immediately comes to life. She is sixty-five years old, a retired army gynecologist. She lives in Vikas Puri, west Delhi, which is an hour and a half away by car, two hours in traffic. Before the Metro Dr. Vandhya would take autos and taxis. Now she only takes the Metro:

"I get a seat ninety-nine percent of the time in the regular coaches. I don't ride the ladies coach; it's a fish market, so much chirping." She tells me that "people are decent enough on the trains," especially "the young generation." But the "car rush" problem hasn't been reduced by the Metro. She likes "Kejriwal's odd-even scheme," which is the Delhi government's once-in-a-while plan to reduce road traffic by limiting who can drive on which days based on their license plate numbers. "People pool; there is a noticeable difference. They allowed women drivers on both days," she tells me before realizing she's sitting at the wrong Café Coffee Day and hurries off to the other one.

Now there is a family of three sitting at the table where the two guys had been. They have downcast glances, and at first, I don't feel like interrupting them, but then we do get to talking and I learn that the daughter, maybe in her early twenties, is traveling to Subhash Nagar hospital in Dwarka. She's here with her mother and brother. The brother looks at me somewhat gravely and says that his sister will travel on the Blue Line once or twice a week to go to the hospital. She will be going for treatment, I'm made to understand. This will be a hospital commute. On this day, they are trying it out, showing her the way.

A little later, another woman is sitting alone next to me, looking down at her smartphone. She ends a call with her son who she was supposed to have met here. She talks to me instead, and in the course of the conversation, lets slip that she comes from a "well-settled" Rajput family but had a love marriage and became part of a Brahmin family.

"My husband met with an accident early on in our marriage," she begins, when I tell her I'm interested in urban transport. "Our son was just a year old. He was driving his car when he was hit by a truck. He lost his memory for two months. He couldn't remember Russian, Spanish, Portuguese, or any of the family, including me. Money is not everything."

Alpana is a college lecturer, a linguist. "The Metro," she says, was at first an example of "the government *not* doing anything for the people." People living "under the bridges," she explains, "cannot approach the Metro. It is meant for working, middle-class people, people who park at stations and then ride the trains." I think of the rows upon rows of motorcycles at stations across Noida, like Vaishali and Botanical Garden. She is right that the Metro is most of all for people who have somewhere to go, and many of those people already have vehicles. The Metro further accelerates their lives.

Alpana sees the city's transport options in terms of the class layers in the city. "I studied at JNU (Jawaharlal Nehru University)," she tells me, "in those days I would drive my father's car. My friends asked me how I could be a Marxist. 'Come on the road,' they would say, 'leave your shoes, and then we'll see if you're a Marxist.'"

Alpana laments the inequality of the Metro. "If thirty-three percent reservations are there for women in Parliament, why only one ladies' coach? Can the average family take the Metro to Gurgaon to go to Dream City? The Metro fare is more than double the bus. The Metro is for ladies who go shopping, you see them carrying large bags on the Metro, but they can't spare a penny for a common person living under a flyover. The city's infrastructures are places for people to live or beg under."

Alpana volunteers at the suicide prevention center, Sanjivini. One day last year while riding the Metro on the Yellow Line to Vishwavidyalaya, it stopped at Race Course station and when the doors opened, she looked across the platform to see a young woman jump in front of an oncoming train. As a volunteer at Sanjivini, she was especially upset by this and wanted to go back, to see to the girl, but the friend she was traveling with cautioned against it. Her friend knew that within fifteen minutes, it would be "all cleaned up."

"Why don't young people want to live?" Alpana asks. "In our families we are not talking in a positive manner with our youngsters." She pauses and then says, "I can convince her to stop from committing suicide, but I can't jump with the girl."

Before Alpana gets up to leave, she tells me one more thing, almost as an aside or salvo, I'm not sure which. "I see my students on the Metro and they are usually with boyfriends or girlfriends. *Theek hai*. That's okay. But they ignore me; they won't make eye contact. Fine, I say, you want to hide your love story."

Thinking about how couples show themselves in the city, I make my way to the other Café Coffee Day across the main concourse and sit next to a couple huddled over a veggie bun. What is revealed and concealed in public? This Café Coffee Day is much nicer than the other one, with a properly fitted ceiling, no droplets of water, stronger air conditioning. I see Dr. Vandhya again; this time she's having a snack with what looks to be her son, his wife, a granddaughter. She waves at me. More couples and groups enter the cafe; it is filling up now as the afternoon stretches on, as the trains keep coming. The walls of the café are covered with black and white photos of trees and a slogan that reads: "Nature loves our coffee." Included is a promise to grow more trees, a pledge that the Delhi Metro Rail Corporation also makes, ten saplings planted for every tree cut. The discourse on nature and greenery is both soothing and strange in this underground space, in this hulking, coughing city.

LOOKS

Several men in their twenties with hard looks line the space between the ladies' and general coaches. A cold stare that looks past and across, at no one and everyone. Next to them a couple squeezed in, looking into each other. Intimacy next to confrontation.

STREET SURVEY

In the lanes of Dakshinpuri, compressed, three-story, concrete dwellings line each lane, with simple grills over the windows, and plants hanging from balconies. There's a constant din of motorbike engines, honking horns, chirping birds, barking dogs, people's chatter. Girls sit on doorsteps of their homes; boys lean on motorcycles.

I've come to meet Seema, and we walk through the lanes near her house. She convinces me that this is the way to "survey" her neighborhood. She knows many of the people we meet, but not all. Most say they don't ride the Metro, which is not surprising since many of the guys are sitting on their motorcycles as they talk to us. Some say they ride it once in a while, which usually means a couple of times a month. The thing about the Metro, they say, is that you have to take an auto to get to the station (Chirag Delhi for the Magenta Line, Saket for the Yellow Line) and that costs twenty rupees. Then you have to go into it, down the escalators, through security. But the real putoffs are the lines to buy tokens, first at counters, now at machines that sometimes don't work.

There is Chanchal, eighteen, a college student who says she uses the Metro sometimes. "I have to come and go a lot," she says, "but I only use it if I have to go to Karol Bagh or Jandewalan. I don't think of anything but to get there quickly. The bus is difficult, sometimes you have to wait for fifteen-twenty minutes. Before, the Metro wasn't expensive, but now it is in the sixty-rupee range. I am a student. I'm doing a BA at JB College in Faridabad. I get there by college cab."

Gayatri, a twenty-eight-year-old IT programmer, says, "Traveling by Metro is very convenient, it's time saving. And if the station is nearby, all the better. Before we went by bus, then auto to the station. I go from Chirag Delhi station to Noida, sector 135. I change at Botanical Garden. Before I went by bus. Now I get there in twenty-five minutes. It's secure in the Metro; in the bus they do snatching. Metro is *sahi* (correct). If I'm with friends, I go in the general coach, otherwise ladies. It depends where I can get a seat. If I'm coming late from office, I prefer to come by Metro."

Nikita, twenty-two, who works in admin for an NGO, remarks, "In Metro there's a big crowd, but we can get anywhere easily. There are a lot of facilities."

Anu, twenty-two, wants to study to be a hospital technician. She compares the Metro to other forms of transport: "In the bus you waste time. Metro is comfortable. You can wash your hands in the stations. On the bus, you can recognize people; on the Metro, you don't recognize anyone. Autos are expensive and then there's the chance you'll be in an accident. Metro is completely safe, nothing can happen."

We turn the corner into a narrow lane where several young women are sitting out on the stoops of their homes, oiling their hair.

Ruksa, nineteen, says, "I go by Metro to college at DU [Delhi University]. Now college is over and I don't go anywhere. I don't have a job."

Shalu, twenty-four, says, "I go to college by Metro to Vishwavidyalaya station. I also go by Metro to visit my relatives. I was afraid of the escalator. I have to take someone's hand. Sometimes I get confused, where to get on, where to get off. But it's easy to take the Metro. You're not sweating. We can charge our phones. It's better than waiting at a bus stand. Sometimes the bus doesn't come. You save a lot of time by Metro. You avoid the traffic. It's not expensive, it's normal. Well, it's a little expensive."

Mumtaz, thirty-four, keeps it simple, "It's good, what else can I say? I never feel afraid there."

Then we encounter Yash, who is twenty-four, and whose path we cross as we get further from the scent of amla oil wafting through the air. He wears clear aviator glasses and a plastic headband pushing back a lush head of black hair. "I feel good in the Metro. I don't get negative vibes there. It's safe. For men and women, both. For senior citizens, too. I take the Metro from Malviya Nagar to Hauz Khas, just one stop. If I go by auto the whole way, it's too far for me. I take a shared auto to the Metro station. It takes me just ten-fifteen minutes to reach there. My school is just two-three hundred meters from the Metro stop." With a wide grin he tells us about his hairdressing course in the Hauz Khas; he is going places.

"I'll finish my course in two-three months. I have only one dream: to be a creative hairdresser. I love doing this. After graduation, they'll provide me a placement; they have a partnership with Looks and other salons. I'm very happy with my course. I'm very satisfied." We feel satisfied too after talking to Yash; maybe because he was so upbeat, maybe because he had a lot to say; maybe because his one-stop use of the Metro counters everything else we've heard.

AASIF

The interchange at Hauz Khas station is one long slick concourse connecting the Magenta and Yellow Lines. It is an awesome space with a sea of people, numbers which I haven't seen on the Metro quite in this way before. The width and length of the concourse shapes the sea into a massive undulating wave. A hum of voices and shuffling feet. And then, after some time, it peters out and returns to a flow and then a trickle. Then emptiness with only the lights bouncing off the walls.

When I reach the Yellow Line, I notice a young man in a wheelchair rolling fast down the platform, pumping up his arms. He's nothing short of exuberant. At the ladies' coach end of the platform, he slows down and is met by a DMRC staff member who helps him maneuver his wheelchair so he can get on the train. I get on and see this man, not in the designated wheelchair area behind the train operator cabin but holding onto one of the metal poles. He has a confident air, and it's clear he's enjoying himself. I decide to approach him and find out that his name is Aasif, that he's thirty-years old and has been riding the Metro for the last year.

"The Metro is great," he says, "a one-of-a-kind transport in the city. No other public transport works for me. One day last year I said, 'I'll go by Metro today.' I wanted to see the accessibility. It was exciting. I bought a token at the ticket counter, and a staff member there asked me, 'Do you need an escort?' The escort took me to the train. It was a very nice experience. That day I realized, I can travel, if connectivity is there.

"In this city, there is hardly a ramp to get into shops. Wherever I go, I try to sensitize people. At Domino's, I tell them, 'Look, get a ramp, people like me will come and also buy your pizza.' We have to go places, to the cinema, to restaurants, wherever.

"Recently, I took a bus, just to see. The bus driver had a hard time lowering the ramp, and then the ramp was in bad condition, as if it hadn't been opened before. The driver told me almost no one ever asks him to open it.

"My only complaint about the Metro is when the lift isn't working. Then I have to take a cab or an auto. Even at big Metro stations, there's only one lift."

We reach the INA Metro stop, where he's getting off. We exchange contact details before he is met by a staff member and quickly rolls away.

E-RICKSHAWS

When I get down from the platform at Majlis Park, it smells of sulfur gas. I'm at the outer edge of the city on a new section of the Pink Line. It is the last stop on the line, the northeastern reach of Metroland. Cows graze in marshy plains. Wheelchair ramps at the station are ample, inviting, but the station itself feels desolate. Outside, several e-rickshaws wait to take people to the surrounding residential societies, mid-rise apartment buildings one after the other, spaced out across empty fields. Outside the station: a small highway and the line of e-rickshaws. No vendors, no people, save the occasional group of schoolgirls with plaited hair. The e-rickshaw drivers tell me they take people to and from these apartment buildings all day, that's all they do, that's where they go. They gesture to the buildings around us in the far distance as if they are close by. The buildings are small islands, while the Metro station is a kind of mainland for the gondola-like e-rickshaws.

On the train back from Majlis Park to Rajouri Garden, Central Industrial Security Force (CISF) officers sit near but not in the ladies' coach. Many people get on at Azadpur. The train goes aboveground at Shakurpur. A guy squats in the gangway between the coaches, talking on his mobile. A woman in a frayed mint green sari travels with her son. The PA systems tells passengers there are sockets for charging laptops and mobile phones in the trains.

Across town at Jangpura station on the Violet Line, another line of e-rickshaws wait at the station exit. Abdul, Anil, and I sit in Anil's empty open-air vehicle. An e-rickshaw costs one lakh sixty thousand, but most drivers rent them for Rs. 350–400 a day. They can only ply in colonies, planned residential neighborhoods, and will get fined 4,500 rupees by the police if they're caught elsewhere, so they're afraid to go anywhere. Abdul used to work in a "steel fabrication factory," but now that he drives an e-rickshaw, he can make 500–600 rupees a day, a thousand, if he's lucky. Both men have a sense of resignation. The informality of this job is its allure and limitation.

Electronic rickshaws first came onto Delhi's roads in 2008. Then chief minister Sheila Dikshit was a proponent of them, since they ran on batteries and emitted no pollution. Rectangular in shape, they have a jeep-like quality to them, but are much closer to the ground. They replaced the exhaust-happy tuk-tuks that you used to see ferrying people from Old Delhi to Connaught Place. Like tuk-tuks, e-rickshaws can fit four to six passengers and pile on a few more if necessary. The driver sits up front and collects anywhere from ten to twenty rupees from each passenger,

Figure 20. Lal Quila station, Violet Line, 2018. Like the newspaper and phones depicted in this photo, the Metro relays information along with people.

usually for a few kilometers' ride. They ply known routes within neighborhoods or to and from Metro stations and markets. The vehicle has almost no shock-absorber system, so riding in one can be a shock to the system. They feel frail and bumpy, like riding in a frame of a vehicle rather than in the vehicle itself.

E-rickshaws are the cousin of the ubiquitous auto rickshaw, the triangular, three-wheeler that runs on compressed natural gas. Auto rickshaws may be open to the elements on the sides, but they have a hard shell overhead and a slightly more solid shock-absorber system on the three-passenger bench behind the driver. Autos can flip over though, as once happened to one of my aunts. The auto rickshaw she was riding in was hit by a car; it flipped, but she and the driver were okay. She said it was like being trapped upside down in a turtle.

E-rickshaws are considered "intermediate public transport"—vehicles that are used on hire for flexible passenger transportation but that do not follow a fixed time schedule. The government gives few permits for e-rickshaws to ply on roads, even though politicians like to talk about how good they are for last mile connectivity and for their nonpolluting ways. Bus and car drivers find them a nuisance, much like their view of cycle rickshaws. E-rickshaws add a dimension to the transport scene but have had only a small impact thus far.

Across the Yamuna River, in east Delhi, Tarun sits on his blue e-rickshaw, waiting for passengers to get on board. He seems to delight in his command over this vehicle. He has just taken me from the adjacent neighborhood of Trilokpuri to the Mayur Vihar station. He is from the locality, he tells me, a point of pride. Now he'll do the return journey once the vehicle is filled. Tarun says he can make 800 rupees a day, and that 400 of it goes for rent of the vehicle. He says he can work in a factory or in a tea stall or do this.

Transport is about speed but also about insulation between the passenger and the vehicle, the vehicle and the road, the driver and the city. It is about a bumpy ride, a bumpy life, an exposure to elements, a closeness or distance to the road.

LOVE MARRIAGE AND A HEAD INJURY

DAY ONE. It is the wedding of Seema's niece, Isha, to a boy named Amitabh. For months I had been hearing from Seema, the house cleaner of my upstairs neighbor, about the stress in her extended family over the relationship her niece was having with a boy she had met in college. Seema's brother (Isha's father) was trying to convince his daughter that she was too young to marry. Isha threatened that she would run away. The family was up in arms about what to do. They were also aware of where these kinds of conflicts might lead, such as an elopement or a pregnancy. The family may have been anxious about the couples' caste difference, but it seemed they were more concerned with the girl's future prospects, her upward mobility. The women in Seema's extended family who were in their thirties, forties, and fifties tended to do some kind of domestic work or work in beauty salons. Their kids were all getting educations, and the expectation was that they would do better. Seema says that it is Isha's age and not the fact that the two are of a different caste that is the issue.

On the morning of the wedding Seema meets me in front of my building, and we take an auto rickshaw together to the marriage hall at an Arya Samaj temple in Greater Kailash II. It's just down the now-defunct Bus Rapid Transit corridor, twenty minutes away, but somehow as we get closer, we can't find the venue, so we stop at street corners and ask our auto driver to ask for directions. We loop around the colony. Some entryways to the colony are closed even in the daytime, which confuses our driver. We loop some more.

When we finally find it, when we finally get there, the couple has yet to arrive. We go inside and most of the women are seated in folding chairs that have been arranged in two rows to one side of the room. On the other side of the room is a buffet, with large stainless-steel containers and a tray of small plastic cups of Coke and Limca. I already know her sister, Kamala, but Seema introduces me to her mother, her other sisters, their husbands and children. I sit with the women on the folding chairs; they seem happy.

The couple has known each other for two years, but they are both too young; both families agree on this point. One sister tells me that it is the first love marriage in their extended family. Another says they are "just eighteen" and still in college. Someone else mentions that the boy's family has "two-two cars."

The couple arrives and sits on the dais on matching throne chairs. Isha is very slim and wears a sparkly purple sari. Amitabh wears a cream-colored kurta pajama and sports a garland of ten-rupee notes. As per tradition for brides, Isha is crying through much of the celebration, a soft teary cry, not a sob.

DAY TWO. Seema is hit by a motorbike while getting onto a bus on her way to work. She is in emergency with a head injury. It's not too serious, and she is sent home by the end of the day.

When I visit her at her home later, in the lanes of Dakshinpuri, we eat chicken biryani that her daughter has made, and while I lament her accident, she is more interested to tell me that "the dividing line" in life, socially and economically, is whether you own your own place. Seema does not, while her brother, living a few doors down on the same lane, does.

DAY THREE. Seema's sister, Kamala, says Isha wanted to marry quickly so that, one, Amitabh did not find another girl, and two, her parents did not find her another boy. Marriage, she tells me, was a strategy as well as a risk.

FARE HIKE

At the beauty salon near Amar Colony again, it is less than a year after the Metro fare hike, which raised fares by 50 percent. The ruling Delhi Aam Aadmi Party sided with "the people" in this case, demanding that the DMRC and the Bhartiya Janata Party–led central government reverse the increase. This didn't happen, and by the summer of 2018, about a year after the hike in fares, Metro ridership had fallen by about 30 percent. Indrani, Revati, Arun, and Vikram all still take the Metro, but the fare hike has hit them.

Indrani explains, "I started to take the bus for a few days, but it's slow, it takes more time, and it's closed in."

"What was eight or ten rupees became eighteen or twenty," says Arun. "A few rupees more would have been okay, but this really pinches. Long journeys are okay, but short journeys are too expensive."

Neelam, new to the salon, lives close by in Nizamuddin. She takes the bus to work since it only costs ten rupees. If she took the Metro it would be thirty-five rupees, fifteen for the Metro and twenty for the cycle rickshaw. The bus is point-to-point. Neelam is in her early twenties, and her surface demureness quickly falls away once she starts to speak, with clarity and some passion. She has been working at the salon for a year; before that she completed a beauty course in Lajpat Nagar.

"I know how to ride the bus," she tells me, "how to deal with men who are sometimes drunk. The bus is okay until eight at night; after nine, ten, it can be bad, especially if there aren't many people on it. I only get on a bus if there are a couple of other women on it. Ever since the 2012 bus case, people are scared."

I commute home with Indrani that evening. We all leave together—Mrs. Khanna, Indrani, Revati, and I—and exit through the back of entrance of the salon and walk a few minutes to the Moolchand station entrance. Mrs. Khanna and I take the stairs up to the station.

Indrani and Revati go to a different entrance that has a lift. I get the feeling that because there's a lift, they feel they want to use it. We meet up aboveground, and Indrani proceeds to mock-search me, joking how "physical" the security searches have gotten these days. We all go through security and the ticket gates, and Indrani and I say goodbye to Mrs. Khanna and Revati, who are traveling northbound. Indrani and I get on the ladies' coach of a Badarpur-bound train. We stand at first, then Indrani gets a partial seat, squeezed in between two other women. I stand holding a metal pole in front of her. Soon a girl on the opposite side of the coach gets up and I take her seat. We ride. Indrani is looking at the phone of the young woman sitting next to her and then she's absorbed in her own phone. As we approach Kalkaji Mandir station, Indrani says, "Quick, look outside!" The whole mandir is lit up against a darkening sky. A woman in her twenties, sitting next to me, asks me if it's my first time on the Metro, since she saw Indrani pointing things out to me. I laugh and say, no, I've been riding it for years. We start to chat. Her name is Latika; she is friendly, cheerful. She works in Lajpat Nagar where she makes applications for iPhones and Androids. She travels home by Metro every evening and lives at the Badarpur border, a few minutes' walk from the station.

"When I used to take the bus anywhere it would take hours," Latika says. "Now, it's fast."

"Super-fast," Indrani chimes in with a big smile. There is a sense of mastery in her words and expression, a sense that this super-fastness is hers, that it is for her too.

"How is your experience commuting by Metro?" I ask Latika.

"Sometimes I see Metro riders using the apps I've made and that's cool," she says.

When I ask her about her accent, which seems slightly foreign to me, she replies, "I'm from Delhi and only Delhi. But my boyfriend is a foreigner. He is from Africa. Maybe that's why."

Her face lights up when she starts to speak about him and how they met through a friend from college. I can sense Indrani has become distanced from our conversation, with Latika and I speaking English at a fast clip.

As we three exit the train together at Badarpur, I say goodbye to Latika and continue walking with Indrani, who hurries me into a convenience store on the station premises. She insists on buying me chips and a drink because she can't have me over to her house. I never expected to go to her house, but then I realize she thinks I may have had that expectation.

"My house is not fully made, there is little furniture," she tells me.

"We don't have to go to your house, I was going to just go home now anyway," as I protest her offer of buying me snacks. Then I see that I may risk offending her. I decide not to refuse her hospitality.

We sit at the station, eating chips.

"I have worked at the salon for seventeen years, but I had a break of nine years in between," Indrani begins. "Ma'am [Mrs. Khanna] knows my story of trying to get a better house."

"What about your husband, your children?" I ask, somewhat tentatively.

"Of my three kids, one is not good with studies but he works in the Looks Salon. The other two, younger ones, are studying. My husband is a security guard in a hotel in Defence Colony. He makes the dinner each night with the vegetables I've cut in the morning. Then he works the night shift."

Talking like this at the busy station during the evening commute feels like a pause. It occurs to me that only here, not at her place of work, not in the Metro with others, and not in her own home would Indrani have been able to tell me her story, or her situation, at least. It is fragmentary and full of pauses, and I don't feel like quizzing her. And yet, there is a kind of urban intimacy that happens in the station, even between people like Indrani and me, who don't know each other well but wish each other well.

When we say goodbye, she pushes me toward the security line, worried about my safe return home. I make as if I'm going in, but then watch her descend the long staircase to exit the station. At the bottom of the stairs, she gives a coin to a beggar before hurrying along to the auto stand. She never looks back to see that I am lingering at the end of the security line; she thinks I've gone in.

AT HOME IN DAKSHINPURI

Aditya has a five-day-old beard, one by design I'm pretty sure. We are sitting in his parents' house in Dakshinpuri, a working-class area of south Delhi, where he lives, and where his sisters lived until they got married. "If you see," he says, "this is a twenty-five-yard house, so we have less space. Luckily, we have a good place to live; we have a park outside; we don't have buildings just across. Another good thing, we are going to have a six-hundred-bed government hospital just a walk away. They have been building it for the last six-seven years, and it's going to be completed in the next two-three years."

Aditya is the nephew of Seema, who lives a few houses away on the same lane, and Kamala, who lives in east Delhi. It is because of his aunts that I have come to know him. Aditya works in Noida at an IT company. Unlike his aunts, he speaks in English. I start by asking him about transport, how he gets to work. He drives his motorcycle each day. Metro stops form part of the landscape for him, but he doesn't ride it. Soon our conversation turns to where we are rather than where he goes.

"The drawback is the area. People think Dakshinpuri is not a good place to live, people who live in posh areas like Malviya Nagar. I have many friends who live in other localities, and they think Dakshinpuri is not a good place to live. But if I think of myself, I find everything I need here. If you go elsewhere, to Noida, you won't find the culture of neighborliness we have here. There people are stuck to their house; here people ask you things." As I watch Aditya talk, sitting on his sofa in his small house, he seems out of place; his ambitions are beyond this place, even as he is anchored by it, proud of it. And then he happens to say,

"In the future I may shift to another place, but my mother wants to stay here where she knows everyone. You want a place where your kids can play safely. Whether you are in Dakshinpuri or GK [Greater Kailash], things can happen anywhere. But crime is more here. Younger people get motivated to do bad things, illegal things. Maybe they are not educated enough; they don't have friends or a good background or good lifestyle, and then they have the same kind of people attached to them. If they have a problem with people, some negotiate with talk, others with fists. There is much hope things will get better."

Mobility isn't just about where you are going, but also where you are from, even if that place isn't static.

"Dakshinpuri has changed in terms of facilities and in terms of standard of living and in terms of people's perspective; it got changed. But I still feel it has much scope, a wider scope to improve the society, because in Dakshinpuri people are from a low background or if I were to talk about the caste, we are from SC [scheduled caste] / ST [scheduled tribe] and not from a big background.[13]

"People got these houses because earlier they were living in slums; they came from slums to this place. We have good facilities in Dakshinpuri, there is water logging. If you go to other areas, you have rain for an hour and you see things get clogged. It's the municipal government that is in charge of that. Water logging is a unique feature of this colony. We also have nearby hospitals, malls, and three Metro stations: Malviya Nagar, Chirag Delhi, Saket, on two lines, Yellow and Magenta. And if I have to get an electronic item, we have Nehru Place."

I ask him if this was his family's first *pukka* house. "Yes, but our family was not living in slums. We came from Bijnor, where our grandparents were doing small jobs, working in houses. Now my grandfather has passed away, and my grandmother lives with my uncle. My father joined the army a long time ago. That changed things for my family; we got the opportunity to study. My brother, sisters, we all studied in the Kendriya Vidyalaya government schools. After that my brother was doing Economics honors from Dayal Singh College. He had a passion to go to the army; now he is posted in Patiala; he has one child and lives his own life. He's not in a very good position in the army, but he's happy; he has everything he wants to have. My younger sister, she studied till tenth standard; she's not much good in studies, so she quit. Yeah, it's too bad she doesn't want to study more. Through distance learning she did her exam for tenth standard from Open University. At age twenty-two–twenty-three she got married; she doesn't have plans. To go outside [abroad] you have to have some kind of talent or passion. We found a good family for her, from a good background in monetary terms, and in terms of values."

"What's a good family?" I ask.

"From an Indian perspective, we thought of 'good background' in terms of wealth, the person should have a good job, what his father's doing, what his brother's doing. They are not wealthy, but if I compare them to our family, they have a little bit 'up' status," Aditya says, using both hands to gesture up as if he's about to lift a ball.

"Every father, every brother wants to have something a little better for his sister. She is happily married; she lives nearby, five hundred meters away. All things come from the family; society is not going to tell you anything. People in their fifties and sixties, they have set thinking; at the same time younger people have their own thinking. Lack of education is not the fault of the teachers but of the family. If I am a father and my son does not want to go to school, it is my job to take him to school."

Aditya's own education has taken him into the call center world. "I did B. Comm from Delhi University, College of Commerce. After my graduation I got a call from a friend saying there were some jobs in Gurgaon, eight-hour jobs. After two days I went for that; otherwise jobs are contractual. After taking that job, they saw something good in me, so they extended my contract, one year, two years. Then I moved to another company, working night shifts because of the U.S. market. They wanted me to go to the U.S. for a work trip, but I had only been at the company for one month, so my visa was rejected."

DILLI HAAT

Aasif and I decide to meet at Dilli Haat one afternoon. It's one of the most accessible public spaces in the city, he tells me, and I remember that when we had first met on the Metro, he had gotten off at INA, which is the station for Dilli Haat.

I get to the Nagaland eatery where we had agreed by text to meet, and within a few minutes I see him approaching in his wheelchair. We install ourselves next to a cooler and order fresh lime sodas. It's been about a week since we first met on the Metro, and our conversation seems to easily pick up from where we left off.

"Disability is different in this country," he says. His mother had to fight with schools so he would be let in. "They thought I would be a burden. She had to convince them I was a fine child."

Aasif's father works on the grounds of Jamia Millia Islamia University, and so the family has always had quarters there. Aasif did his schooling at Jamia and ultimately completed his postgraduate study in Social Exclusion and Inclusive Policy. "The person you're seeing now," he says, "is not the person I was."

Aasif goes on to explain how his life changed two years ago when he started working. Before that, he says, "So many barriers were in place by society and technology." In July 2013 he became a field officer for the Chintan Environment Research and Action Group, based in Lajpat Nagar. He recounts how he did fieldwork with ragpickers across twenty-eight clusters where they were living. "I went there to mobilize them. To teach them about waste management, hygiene, government policies. When I left, they would call me and ask, 'Why did you leave, you are so good, you are our friend, you share our pain.' This was a good experience, I got love from them. My confidence level went way up. I met people. I'd been a tough guy since childhood. The ice started to melt."

One time when the elevator at a Metro station he'd gotten off at was not working, he describes going up an escalator in his wheelchair. He smiles. He relishes these adventures. A way to push boundaries for himself but also create new images for society to witness. The more we talk, I realize this urge of his, and the exuberance, comes perhaps from having had limits continually placed on him.

"Earlier I didn't like to talk about disability, in the social environment I was in. People always ask you about your disability, not your name, not your education. Now I have an answer for people when they ask me what happened. I tell them I was taking a selfie on the Eiffel Tower and fell all the way down and look what happened!

"You don't see people with disabilities active, enthusiastic. I don't want sympathy. I don't like that. You are facing challenges; I am facing them too. See me as a person first. Somewhere everyone has a disability. I can't walk, but I can roll. I can propel myself for two to three kilometers. I can move faster than most. There's a difference in how people see me based on their level of education. On the Metro, women in traditional sari, they look at me in disbelief."

Aasif's legs stop at the knee, a congenital condition. He doesn't use prosthetics. For the last two years he's been working for the start-up, v-shesh.com, in the disability sector. "Till the end, I want to be in this field only, working in technology and innovation," he tells me.

Aasif rides mostly alone on the Metro, though sometimes with friends. At the security gate, a guard opens the barricade for him, he opens his arms wide and they check him with an electronic wand. "I always tell people with disabilities to travel by Metro. The more there are of us, the better. The more we use the facilities, the more they'll keep them up. It's easy for me to come to INA station, but everything has to work."

He likes being able to ride in the ladies' coach since it's more comfortable. Once while he was riding in a general coach, a Brahmin priest, in traditional attire and a topknot, made the sign against the evil eye when he saw Aasif. "I started laughing," he recounts, "as did others. The *panditji* looked ashamed. Earlier people would say to me, 'You've done a very bad thing in your previous life.' Now I say to them, 'Tell me about *your* past, bro.'"

PINK LINE

By 2019 the Metro system has expanded to such an extent I start traveling in loops around the city. One day I take the Pink Line from Vinobapuri in southeast Delhi to Azadpur in north Delhi, then get on the Yellow Line down to Rajiv Chowk, followed by the Blue Line to Mandi House and the Violet Line back down to south Delhi. Delhi's ruling Aam Aadmi Party had just announced their intention to offer free transport to women traveling on city buses and the Metro. The central Bhartiya Janata Party (BJP) government and the DMRC immediately criticize the idea, citing financial concerns. Former Metro project manager E. Sreedharan writes Prime Minister Narendra Modi a letter urging him not to allow the proposal, arguing that differential fares go against the whole idea of a metro system.[14] Around the same time, in a newspaper interview Sreedharan says the Delhi Metro is a "social service" that shouldn't only be subject to "business considerations."[15] Meanwhile the op-ed pages and blogosphere light up with perspectives arguing for and against. Some say that it is a timely step toward gender and class equality, a way for all women to be invited into the city's public spaces like never before; others argue that it's a populist measure that won't really help women, only imperil the city's transport system.

I ask a fellow woman passenger I happen to be sitting next to in a general coach what she thinks of the "free transport for women" proposal. She responds as if she'd been thinking about it already for a long time: "Women have been excluded. Women will come out of their houses." She tells me she is "self-studying" for the IAS (Indian Administrative Service) exam and rides the Metro "from time to time."

I get a quite different response on the Lajpat Nagar platform, where I chat with three women students from Gargi College, Dayal Singh College, and Polytechnic for Women. They are eighteen-nineteen years old, wearing jeans, decorated T-shirts, and makeup; they are studying to go into medical tourism, interior design, and teaching. One of them quickly responds, "It will be unfair to the guys. Women can pay for it. It should not be free. If they're going to reduce the price, they should reduce it for everyone." Her friends agree with her and echo her thoughts. I get a strong sense that the idea of a subsidy for women seems to put a blemish on their ideas of their own womanhood and desire for equality.

Later, back on the train, I talk to Kajal, who is twenty-four and studying home science. She's wearing a mustard yellow salwar kameez and has her hair pulled back in a ponytail. We speak entirely in Hindi. "Yes," she says, "they [the government] should have free transport for women. In families, not all women are independent." Kajal thinks the initiative will encourage them. "More women will ride the Metro, so more women will be safer. If women don't get ahead, that will be bad for all society. There are women in all families, so it will benefit everyone in the family." Kajal makes the point that a subsidy for women is a subsidy for the whole family precisely because of women's diminished position in many families. "If women pay less, the family saves. If there is free transport, more women will come on the Metro for sure. Whether the government pays or women pay it doesn't matter. Women come to Delhi to work, to stay in hostels; the more they travel on the Metro the better. I travel alone, till 10 or 11 p.m. in ladies or mixed coach; it is safe." Kajal's comments start within the space of the home and domestic economy but then quickly become about women in urban space and how safety is also a numbers game.

Figure 21. Vinobapuri station platform, Pink Line, 2019. One of the lines built in the third phase of Metro construction, Pink Line stations feature new graphics and platform safety doors.

Further along on the Pink Line, past Rajouri Garden, I interrupt Diksha, a third-year Bachelor of Science student who is reading on her phone. When I ask her about the free transport for women idea, she says, "I don't think it's a good idea. Obviously if it's free, people will misuse it. We should travel less and promote bicycles. The Metro uses a/c, electricity, burning coal—it's bad for the environment. I will go somewhere by Metro when I can eat from nearby instead." Her point is that the Metro encourages people to travel longer distances when they might not need to. This was an argument I'd heard from transport researcher Geetam Tiwari as well. Diksha continues, "It's not a right to have free transport. Men will then have to pay more." For greater equality between the sexes, she says, there should be more jobs for women, not reservations [quotas]. Diksha shifts from talking about free transport for women to preferential treatment of women on the Metro. "I don't go and ask for a seat, I don't do that. The ladies' coach is fine; some feel more comfortable in it. I'm not against women; I want equality. The more people on the trains the better, since then there are more trains and less waiting time."

Diksha travels seventy minutes each day to get to her college. She had a bad experience on the Metro early on: A man grabbed her breasts from behind on a Rajiv Chowk station platform. "You can't stop in your life due to bad experiences," she tells me, "you have to fight. In buses, there are all kinds of experiences like this; it's kind of a normal part of your life. In the Metro, people stand up for you. In that incident, someone called the Metro staff; they'd seen what had happened. People are more helpful, better than on the DTC (Delhi Transport Corporation) buses. Instead of free transport, we need to earn more, we need more opportunities."

Diksha says that her family is supportive of her moving around the city. "When you are in college you want to try everything. I have the same rules as my brother, though not the same as compared to boys outside my family. I have to enter my house by eight p.m., sometimes nine p.m. is okay."

CITY PARK

City Park station marks the end of the Green Line. I pass through twenty stations to get to the end of the line. At City Park, things are quieter, less crowded with people and the whir of traffic as compared to Mundka, where a couple of years ago the line used to end. I take the open-air escalator down from the station. To my surprise, the first thing I see, in a small park adjacent to the station, is a photo shoot, something I might associate with tonier areas of the city. Two young men, dressed in jeans and white shirts, are doing the posing; another man with a large, professional camera with a telephoto lens is taking the photos. I keep going down and reach street level where I see the same National Highway 10 that bypasses Mundka station. Here there are only a couple of street food vendors but no rickshaw stand; the area around the station is still being built up. I meet a lone woman who is standing by the side of the road trying to catch one of the big buses that keeps passing us by. She tells me that she usually gets picked up by car from the station but today she has to find her own way. She is headed back to Rohtak, the next major city, forty kilometers away.

I cross the road that bifurcates the Metro station and come upon two security guards sitting on plastic chairs on the edge of the station premises; they say they work for the DMRC, and I can see from the insignia on their blue uniforms that they are contract security, not the Central Industrial Security Force (CISF) guards you see on the trains and in stations. These guys are relaxed.

A young man in faded jeans with a light blue backpack and slightly disheveled hair comes up to the guards. His name is Gulshan; he's come from Rohtak and is headed to Ghevra station, just a few stops away on the Green Line. There is a kind of gentleness to him. He is asking the guards about job opportunities as a security guard. They start talking about when this Metro line will reach Rohtak. The guards are sure it will, it's only a matter of time. Gulshan says, "Who knows if it will, it's up to the government; just like this one came, we didn't know it was coming." The guards venture, "If Congress comes, it'll come quickly. Congress brought the Metro in the first place; if BJP, it will take time." I'm a little surprised to hear this assessment, since Narendra Modi's BJP government, in power since 2014, has taken credit for the Metro through advertisements and ribbon cuttings with each new line opening and extension.

I walk with Gulshan up to the Metro station. He's come today looking for a job and will head to Ghevra where there might be some possibilities. He tells me he is studying for the entrance exam to be a policeman in another city—Chandigarh—but he keeps having to pay for coaching for the exam. He might be a security guard until he finds something else. "Who knows, let's see what my luck will be," he says.

Here, an hour and a half by Metro from central Delhi, I feel I am farther and farther away, and that the city is expanding. But as I talk to Gulshan I see that for him, coming from Rohtak and hoping to find work in Delhi's periphery, the city is contracting. He has reached the beginning of the line.

Epilogue

The Metro is an ongoing and recurring narrative, one with stops and starts, and loads of unfinished business, ethnographic vignettes whose endings are not necessarily seen by the ethnographer or the reader.[1] New ways of experiencing time and space because of the existence of the Metro produce new kinds of narratives. This newness is captured and expressed in the wanderings of the contemporary Delhi Metro commuter, riding en masse.

By the later 2010s, the narrative time of the Metro, the system's place in the history of Delhi, was being felt in yet another way. I started meeting people in their twenties who had no memory of the city before the Metro. At first this took me by surprise; then I kept meeting more of them, people who had this perception that the city had always moved in this Metro way.[2]

The subplots of *The Moving City*—such as those about urban planning, architectural design, what it means to develop, the spatiality of class, gendered experiences of the city, how love and despair happen in and through the urban—point to the ways mobility is an experience through space and a marker of time. But mobility is also a social experience that is often not linear and does not move at or with the same speed as the trains. This book has meant to capture and contrast the mobilities of society and of transport as people get located on the trains, in urban discourse, and in the midst of their lives. Despite the mostly linear progression of the three phases of the Metro's construction, the rest is hopscotch.

The subplots are also a catalogue of how the Delhi Metro frames in multiple ways: on the landscape and as landscape; social spaces in the trains, at stations, and around them; how spatial inequalities map onto peoples. Infrastructure is not only plans, coordinates, capital, design, governance, power, hierarchy, and bureaucracy (even if it is all those things); it is also a space of negotiation and possibility, of imagining and reshaping, of the dichotomous relationship between old and new, then and now. Following infrastructure is to be always in-process and always aware of the unfinished portrait of urban life. The disparate plots in this book have meant to make a story of the Delhi Metro, of the moving city.[3]

All the while the Metro makes "the everyday" a more exalted realm, simultaneously reproducing social divisions, leveling them, and bringing out the particulars of how they are known and felt. Metro and other urban transport systems encapsulate many of the ideals and struggles of urban living in a global context. *The Moving City* has meant to forefront local voices, perspectives, arguments, and experiences from the ground up— and in this case, the underground up.

On the Metro, commuters study the crowds but also the city through its many glass-paned windows. They are invited into a new commodity world represented diffusely as points on the Metro map to choose from, go to, discover, and long for. People may also be overwhelmed as they are subjected to this map and new form of ordering, which requires a new reckoning with the city and their place in it. For Metro riders in Delhi, what is public about the Metro, as a space and form of transit, becomes intimately linked to their own sense of mobility.

The value of a Metro public is the meeting or at least commingling of people across social classes and experiences. There is a sense that the Metro naturally accomplishes a kind of social work involving cross-class recognition. But that view of the Metro would also assume that it is a kind of tabula rasa, a blank slate for such commingling, when in fact it is already a globalized, middle-class, male-dominated space (because 75 percent of Metro riders are male but also because the Metro is a place where a female safe space must be carved out in the form of a ladies' coach). The Metro public then is one that has already conformed to these requirements.

A public is not necessarily connected to a reality in the here and now, but rather to life experiences and circumstances beyond a physical grouping. It is an idea as much as it is a lived reality, and on the trains, a mix of ideas as much as actual bodies. And it is for this reason that I see public transport as a potential place of social transformation. Metro crowds are composed of different publics, even discordant publics, with different political interests and proclivities. The crowd *does* coalesce into a public in moments and scenes; however, publics are multiple and also evanescent.

Publics come into being through discourse, such as how the DMRC and other corporations address Metro riders through signs and advertisements to how Delhi newspapers write about Metro commuters. The discourse on the Metro public is often framed in terms of the ameliorative affect the Metro is meant to have on "unruly" publics. The idea is that the Metro's order and cleanliness will rub off on people and make them more in touch with their civic sensibilities. Fittingly, this idea is further supported by the many ads on trains and platforms promoting good hygiene and beauty products. An appeal to publics and also public selves.

The Metro, like all such systems, is a space of surveillance, modern governance, and conformity at the level of the self. At the same time, the kind of visibility and invisibility I have documented in these pages has not only to do with what goes on in the trains, how people behave vis-à-vis the CCTV cameras and other passengers, for instance, but also how the Metro as a system works on the urban landscape, as a visible structure that also covers up. I have emphasized the idea of visibility to highlight issues of inclusion and exclusion, which are central to citizenship-making in the Indian capital and most cities in the world today.

The stories and scenes of Delhi's Metro are a mixed dialogue. The politics of urban space begins with land acquisition and management and the government and upper-class interests that direct those processes. Before public space can be created it has to be designated. Land and public space are reflections of class relations in the city. But class is something that is also performed by individuals—in offices, on Metro trains, on roads, etc.— while class narratives take hold of people's imaginations. This taking hold is powerful since it spreads ideas about who should get what, when and where. People don't just want the Metro; they want the rest of the city, the other infrastructures they depend on like roads, water, and electricity, to be more like the Metro. The emergence of a Metro public emboldens and encourages similar forms of urban development in the city. It serves as an example and is now routinely referred to as the city's "lifeline." One hopes that the idea of a lifeline would encourage public works that go beyond the Metro in terms of the inclusion of more crowds and the creation of more publics to address the ever-widening gap between them. The goal should not just be about safe or "smart" digitally managed spaces and services, but instead about ones that address the needs of a mixed population and that work toward closing the gap between those who have "natural" rights to the city and its services, and those who do not.

~

What kind of moving city then does the Delhi Metro forge? The Metro incorporates what Rahul Mehrotra has called the "static" and "kinetic" qualities of Indian cities, the state-sanctioned built environment of steel, brick, and concrete versus the energy and "indigenous urbanism" of the street.[4] The Metro in my reading is an example of where the static and the kinetic meet and intermingle, what I have been calling "the interface" between the Metro and the street. It is a space that invites local populations from different classes to try out and interact with a new technology, an invitation to a globalized experience of speed, mobility, and high-tech ambience, and a place where women can hold their own spatially in an otherwise male-dominated social space. The Metro attempts to close certain gaps of experience in the city, even as it is also an imposing space that excludes many of the "indigenous" activities of the city. You have to be and act a certain way to get on the Metro; you have to go through security and have your bags checked; you have to line up and pay for a token to enter the system. The Metro is off-putting to many, even if they are awed by it, and because they are awed by it.

What unfolds in the space of the Metro is not just a blurring of the static and kinetic, but a relationship between them, a meeting of multiple mobilities. The street vendors who pack their materials and setups and get

Figure 22. Lajpat Nagar station, 2019, Violet and Pink Lines. This portion of the Violet Line is elevated, while the Pink Line intersects it underground.

on the Metro; the lovers who meet on the train to find a place of pause and connection; the IT worker who crosses the city in a packed ladies' coach of suits, heels, and salwar kameez. Where once we might have spoken of the pleasures of the street, with its plethora of foods, sights, and smells, today most Metro riders speak of the pleasures of a fast, cool ride that takes them from one part of the city to another in record time. People of different walks of life ride the Metro, and bring their ideas, experiences, and hopes with them. Yet the Metro is not quite a "cultural" experience in the way some streets and bazaars still are. There are more things that you cannot do (spit, smoke, eat) than you can do. And there are those things you are told not to do (stop the door with your hand, take photographs, befriend strangers) that you *do* do. It is a public space and yet still a space apart.

The Metro is also a lesson in the spatial geography of the National Capital Region. The system does not reach out to the hinterlands so much as it joins them. Delhi is reflective of what is around it, linguistically and culturally, making for shared social and cultural attitudes. This is especially true when it comes to the gendered space of the Metro. The Metro does provide a more fluid space for women and that fluidity extends to bodily comportments, dress, and ways of being. But patriarchal notions of women's safety also get reproduced in the space of the Metro. Women feel safer at night on the Metro than in any other public space, and yet they are still contained (whether they ride in the ladies' coach or not) and still subject to questioning about their timings and whereabouts by their families, the police, and society at large. Women's "right to the city" is certainly widened and emboldened because of the Metro, and yet to change their place in the city, their place in a gendered hierarchy, women would need to be in the city's public spaces in even greater numbers than they are now.[5]

The Metro has changed the geography of Delhi, but not for all time. The city is a constantly changing geography and will continue to be so in the years to come. Metro stations and even lines will gain new meaning as people make new and different kinds of connections on and through them. By early 2020, as the nationwide protests against India's Citizenship Amendment Act continued to convulse the city, the women-led sit-ins at Shaheen Bagh in south Delhi and marches in northeast Delhi created a new imagining of the city once more as ideas of citizenship and who belongs in the national imagination led to actions meant to reshape parts of urban space and street life. The Metro in this case became a way to reach protests (or be cut off from them when certain stations were strategically closed), and when the protests in some areas turned riotous and led to violence, the Metro became a way for health and social workers to reach those in need. In this sense the Metro extends and connects what is happening in different parts of the city; places become less remote and part of the imagination of "the city," as well as information points, where people come to find out what's going on. And yet certain places can also be where the Metro is neither crowd nor recognized public, but a population to be managed. The Metro makes it more difficult, though not impossible, to spread misinformation about what is going on. It becomes a competing institution, one with many voices, and then when station exits are closed, one with no voice.

~

In March 2020 the Metro started to come to a stop, like so many other things in the face of the Covid-19 pandemic. All of a sudden, the Metro became a place of too much closeness, too much proximity. Crowds were not to be endured, but avoided, as the Metro itself became a possible and likely vector of illness. The Orange Airport Express Metro line went from symbolizing Delhi's connections across the globe to being seen as a portal for the virus to enter the city from foreign destinations.

Metro authorities first recommended social distancing, advising passengers to let packed trains pass, as they were doing in so many cities around the world. Then trains only ran during rush hour for essential workers and trips, with random thermal scanning at stations. With the "*janata* curfew" (people's curfew) called by the central government, the Metro closed for the day. By March 23, the system shut down completely, with officials declaring that service would return on March 31. There would be internal operations and security measures in the Metro system, but no public interface, no trains running.

The Metro's closure ended up lasting more than five months. You could say the city stopped, not only because of the Metro but also due to the halting of buses, rickshaws, trucks, and cars. The roads emptied out, and an unusual and eerie quiet came over the city. The skies started to clear as the city's pollution levels dropped to their lowest levels in years. Meanwhile, stories of the moving city became the ones about migrant workers fleeing Delhi by foot, an exodus of people who could not work from home but who needed to get home. They had little if any infrastructural help from the government, as many stood in long, cramped lines to get on interstate buses. The contrast between who could shelter at home and who had to keep traveling to get home said everything about the structural relationships of Delhi—a floating population in the moving city. In the more lethal and widespread second wave of Covid-19 in the spring of 2021, the Metro closed again for several weeks, amid news of families circling the city in ambulances in search of oxygen for their loved ones. By summer select Metro stations doubled as vaccination centers.

People lamented the Metro's ongoing closures as they engaged in DMRC trivia quizzes on social media and shared memories of riding the trains. The "culture" of Metro riding has taken hold in the last almost two decades, a dream world that has become linked to the unconscious of many Delhiites. The city did not all of a sudden get "unmapped" when the Metro closed, even if the daily ridership of it came to a halt. The city had already been recodified by the Metro. The Metro map did not do this alone, nor did the concreteness of the stations and viaducts. Rather, it was and is people's own experiences of the trains, their own itineraries practiced again and again.

Acknowledgments

The research for this book was launched thanks to a fellowship from the American Institute of Indian Studies. The book was completed thanks to a grant from the National Endowment for the Humanities (#FT-264777) and fellowships from the American Council of Learned Societies and the Weatherhead Foundation / School for Advanced Research (SAR). I am grateful to all of these generous funders. I wrote in several places, often in Delhi, but the book took shape and was finished in the open expanse of New Mexico, where I was a resident scholar at SAR in Santa Fe. Special thanks go to Michael Brown, Paul Ryer, Maria Spray, C.J. Alvarez, Patty Crown, Fátima Suárez, Davina Two Bears, Katherine Wolf, Leslie Shipman, Robert Lujan, Elysia Poon, Steve Feld, Carol MacLennan, Nancy Owen Lewis, and Deb Winslow for making the year there such a good one.

At George Mason University, many thanks go to my colleagues in the Department of Sociology and Anthropology for all of their support over these years; to the Cities and Globalization working group and Global Affairs faculty for reading early papers; and to the College of Humanities and Social Sciences and the Provost's office for summer grants and research leaves. Having students from all over the country and world in my social theory, urban anthropology, and India courses has been one of the joys of teaching—to interact with them and learn from their own worldviews.

At the University of California Press, Kate Marshall took an interest in this book as it was coming together and gave valuable feedback throughout. Two peer reviewers gave generous comments while Enrique Ochoa-Kaup managed all the details. The three maps were drawn by Bill Nelson.

Some of the ethnographic material that appears in this book was first published as a chapter, "Regarding Others: Metro Crowds, Metro Publics, Metro Mobs," in *Crowds: Ethnographic Encounters*, edited by Megan Steffen (Bloomsbury Academic, 2020), and in articles of mine in *City & Society* ("'We are visioning it': Aspirational Planning and the Material Landscapes of Delhi's Metro," 2018), *Anthropology and Humanism* ("At the 'Love Commandos': Narratives of Mobility among Intercaste Couples in a Delhi Safe House," 2018), *Seminar* ("The Metro and the Street," 2012) in an issue edited by Curt Gambetta and Ritajyoti Bandyopadhyay, and *Economic and Political Weekly* ("The Delhi Metro: An Ethnographic View," 2010).

Thank you to those who invited me to give lectures on my Metro research and the audiences who engaged with them at the India International Centre, the Nehru Memorial Museum and Library, Delhi's School of Planning and Architecture, Ambedkar University, Delhi University, the Centre for Policy Research in Delhi, University of Paris-West at Nanterre, Yale University, George Washington University, University of Karachi, Princeton University, and The New School's India-China Institute. I was able to work out some of my ideas at workshops I was invited to at the University of Hong Kong and Rutgers University, and through panels and symposia over the years at the Annual Conference on South Asia in Madison, Wisconsin.

My Delhi home base has sustained me for many years and made this book possible. Padma Narayanan, the late R.I. Narayanan, Harini Narayanan, Gautam Modi, and Alli Roshni fueled me year after year with good food, good cheer, and good counsel, while Promilla Mathur, Veena Naregal, and Sunila and Promod Sharma and family were there from the early days as I shuttled between north and south Delhi.

In Delhi, there was also, in pivotal moments and times, Aparna Balachandran, Anindita Chakrabarty, Vasudha Dalmia, Geeta Rai, Priya

Sen, Nishant Lall, Swati Mantri, Smruti Shah, Anjali Modi, Rathin Roy, Ananya Vajpeyi, Mahesh Rangarajan, and Narayani Gupta, who gave professional support, research contacts, and more. Lawrence Cohen and I rode the Metro together more than once, which brought everything full circle.

In the United States, Rachel Heiman, Ilana Feldman, Sarah Pinto, Miriam Ticktin, Stéphane Tonnelat, Amy Best, Andy Bickford, Johanna Bockman, Indigo Eriksen, Leeya Mehta, Ryan Tuggle, Falu Bakrania, and Priya Doraswamy read and supported this work and me in more ways than I can count. That Miriam managed to come to Delhi was an added bonus.

My mother, Veena Sadana, surely planted the Delhi bug in me early on when she first brought me to the city in 1971. I thank her and Suren Sadana, Ritu Sadana, Jacques Bury, Jacques-Kabir Bury, and Gitanjali Eva Sadana for all they do but mostly just for being there.

Vivek Narayanan and I first met in New York City and then again, by chance, several years later in Delhi around the time I started doing the research for this book. That Ambika was born in the shadow of the Violet Line was somehow fitting. We have seen her grow and the Metro grow over the last twelve years.

Finally, my heartfelt thanks to the people of Delhi. They are the "social life" of this book, the Metro public I discovered. I always looked forward to going into stations and getting on trains, not because of the technology so much, but because of the people I knew I would meet there. The people who ride the Metro kept me going for many years as there were always new lines and stations coming up, new possible itineraries, and new people to watch or interact with. There still are.

Notes

1. Haryana has the lowest ratio of women to men, according to the 2011 Census of India. There are 877 females to every 1,000 males in the state, whereas the all-India rate is 940 females to 1,000 males. See the Government of India 2011 census website: www.census2011.co.in/sexratio.php.

2. On the topic of women's safety in urban India, Kavita Krishnan writes in *Fearless Freedom* about how the discourse on women's safety is part of a patriarchal discourse, one that impinges on Indian women's freedom of movement and sense of autonomy. In a related manner, Shilpa Phadke, Sameera Khan, and Shilpa Ranade build an on-the-ground feminist politics out of the question of women in Indian public space in their book, *Why Loiter?* To loiter, they argue, is to normalize the female presence in public spaces; it is to push for a new way of thinking about, being in, and claiming the city, without hesitation or apology. They defend and define women's right to be in public space *for no particular reason* and to "court risk" as they see fit (110). Theirs is a complete reversal of the discourse on women in public in India and most other places in the world, a discourse that tells women to police and modulate their behavior in public so that men don't harass or attack them. The onus is on women to keep safe and ensure their bodily integrity. Phadke, Khan, and Ranade oppose this patriarchal narrative on women's safety, whereby women are viewed "as property rather than as citizens with rights" (110). How women and girls come to occupy urban space in the everyday becomes

a way to counter this narrative. Their demand is nothing short of a new social contract, and they see each individual woman as a potential agent of this change, hence their encouragement and challenge to women to loiter in public. For current reports on the issue of women's safety, see the work of the Delhi-based Jagori (www.jagori.org/), a nongovernmental organization that offers counseling services to women, as well as engages in the analysis of women's right to the city and the issue of violence against women in their homes and on the street. Kalpana Viswanath and Surabhi Tandon Mehrotra call this "the violence of normal times" in their article, "'Shall we go out?' Women's Safety in Public Spaces in Delhi." See also Leo Coleman's "Inside and Outside the House: A Narrative of Mobility and Becoming in Delhi." In the story of a male domestic servant in a south Delhi home, Coleman writes of the "hierarchy of values by which urban spaces and the bodies that move across them are evaluated and controlled" (700).

3. The 2011 Census of India shows that 68.4 percent of Indian workers are male and 31.6 percent are female; however, the percentage of female workers is highest in rural areas; more women in cities stay at home. For a discussion of the increase in the female urban workforce since the liberalizing of the Indian economy in the 1990s, see Shriya Anand and Jyothi Koduganti, "Urban India and Its Female Demographic Dividend." Using data from the 2011 National Sample Employment and Unemployment Survey, they show that the total number of women in the Indian workforce increased threefold between 1991 and 2011, while the number of women seeking work increased eightfold. Looking at workforce data in India, Pritha Chatterjee shows how women's work participation is an important indicator of their worth in society, and while Delhi may be cosmopolitan, it is embedded in a more patriarchal and regional North Indian socio-spatial context, as compared to even southern Indian cities such as Chennai. She calls this a "regional spatial hold on women in Delhi," which includes fears families have of their daughters traveling alone across town and being out at "odd hours." See Chatterjee, "Embedded or Liberated: An Exploration into the Social Milieu of Delhi," in *Marginalization in Globalizing Delhi*, 172.

4. You can see the official Delhi Metro network map on the DMRC's website: www.delhimetrorail.com/Zoom_Map.aspx. Delhi's metro map joins the tradition of transit maps that deviate from "mimetic priority," that is, a scaled representation of geographic points and distances. This deviation comes with the realization that people use transit maps differently than road maps; see John Schwetman, "Harry Beck's London Underground Map: A Convex Lens for the Global City." What's important in the Metro map are the stations and their relations to one another, hence it becomes okay, practical even, to simplify reality. Schwetman shows how this tradition begins with Harry Beck's creation of the London Underground map in 1931, which came to be a symbol of global urbanity and a premier example of information design. See also Janin Hadlaw, "The London Underground Map: Imagining Time and Space," and Janet Vertesi, "Mind the Gap: The London

Underground Map and Users' Representations of Urban Space." Meanwhile, Patrick Joyce, in *The Rule of Freedom*, describes how maps are a mechanism of liberal governance; they are a modern abstraction whereby "people and things were identified so that they might be brought within the view of government" (260). Paul Virilio sees transport systems themselves as technologies of space and hence an expression of modern governance (*Speed and Politics*, 11, 8).

5. Throughout this book I have followed the place name spellings used by the Delhi Metro Rail Corporation.

6. The Haryana government changed the name of Gurgaon to Gurugram in 2016, but in the period of the research for this book, people were still calling it "Gurgaon" even as signage was starting to change. I have retained "Gurgaon" in people's speech and as it relates to their stories if they use the old name. The core of Delhi, encompassing Old and New Delhi as well as suburbs within the Outer Ring Road, is officially known as the National Capital Territory and had a population of 13.5 million according to the 2011 census of India (estimated now to be twenty million). The National Capital Region includes nineteen districts in the neighboring states of Uttar Pradesh, Haryana, and Rajasthan, and covers 46,000 square kilometers. The 2018 figure for the population of Delhi's National Capital Region is 28.5 million according to the United Nations, *World Urbanization Prospects: The 2018 Revision*, 77.

7. Norma Evenson (*The Indian Metropolis*, 189) cites the class divide in Delhi's spatio-geography as having originated in the colonial period and as having been marked by a difference in modes of transport: "Colonial New Delhi was planned by, and essentially for, the automobile-owning class. Post-independence planning continued this pattern, promoting an extended urban fabric of relatively low density based on a system of road transportation. In what one critic called 'the world's most energy inefficient city,' most citizens would remain condemned to tedious hours of commuting on a notoriously inadequate bus system."

8. There are a number of important histories of Delhi as an ancient and modern monumental space, such as Upinder Singh's *Ancient Delhi*, Narayani Gupta's *Delhi between Two Empires, 1803–1931*, and Percival Spear's *Delhi: Its Monuments and History*.

9. The "imageability" that the Metro gives Delhi resonates with Kevin Lynch's account (*The Image of the City*, 9) of how certain public structures create an image of the city that evokes something in people that makes them associate the structure as emblematic of the city. The Delhi Metro has this effect, but it is happening slowly, over time, which makes it an especially useful object to study.

10. On Delhi as a gendered space, see Urvashi Butalia, "The Fear That Stalks: Gender-Based Violence in Public Spaces," where she discusses how the very notion of "public" assumes to be a right for men to be able to claim and a kind of transgression for women. Thinking about space more generally, I draw here and going forward on Henri Lefebvre's (*The Production of Space*, 11) notion of space

as an analytical tool encompassing three fields: physical, mental, social. Space, which is always social in Lefebvre's rendering, is a concrete materiality continuously produced by thinking, acting, experiencing subjects. My understanding of space is also influenced by Daphne Spain's connection of architecture to social status in *Gendered Spaces*, David Harvey's analysis of time-space compression in *The Condition of Postmodernity*, and Wolfgang Schivelbusch's depiction of how nineteenth-century trains carved out new landscapes and created new compartments in which to exist in *The Railway Journey*.

11. Jennifer Robinson's *Ordinary Cities* tackles this issue by trying to level the playing field between cities through a rejection of a European-based "universal" theory of urbanism and by embracing a more radical comparative urbanism that eschews arbitrary hierarchies of cities and the ways of being in them. Central to her comparative urbanism is a recognition that modernity is always borrowed (across cities globally and through time) and that "urban innovation" is and always has been "cosmopolitan interdependence" (77). Charles Taylor (*Modernity and the Rise of the Public Sphere*, 251) states this in a different but related way: that the idea of modernity only being Western is simply an ethnocentric way of seeing things. In recent decades urban anthropology has become a place to compare cities in this manner: to refuse the idea that one city is a precedent for another without resorting to exceptionalism, and by replacing the idea of alternative modernities with multiple and comparable ones.

12. See Sanjay Srivastava's *Entangled Urbanism* and Christine Brosius's *India's Middle Class* for detailed studies of Delhi's new urban consumer spaces such as malls. And see Mark Liechty's *Suitably Modern* for an important discussion of what it means to study middle-classness (21–30). Like his study, this one views class through the prism of both performativity and narrativity, whereby class is a process.

13. In *Living Class in Urban India*, Sara Dickey makes the important point that "everyone creates class" (15), and I would add that every space creates class as well. On aspiration, see Dimitris Dalakoglou and Penny Harvey, "Roads and Anthropology: Ethnographic Perspectives on Space, Time, and (Im)mobility," for their discussion of roads as the "most aspirational of social infrastructures" (463). See also *The Promise of Infrastructure*, where editors Hannah Appel, Nikhil Anand, and Akhil Gupta write ("Introduction," 11) of how infrastructure is "the slowness of the process of speeding up." Their phrase nicely captures the paradox of the *longue durée* of spatial expansion and construction with shrinking travel times, but I also like this phrase because it captures a dynamic of social mobility as experienced by many riding the trains. I would argue that today's transnationally built urban metro rail systems are an equally apt example of an aspirational infrastructure that holds promise, maybe more so. These systems are generative of different forms of mobility, like roads, but because of the outsized capital investment required to make metros and the widespread physical construction-destruction

that goes into its transformation of the urban landscape, the aspiration is at an individual and especially societal level to a greater degree. And then there is Valeria Luiselli (*Sidewalks*, 66) who writes, "Cities, like our bodies, like language, are destruction under construction."

14. Sanjay Srivastava (*Entangled Urbanism*, 209) has identified "the making of a moral middle class," referring to the way in which people manage their "anxiety" about consumer society and how it relates to "the meaning of Indian-ness." In this respect, I chronicle how Dilliwalas embrace the hypermodernity of the Metro system and the myriad ways in which they square it with the many identities they have.

15. The Metro's role as property developer is mentioned early on, in the first detailed project report (*Integrated Multi-Modal Mass Rapid Transport System for Delhi*) prepared in 1995 by RITES, the Government of India consultant to the project. In the "Financial Analysis" section (xxxix) of the report, it states, "It is seen that urban mass transit systems throughout the world are not commercially viable. Hence, there is a need to charge both the user and non-user beneficiaries of the MRT systems." The report goes on to say, "It is proposed to raise an amount of Rs 2550 crores [USD 343 million] at current prices through property development" (xl).

16. Anupama Mann, "A Megaproject Matrix," xxii. See also her discussion of how property development was imagined by the Delhi Metro Rail Corporation early on in the project planning stage (184–93). The DMRC also lists some of its property development on its website: www.delhimetrorail.com/Property_Develo pment/pd_workundertaken.aspx.

17. The idea of citizenship in India has become especially fraught since 2014 as the Bhartiya Janata Party–led central government has mainstreamed Hindu nationalism, or Hindutva, in its strategies for governance and everyday political actions, which have routinely included the intimidation and disenfranchisement of Muslim, Christian, and Dalit communities and individuals in order to further bolster the pride of the 85 percent majority Hindu population. See, for instance, *Majoritarian State*, edited by Angana P. Chatterji, Thomas Blom Hansen, and Christophe Jaffrelot, for multiple examples by a range of authors. The Delhi Metro may be a somewhat neutral, technocratic space, yet it is involved in the city's circulations and all they entail. As James Holston and Arjun Appadurai write ("Cities and Citizenship," 188), cities engage "the tumult of citizenship": "Their crowds catalyze processes which decisively expand and erode the rules, meanings, and practices of citizenship. Their streets conflate identities of territory and contract with those of race, religion, class, culture, and gender to produce the reactive ingredients of both progressive and reactionary political movements. Like nothing else, the modern urban public signifies both the defamiliarizing enormity of national citizenship and the exhilaration of its liberties."

18. Brian Larkin, "The Politics and Poetics of Infrastructure," 329. Larkin also

details how infrastructure "offers insights into other domains such as practices of government, religion, or sociality" (328). Metro systems can also make more than one statement or change statements over time; for instance, see Alaina Lemon's article ("Talking Transit and Spectating Transition: The Moscow Metro") on how the Moscow Metro stands for political utopia *and* totalitarian oppression and may be a sign of both conformity and being cultured.

19. The per capita (annual) income of 303,073 rupees (4,008 USD) is an estimated figure for 2016–17 for Delhi's National Capital Territory, as reported in the *Delhi Statistical Abstract 2016* (112). The percentage of Delhiites living below the poverty line is 23.3 percent (114).

20. It should be noted that the Indian Railways, built in the nineteenth century during British colonial rule, were also seen (by British officials) as a "civilizing technology" that would "wither away" caste distinctions as people traveled side by side in train compartments across regions of the country, as discussed in Manu Goswami, *Producing India*, 106. Goswami writes, "As pedagogical and disciplinary nodes of colonial governance, railways were figured as the progenitors of an abstract, homogenous space of production and circulation, and as the incubators of modern subjects liberated from entrenched prejudices and customs" (106). However, this colonial narrative intersected with the reality of railway space that instituted a class and racial hierarchy reflected in everything from carriages, rolling stock, platforms, and stations (118–19). See also Marian Aguiar's *Tracking Modernity*, where she argues that the Indian Railways were meant "to establish rational and unified public spaces that were culturally secular so as to subsume religion into the order of the state" (xvii).

21. As Goswami, *Producing India*, and Aguiar, *Tracking Modernity*, point out in their respective studies of the implementation of the colonial-era Indian Railways system, the idea of a separate space on the train for women was key to the emergence of middle- and upper-middle-class women into public spaces. So, the idea of a ladies' coach on the Metro is a familiar response; it is nothing new, and yet many women in urban India today have different expectations for how their public presence should be registered by society.

22. Mina Saidi-Sharouz offers an interesting point of comparison in her paper, "Le Métro de Téhéran: Une gestion publique des relations de genre," about the women-only car of the Tehran Metro. She shows how the women's car necessitates the "feminization" of the transit space since officials are tasked with making sure that Islamic laws are respected for both sexes while traveling. Meanwhile, Stéphane Tonnelat and William Kornblum, in their discussion of gender relations on the New York City subway, point to the high incidence of groping (*International Express*, 138–69). See also Shelly Pandey, "Reinterpreting Gender in Globalizing India: Afghan Sikh Refugees in Delhi City's Built Environment," for her discussion of female refugees in Delhi and their use of the ladies' coach as a space of urban mobility; Tara Shelly, "Private Space in Public Transport: Locating Gender in the Delhi Metro"; and Shilpa Phadke, "Gendered Questions of Access in Mumbai."

23. See Dinesh Mohan, *Mythologies, Metros, and Future Urban Transport*, and Geetam Tiwari, "Metro Rail and the City: Derailing Public Transport."

24. Bruno Latour's *Aramis, or the Love of Technology* innovatively explores this theme in his ethnography of a French point-to-point urban transport system that ultimately failed.

25. In Louis Firth's classic essay, "Urbanism as a Way of Life," he makes the point that "the urban" is not merely about the size of population or the delimitation of a geographic area but rather is a host of qualities expressed as an observable "set of attitudes and ideas" and a "constellation of personalities" (19). From a twenty-first-century perspective, Firth's idea of urbanism seems almost generic, and I think this is because there are as many ways to be urban as there are sets of attitudes, ideas, and personalities. How these "sets" coalesce in cities around the world make the basis for the study of a more robust urbanism.

26. See Michael Warner's "Publics and Counterpublics," his influential article on how publics get created by being addressed. While Warner's focus is on publics that are addressed through the circulation of texts, I am extending his idea to include the Delhi Metro as a kind of text that circulates in the city and "speaks to" those riding it and living in its midst. See also Francis Cody, "Publics and Politics," for a discussion of Bruno Latour's idea that publics might be created through "material infrastructures of communication" that extend beyond printed texts and may include buildings, political rallies, literary salons, coffeehouses, and tea shops, etc. (47), what Latour calls "an object-oriented democracy" in "From Realpolitik to Dingpolitik, or How to Make Things Public" (8). By comparison, in *Lines of the Nation*, Laura Bear writes of the emergence of an "Indian traveling public" who were under the surveillance and discipline of the colonial government's Indian Railway Acts and hence railway staff, which was not the case for train passengers in Britain (41). Whereas the Indian Railways created a new national imaginary, the Delhi Metro creates an urban *and* global one, which will be detailed in the pages that follow.

27. Alondra Carrillo Vidal, as interviewed by Amy Goodman on *Democracy Now*, October 28, 2019.

28. Sangeeta Ojha, "Delhi Metro Latest Update: Currently, 16 Stations Closed. Here Is Full List"; Press Trust of India, "Women Gather Near Delhi's Jaffrabad Metro Station to Protest against CAA, NRC"; Poornima Joshi and A.M. Jigeesh, "Anatomy of a Riot in North East Delhi," *Hindu Business Line*. In "Talking Transit and Spectating Transition: The Moscow Metro," Alaina Lemon shows that even earlier, in the 1991 coup that led to the breakup of the Soviet Union, as mainstream media outlets were shut down, Metro underpasses became places where people gathered to share information and Metro walls were used to post accurate information that then traveled to the edges of the city (21). The extent to which the Delhi Metro is a democratic field of engagement is debatable precisely because its spaces are controlled by the state, but it is certainly a symbolic space of struggle and conveyor of information.

29. I refer here to Laura Nader's call for anthropologists to study those in power, "the institutions and organizations that affect everyday lives," in "Up the Anthropologist: Perspectives Gained from Studying Up" (286). Most anthropologists do this today—they study up, down, and all around. Nader's point was particularly salient for anthropologists in an era when they were mostly studying village societies and social structures but starting to shift toward the study of complex societies and urban areas. I would place her idea of studying up in the history of an evolving urban anthropology from the 1970s onward.

30. See Melissa Butcher, "Cultures of Commuting: The Mobile Negotiation of Space and Subjectivity on Delhi's Metro," for her description of middle- and working-class commuters on the Delhi Metro. See Rachel Heiman, Carla Freeman, and Mark Liechty, eds., *The Global Middle Classes*, for a primer on the idea of the global middle classes; and Amita Baviskar and Raka Ray, eds., *Elite and Everyman*, on the vagaries of the Indian middle classes. Baviskar and Ray's volume does not mention the Delhi Metro in the text of the book, but it does feature a photograph of the inside of one of its trains on the book's cover.

31. See, for instance, Zachary Schrag's history of the Washington, DC, metro system, *The Great Society Subway*.

32. Marc Augé, *In the Metro*. See also his follow-up, *Le Métro revisité*. For a more recent ethnographic study that centers on the Gare du Nord, as train station and Paris Métro stop exchange hub, see Julie Kleinman's *Adventure Capital*.

33. UN Habitat has started calling cities that have thirty million in population "metacities," which are so big that they change the very dynamics of urbanization. Delhi is the second-largest urban agglomeration or "metacity" in the world, after Tokyo and before Shanghai (United Nations 2019, 75). This transformation is not just about the size of the population but also about how the city is imagined.

34. For this reason, I don't see the Delhi metro as a "non-place" in Marc Augé's sense of nondescript places such as hotels, airports, and mass transit systems in his *Non-places*. But like him, I do think "place" and "non-place" give us another way to think about the relation between "space" and "place" (64)—imbibing qualities more than hard-and-fast designations. The Delhi Metro is a non-place in the sense of how it symbolically connects to other metro systems in the world, but not in terms of the way the system operates and the place it occupies in Delhi itself. The traveler's space, Augé says, is "the archetype of *non-place*" (70), as there becomes a "shared identity" of passengers and customers based on identities made and registered by credit cards, tollbooths, ticketing, etc., as well as "entirely new experiences and ordeals of solitude" (75). So there is an idea of what is contained in a non-place and what it affords those who have been admitted to it. Transport and transit are examples of spaces "formed in relation to certain ends" and where individuals come to have relations with one another that are specific to that space (76). The Delhi Metro would of course be an example of this kind of space—once you pass through the electronic turnstiles, you are registered as a passenger and

free to move within the space of the station and get on a train to reach a particular end or destination. Augé concludes by saying, "In the concrete reality of today's world, places and spaces, places and non-places intertwine and tangle together," and then more intriguingly, "The possibility of non-place is never absent from any place" (86). Meanwhile, David Ashford argues that the London Tube, which began running in 1863 and went underground in 1890, "foreshadows the international non-places of our increasingly virtual world," in *London Underground*, 2. For another take on the refusal of the distinction between space and place, see Doreen Massey's provocative *For Space*, which among other things points to space as being "the product of interrelations; as constituted through interactions, from the immensity of the global to the intimately tiny" (9).

35. See, for instance, Anru Lee, "Subways as a Space of Cultural Intimacy: The Mass Rapid Transit System in Taipei, Taiwan."

36. This process of how the Metro is being integrated into Delhi's landscape and people's psyches may be contrasted with Michael Fisch's *An Anthropology of the Machine*, a study of the seamless "technicity" of Tokyo's metro. Unlike the Delhi Metro's state of becoming with the city that I recount here, whereby the interface between the Metro and the city is being worked on and worked out, the separation of Tokyo's commuter train network from the city of Tokyo, Fisch says, is "unthinkable" as the two "have realized a certain functional coherence to operate together as a single associated milieu" (41).

37. See Mann ("A Megaproject Matrix," 133) for a description of how the idea of urban mass transit developed over successive five-year plans, with the first mention of mass transit for Delhi coming in the fourth five-year plan from 1969–74.

38. Yumiko Onishi, *Breaking Ground*.

39. Susan Caba, "Calcutta Metro Instills Pride and Cuts Commute"; Bish Sanyal, "Calcutta's Metro: Desperate Symbol of Middle-Class Hope"; Jayanta Sarkar, "Calcutta's Metro"; Nick Haslam, "Notes from the Underground—Metropolis."

40. Aveek Sen, "Notes from the Underground—Private Faces in Public Places."

41. Onishi, *Breaking Ground*, 3.

42. Sundaram, *Pirate Modernity*, 170, 141.

43. Amelia Gentleman, "Crackdown on 'Killer Buses' Strands Delhi Commuters," A6.

44. My idea of the fragment is comparable to Rebecca Solnit and Joshua Jelly Schapiro's idea that "fragments make the mosaic we mean by city, and each of us grasps and inhabits only part of the pattern." See their *Nonstop Metropolis*, 1. In the case of the Delhi Metro, we could also think of the system as a new pattern that has been set onto the urban landscape.

45. Writing about his own choice to focus on the vignette form in his ethnography of village life in the Philippines, Jean-Paul Dumont (*Visayan Vignettes*, 4) explicitly responds to the mid-1980s "*Writing Culture* moment" in anthropology by questioning the social truths that anthropologists construct through their field-

work and "the totalizing models of explanation or interpretation." My own use of vignettes echoes some of Dumont's concerns and reasoning about the nature of ethnographic knowledge as well as Lila Abu-Lughod's idea ("Writing against Culture," 149) of "the ethnography of the particular" as a way to stop "othering" people and to unsettle fixed notions of culture. Dumont (*Visayan Vignettes*, 1) also reminds his reader that "vignette" means "small vines," which for him conjures fragmented, nonlinear tales. I like the visual of vignettes as small vines since they echo the lines as shown on a metro map. But the point of formal experimentation, at least for me, is to fiddle with the genre of ethnography as a mode of perception.

46. I see the "affective realm" as including the ways in which the built environment of the Metro, including its surfaces, lighting, seating, entry gates, but also the look and plan of its stations, viaducts, bridges, etc., evokes emotional responses by those coming in contact with the system. And what is evoked becomes part of the very transformation of the city and people's senses of self. This relates to Setha Low's idea (*Spatializing Culture*, 154) that "the built environment produces affect and feeling but also that affect, in part, produces the built environment." I also draw here on Gilles Deleuze and Felix Guattari's idea (*A Thousand Plateaus*, 8) of the assemblage as an "increase in the dimensions of a multiplicity that necessarily changes in nature as it expands its connections"; and Stephen Collier and Aihwa Ong's description ("Global Assemblages, Anthropological Problems," 4) of how a global form becomes "territorialized" and leads to "new material, collective, and discursive relationships." Like a global assemblage, Delhi's Metro is "not reducible to a single logic" suggesting its "inherent tensions." The idea of the Metro as an assemblage works in a couple of ways: First, in the literal way in which the system grows as new lines and stations are built; with each addition the system changes in a particular way but also as a whole. The second way has to do with the multiple logics of the system. These logics are shifting and harder to pin down and map out, and yet they become documentable in scenes and instances.

47. On the limits and possibilities of connection: "The city must never be confused with the words that describe it," writes Italo Calvino (*Invisible Cities*, 61). "And yet between the one and the other there is a connection." I have also thought about how things connect in Walter Benjamin's *The Arcades Project* (1999), a tome on the city made of fragments in language, thought, and feeling. More practically, I have been inspired by Kathleen Stewart's unassuming yet startling use of micro-stories in *Ordinary Affects*. Initially I just liked the shortness of them and the one-by-one of them, disparate scenes acutely rendered and then almost abandoned; and the way they slowly add up to something without insisting on adding up. Then I saw how her form is also the message: "public feelings" registered as a set of "intensities" and "a set of sensations that incite," "a tangle of trajectories, connections, and disjunctures" (10, 93, 5). And indeed, there is a cumulative affect that resonates by the end. Stewart describes "affect" as "public feelings that begin and end in broad circulation, but they're also the stuff that seemingly intimate lives are made of. They give circuits and flows the forms of a life" (2).

The use of micro-stories or vignettes is also a way formally to highlight the everyday, or as Veena Das puts it (*Life and Words*, 8, 3), to see "the everyday itself as eventful" and to recognize "the voice in the everyday" as both more and less than what is simply just said. What I find most appealing about the anthropological study of infrastructure is the way in which the everyday is "both a key domain through which practices are regulated and normalized as well as an arena for negotiation, resistance and potential difference," as described by Stephen Graham and Colin McFarlane, *Infrastructural Lives*, 2. My study is also motivated more broadly by Gillian Rose's (*Feminism and Geography*, 17) notion of feminism *as* the politics of everyday life.

48. Visibility is also, of course, central to the disciplinary mechanisms of modern power. Nevertheless, I think it would be too easy *only* to cast the Metro as a disciplining institution in the Foucaldian sense, as rich and complex as that is. See, for instance, his discussion (*Discipline and Punish*, 201) of "permanent visibility" and "automatic functioning of power" in relation to the Panopticon.

PART I. CROWDED

1. The Delhi Development Authority (DDA) is the main planning body for Delhi; however, it operates under the auspices of the Central Government of India. See the vignette "Infrastructure by Example" in Part Three for more about the DDA.

2. I have mostly changed or abbreviated the names of people I interviewed to protect their privacy.

3. Matti Siemiatycki, "Message in a Metro: Building Urban Rail Infrastructure and Image in Delhi, India," 286.

4. In this regard, Dolores Hayden (*The Power of Place*, 9) writes that urban landscapes are "storehouses" for "social memories"; and that they "frame the lives of many people and often outlast many lifetimes." She sees a power in the idea of the ordinary landscape in particular; this power is a way to "nurture citizen's public memory" and "to encompass shared time in the form of shared territory."

5. Steven Feld, "Waterfalls of Song: An Acoustemology of Place Resounding in Bosavi, Papua New Guinea" (100), describes how space is audibly fused with time in the progression and motion of tones and as a result "places make sense, senses make place" (91). This approach to place-making echoes Lefebvre, when he writes about "the rhythms" of a city and its people—"the murmurs, noises, and cries." To capture this feeling of the city (what he calls "spectacle") is to be attuned to the "temporal and rhythmical." Lefebvre, *Writings on Cities*, 223.

6. Menon's idea of the public as profane recalls the distinction made by Sudipta Kaviraj ("Filth and the Public Sphere: Concepts and Practices about Space in Calcutta," 90) between the Western idea of the public as signifying universal access and individual rights, and the Indian idea of "spheres of restricted inclusivity" that

are "governed by the logic of segregation." Writing about colonial Calcutta, Kaviraj asserts that in the Hindu schema, large and even massive numbers of people don't count for universality: "What is precisely missing in these traditional Indian contexts is the notion of universality of access, the idea that an activity is open to all, irrespective of their social attributes."

7. Metro Bhawan was designed by the Delhi-based architectural firm Raj Rewal Associates. The building first reminded me of the Westin Bonaventure Hotel in downtown Los Angeles, with its relatively short, wide stature and defining conical structure, exposed elevators, and mirrored exterior, both reflecting the city and standing apart from it. In his classic take on the Westin Bonaventure, Fredric Jameson (*Postmodernism, or, The Cultural Logic of Late Capitalism*, 40) writes of the hotel as a "total space, a complete world, a kind of miniature city." Metro Bhawan is not a total space in the same way since it is an office building with fixed hours; however, it does symbolize the Metro system as a whole. Moreover, the Metro itself is a kind of miniature city within the city—a complete world with its own lighting, protocols, surveillances, and pleasures. For more on contemporary takes on Delhi's architecture, see *Learning from Delhi*, a volume of essays edited by Pelle Poiesz, Gert Jan Scholte, and Samme Vanderkaaij Gandhi.

8. See Anuj Dayal, *25 Management Strategies for Delhi Metro's Success*, for a complete rendition of how the Metro was built on time and under budget from the perspective of its managers. The strategies include issues of integrity, competency, and punctuality to cleanliness, vigilance, and delegation of power.

9. Joseph Alter, "Yoga, Modernity, and the Middle Class: Locating the Body in a World of Desire," 154.

10. The "timed subject" is similar to but ultimately different from Antina Von Schnitzler's ("Citizenship Prepaid: Water, Calculability, and Techno-Politics in South Africa") idea of the rise of "calculating subjects" through water meter infrastructures in South Africa. On the one hand, Indian Metro riders are encouraged through the Metro infrastructure to be "calculative citizens" in this new form of public transport whose hallmark is timed trains. On the other hand, what is being calculated on the Metro are the intangibles of time and space rather than water, which is a necessity that can be turned off by the state in Von Schnitzler's example. In the case of the Metro, people have to pay up front before entering the system; you are allowed to stay in the system for seventy minutes before your ticket expires. The Metro is a prepaid system, yet it does instill a new form of mobility calculation vis-à-vis the state. For instance, commuters who have more steady access to cash will pay up front for a Metro Travel Card, which requires a 50-rupee deposit and a minimum of 100 rupees that you can put on the card, so a minimum of 150 rupees at the outset. Those with less cash on reserve tend to buy tokens (starting at 10 rupees a ride) and pay for a single ride at a time.

11. Adam Low, *The Strange Luck of V.S. Naipaul*.

12. The question of behavior in public spaces and notions of civility and

cleanliness is linked to the history of urbanization and colonialism, most often as articulated through issues of caste and class. In his discussion of the colonial-era bazaars and parks of Calcutta, Dipesh Chakrabarty (*Habitations of Modernity*, 77) describes a colonialist/nationalist "call to discipline, public health, and public order" in public spaces that went unheeded by most Indians, spurring him to ask: "Can one read this as a refusal to become citizens of an ideal, bourgeois order?" In the case of the Metro, which is a highly managed space, there is little scope for refusal.

13. Dunu Roy's views are supported by Llerena Guiu Searle's ethnography of real estate in Gurgaon in her book *Landscapes of Accumulation*, in which she shows how Indian real estate became a transnational commodity in the 2000s, as actors in the market shifted from government to private sector elites, and land came to have a standardized value for global markets. Central to Searle's story is how the narrative of shining India as an emerging market and repository of increasingly wealthy consumers ("the India story") fuels the speculation and growth in value (5). This narrative correlates with developing Delhi and the National Capital Region into a world-class city (which includes global transport systems such as the Metro) for the purposes of capital accumulation. The Metro sends the message of world-classness. On the drive to make Delhi a global city, see Véronique Dupont, "The Dream of Delhi as a Global City." On the aesthetics that come to inform world-classness in Delhi's case, see Asher Ghertner, *Rule by Aesthetics*.

14. In data obtained through India's Right to Information Act, the Municipal Corporation of Delhi gives figures showing that 669 families were displaced in Phase 1 of the Delhi Metro construction, from 1999–2004, and were relocated to Narela, Tikri Khurd, Bhalaswa, and Holambi Kalan. Although the Red Line of the Delhi Metro traverses northwest Delhi, these areas are far from the Metro line and not well connected to that line. Hence, they form a kind of shadow city. See Hazards Center, *Delhi Metro Rail: A New Mode of "Public" Transport*. These areas in northwest Delhi were developed as informal settlements for the relocation of slum dwellers in the central areas of the city from the 1990s. See Véronique Dupont, "Slum Demolitions in Delhi since the 1990s: An Appraisal."

15. For an interesting comparison of how publics are created in and through particular kinds of activities in urban spaces, see Teresa Caldeira, "Imprinting and Moving Around: New Visibilities and Configurations of Public Space," for her study of young men's practices of graffiti and tagging in São Paulo.

16. See railway blockages protest (*rail roko*) detailed by Lisa Mitchell in "'To stop train pull chain': Writing Histories of Contemporary Political Practice." See also Aguilar, *Tracking Modernity*, and Bear, *Lines of the Nation*, on the cultural politics of the Indian Railways through time.

17. For a literary representation that captures the rhythm of Indian railway train travel and its psychic dimensions, see Mrinal Pande's Hindi short story "Fel-

low Travelers" (the Hindi title is "Hum Safar," which literally means "our journey"), about a mother and son who are jostled physically and mentally by train conductors and fellow travelers in dimly lit carriages.

18. For Elias Canetti (*Crowds and Power*, 75–90), fire, river, sea, rain, and other elements all recall the crowd in one way or the other.

19. Charles Baudelaire, *The Parisian Prowler*, 21. From the first line of the prose poem "Crowds": "Not everyone is capable of taking a bath of multitude: enjoying crowds is an art."

20. See Delhi Metro Rail Corporation publications such as *A Dream Revisited* and *Towards New Horizons...* for a listing of the project's major domestic and foreign contractors.

21. Jane Jacobs, *The Death and Life of American Cities*.

22. See Emma Tarlo, *Unsettling Memories*, 162–70, for government records of, as well as testimonies about, the relationship between sterilization and housing during the Emergency.

23. See Sreela Sarkar, "Women at Work and Home: New Technologies and Labor among Minority Women in Seelampur," for a study of women in Seelampur who receive computer training for these new kinds of jobs.

24. Roland Barthes (*Camera Lucida*, 10) writes, "[O]nce I feel myself observed by the lens, everything changes: I constitute myself in the process of 'posing'...."

25. Andrea Rizvi and Elliott Sclar, "Implementing Bus Rapid Transit: A Tale of Two Indian Cities," 201.

26. Delhi High Court (Case WP (C) NO. 380/2012).

27. Sara Dickey (*Living Class in Urban India*, 6) notes a similar language of class in urban India, whereby people talk about "big people" as a way to distinguish between those who have and those who do not.

28. Ram Shankar's analysis of the social and economic space that the Metro occupies is akin to Leela Fernandes's notion of "the politics of forgetting," whereby urban development excludes the poor and provides for the needs of the globalizing middle classes. For low-income people who see but can't access the Metro, the spatial reorganization that the Metro represents just further highlights middle-class mobility. As in Fernandes's research in Mumbai, in Delhi we see how the Metro can produce an exclusionary form of cultural citizenship, even as it provides new access to the city for some. See Fernandes, "The Politics of Forgetting: Class Politics, State Power and the Restructuring of Urban Space in India."

29. Ram Shankar is referring to the former chief minister of Delhi, Sheila Dikshit. See "Chief Minister" in Part Two for more on Dikshit.

PART II. EXPANDING

1. Mitali Trivedi and Gagandeep Singh, *Please Mind the Gap*. India has long had a cultural space for transgender people, and in 2011, the numbers of people

identifying as transgender (about half a million) was first recorded in the Census of India.

2. Sreedharan's awards include the Padma Shri award in 2001 and Padma Vibhushan award in 2008 from the Government of India and the Knight of the Legion of Honor from the Government of France in 2005.

3. Systra was awarded several design contracts by the DMRC and managed the construction of the first three lines of the Metro. Systra is the consultancy wing of the French National Railways (SNCF) and has worked on dozens of metro systems around the world, including in Hanoi, Riyadh, Mexico, Paris, Turin, Shenzen, Mumbai, Manila, Jakarta, Algiers, Casablanca, Sydney, and more.

4. Old Delhi refers to the sixteenth-century Mughal city of Shahjahanabad, with the iconic Red Fort at one end and the dramatic Jama Masjid at the other, connected by a thriving network of densely packed commercial lanes off the main arterial road of Chandni Chowk. New Delhi was designed by the British and built as a set of stately monuments disconnected from everyday life, what Sunil Khilnani describes as "a modernity that erased every trace of its location" in *The Idea of India*, 123. The form of New Delhi was an expression of a colonial rationality imposed on the city, one that among other things segregated people based on their race and rank. See Stephen Legg, *Spaces of Colonialism*.

5. While new spaces are always being produced, Lefebvre reminds us that "no space ever vanishes utterly, leaving no trace." Space is also an expression of time, whereby "each new addition inherits and reorganizes what has gone before." Lefebvre, *The Production of Space*, 164.

6. *Jhuggi jhopri*, or JJC (jhuggi jhopri clusters) is an official government category for unplanned settlements on public lands. About 15 percent of Delhiites live in JJCs.

7. Sheila Dikshit, *Citizen Delhi*, 16.

8. Before her death, Dikshit apparently requested to be cremated in a CNG (compressed natural gas) machine. See Astha Saxena, "Common Man to Top Leaders Come Out for Final Journey," 4.

9. It's interesting to compare this idea of foreign and local architects and the kinds of symbolic capital they bring or don't bring with the case of China. Xuefei Ren (*Building Globalization*, 13) charts the opposite phenomenon in China whereby hiring foreign architectural companies is seen as a strategy to build competitive global cities. The foreign architect is seen by the state as the globalizing mechanism for local Chinese megaprojects.

10. Matthew Hull ("Communities of Place, Not Kind: American Technologies of Neighborhood in Postcolonial Delhi") describes a comparable situation in Delhi's urban planning soon after Indian Independence. When the Ford Foundation was invited to consult on Delhi's master plan by the minister of health in Prime Minister Jawaharlal Nehru's first postcolonial government, the issue of foreigners consulting on programs for the Indian capital remained politically sensitive (759).

Hull writes, "Nehru himself became furious at one point when the execution of some of his orders regarding slums was postponed to wait for the input of the Ford team" (759–60).

11. www.ericsson.com/in/en/about-us/company-facts.

12. "The languages" in this context refer to the twenty-two Indian languages listed in the Indian Constitution, and that does not include English. See Sadana, *English Heart, Hindi Heartland*, for a Delhi-based ethnography of literary language that analyzes the issues of class, status, and linguistic authenticity that Chaudhuri is referring to when he says that even though he is predominantly English-speaking, he was able to get into the NSD.

13. See chapter 2 of Amita Baviskar's *Uncivil City*.

14. Raqs Media Collective, 18 December 2014–15 February 2015, *Asamayavali / The Untimely Calendar*, National Gallery of Modern Art, Jaipur House, New Delhi. In relation to the idea of the layers of the city, Lefebvre writes of the "unlimited multiplicity" of social spaces. Urban space in particular has a structure, he says, that is more "reminiscent of a flaky *mille-feuille* pastry than of the homogeneous and isotropic space of classical (Euclidean/Cartesian) mathematics." Lefebvre, *The Production of Space*, 86.

15. The Aam Aadmi Party would go on to win the election a few days later, making anticorruption activist Arvind Kejriwal the chief minister of Delhi.

16. See Robert Mackey, "Beating of African Students by Mob in India Prompts Soul-Searching on Race."

17. For one of the videos uploaded to YouTube of the attack at the Metro police kiosk, see "Fight at Rajiv Chowk Metro Station—New Delhi," posted September 28, 2014, accessed May 24, 2017, www.youtube.com/watch?v=0XHBOE93OKs.

18. Tarique Anwar, "Delhi's Everyday Racism: African Students Recount Lynch Mob Attack in Metro."

19. For one example, see "Delhi L-G Gives Nod to Prosecute AAP's Somnath Bharti in Connection with Khirki Extension Raid," *Firstpost*, April 4, 2015, accessed May 24, 2017, www.firstpost.com/india/delhi-l-g-gives-nod-prosecute-aa ps-somnath-bharti-connection-khirki-extension-raid-2378502.html.

20. Rahul Mehrotra, *Architecture in India*, 11. Verma's perspective supports Mehrotra's notion of "statistical architecture," whereby the state "stewards statistics" rather than creates "monumental edifices"—a trend he sees in post-economically liberalized India. Mehrotra does not see this efficiency in design as a laudable trend but rather as evidence of the state's increasingly outsized role in how cities should look and feel.

21. The expertise that Verma gains from his Tokyo sojourn could be seen as an example of the "inter-referencing" that occurs in Aihwa Ong's ("Worlding Cities or the Art of Being Global") notion of the "worlding" of cities, specifically "urban modeling." In her schema, modeling refers to other cities within Asia that are "invoked, envied, emulated as exemplary sites of a new urban normativity" (14). In

the process of worlding, global forms are "recontextualized in the city matrix" (4). Verma, in a sense, is a conduit for this recontextualization.

22. Verma's contrast of riding the bus versus the Metro points to the class-making aspect of each type of transport. By saying the Metro is "comfortable," he is ultimately talking about the dignity one feels riding it and points to the relational aspect of class: The Metro is a place, as compared to the bus, where one has more comfort. See Sara Dickey (*Living Class in Urban India*, 21) on the relationship between dignity and class and how dignity is being seen as "someone who counts," who is "worthy of recognition" and a "full social being."

23. Around the same time as the meeting was held in early 2015, the World Health Organization had reported that Delhi had worse pollution than Beijing, the previously most-polluted city on the planet. This is also when the *Indian Express* began its "Death by Breath" series, an expose that begins by showing how the gains Delhi made in the 1990s with the implementation of buses, auto rickshaws, and taxis running on CNG—compressed natural gas—were "frittered away."

PART III. VISIBLE

1. See Laura Bear (*Lines of the Nation*, 130–31) for a historical perspective on the issue of hierarchy and caste among the officer and worker classes in the Indian Railways, as well as the goals of union members in that organization. Where Bear interestingly highlights the biomoral dimension of the caste hierarchy in the nineteenth and early twentieth centuries, in the case of the Metro, where caste still most often aligns with class, these issues of hierarchy are seen, on the surface at least, as having to do with bureaucracy and corruption.

2. See Shahana Sheikh and Ben Mandelkern, "The Delhi Development Authority: Accumulation without Development," for an analysis of how the DDA privileges high-end amenities in Delhi at the expense of the poor.

3. Land acquisition for urban expansion has been common in India, but also in China and many parts of Africa since the 1970s, as noted by Sumanta Banerjee in *Memoirs of Roads*, 3. Banerjee describes the ironies inherent in this pattern of city-making in relation to road-building in Calcutta when he writes of how land becomes "expropriated from villagers, who have to sell by force or for a paltry sum leaving them destitute, surviving as beggars or daily wage laborers in the city situated on the same soil that once used to be their village homeland." Sanghmitra S. Acharya et al. ("Introduction," in *Marginalization in Globalizing Delhi*, 3) argue that this kind of urban expansion whereby infrastructure "bleeds into high-value agri-lands in neighboring states" gives "primacy to growth rather than development." In the process, Acharya et al. argue that government's role has changed from being "a watchdog and regulator to being a facilitator," whose goal is to ensure efficiency in the market.

4. See Geetam Tiwari, "Metro Rail and the City: Derailing Public Transport."

5. Shekhar Gupta, "Even in an Empty Delhi Metro Coach, Middle-Class Indians Make the Maids Sit on the Floor."

6. The larger question here is about whether a photo can depict a social reality in the first place. And, if so, whose? Susan Sontag (*On Photography*, 168) writes that "photographic images tend to subtract feeling from something we experience at first hand and the feelings they do arouse are, largely, not those we have in real life. Often something disturbs us more in photographed form than it does when we actually experience it." These two observations might explain the gulf in the interpretation of the Metro scene as experienced by the AIIMS doctor and the journalist. The photo takes on a life of its own, as the social tableau gets freeze-framed, which goes against the very nature of sociality. What is typical is that we don't have the perspective of the ayah or "nanny" sitting on the floor of the coach. In her ethnography of photography in Indonesia, Karen Strassler (*Demanding Images*) has shown how the circulation of images becomes part of the struggle for finding authentic truths in the public sphere.

7. Sujata Mody, "A Photo on Delhi Metro Sparked a Debate on Domestic Help. Now Pass a Law to Protect Them."

8. Sweta Datta, "Platform Screen Doors for Automatic Ops, Not to Stop Suicides: DMRC."

9. Ibid.

10. As Michael Fisch (*An Anthropology of the Machine*, chap. 5) has shown in his study of the Tokyo commuter train, suicides interfere with the system, but they also produce new kinds of systematicity. He argues that in Japan the manner in which suicides are detected and dealt with through the subway's advanced technological system conditions the way passengers interpret and think about suicide.

11. This is also the compact thesis of Jocelyn Chua's ethnography, *In Pursuit of the Good Life*, on the rise of suicides of young people in Kerala in post-liberalization India.

12. Extract from *Delhi Metro Rail Corporation Junior Engineer Civil Trade Recruitment Exam (Model Paper)*, (n.d.). Answers: d, a, a, c, c, b, a, c, d, d, c

13. These terms, as defined in the Indian Constitution, refer to the castes and tribes recognized by the Indian government as deserving of positive discrimination (affirmative action) due to these groups' historical marginalization and oppression.

14. Shalini Nair, "Free Travel for Women Threatens Metro Survival, Sreedharan Writes to Modi."

15. John L. Paul, "Metro Man E. Sreedharan on Being a Guiding Force for Infrastructure Projects for More than Five Decades."

EPILOGUE

1. As Elizabeth Wilson ("The Invisible Flâneur," 9) writes, in cities "we observe bits of the 'stories' men and women carry with them, but never learn their conclusions."

2. See Paul Ricoeur ("Narrative Time," 171) for a description of "the plot" as the "crossing point of temporality and narrativity." In this book, I have framed the practice of ethnography as a kind of plot or plotting.

3. Or as Michel de Certeau (*The Practice of Everyday Life*, 129) puts it, "What the map cuts up, the story cuts across."

4. Rahul Mehrotra, "Negotiating the Static and Kinetic Cities: The Emergent Urbanism of Mumbai." Arjun Appadurai ("Street Culture") makes a similar distinction when he identifies the variety and commercial complexity of the Indian street as the "front stage" of cosmopolitanism (which would correspond to Mehrotra's kinetic city with its heady mix of people, storefronts, and occupations). Conversely, Appadurai saw India's more modernized roads and highways as the "infrastructure of cosmopolitanism," a more static city in cultural terms.

5. Lefebvre (*Writings on Cities*, 158) goes as far as to say that "the right to the city" "can only be formulated as a transformed and renewed *right to urban life*."

Bibliography

Abu-Lughod, Lila. "Writing against Culture." In *Recapturing Anthropology: Working in the Present*, edited by Richard G. Fox, 137–62. Santa Fe, NM: School for Advanced Research Press, 1991.

Acharya, Sanghmitra S., Sucharita Sen, Milap Punia, and Sunita Reddy. "Introduction." In *Marginalization in Globalizing Delhi: Issues of Land, Livelihoods and Health*, edited by Sanghmitra S. Acharya, Sucharita Sen, Milap Punia, and Sunita Reddy, 1–18. Delhi: Springer India, 2017.

Aguiar, Marian. *Tracking Modernity: India's Railway and the Culture of Mobility*. Minneapolis: University of Minnesota Press, 2011.

Alter, Joseph S. "Yoga, Modernity, and the Middle Class: Locating the Body in a World of Desire." In *A Companion to the Anthropology of India*, edited by Isabelle Clark-Decès, 154–68. Cambridge, MA: Blackwell, 2011.

Anand, Shriya, and Jyothi Koduganti. "Urban India and Its Female Demographic Dividend." *India Spend*, E-paper, July 30, 2015.

Anwar, Tarique. "Delhi's Everyday Racism: African Students Recount Lynch Mob Attack in Metro." *Firstpost*, October 2, 2014. www.firstpost.com/living/delhis -everyday-racism-african-students-recount-lynch-mob-attack-metro-1739881 .html.

Appadurai, Arjun. "Street Culture." *India Magazine* 8, no. 1 (December 1987): 12–23.

Appel, Hannah, Nikhil Anand, and Akhil Gupta. "Introduction: Temporality, Politics, and the Promise of Infrastructure." In *The Promise of Infrastructure*, edited by Nikhil Anand, Akhil Gupta, and Hannah Appel, 1–38. Durham, NC: Duke University Press, 2018.

Ashford, David. *London Underground: A Cultural Geography*. Liverpool: Liverpool University Press, 2013.

Augé, Marc. *Non-places: Introduction to an Anthropology of Supermodernity*. Translated from the French by John Howe. London: Verso Books, 1995.

———. *In the Metro*. Translated from the French by Tom Conley. Minneapolis: University of Minnesota Press, 2002.

———. *Le Métro Revisité*. Paris: Éditions du Seuil, 2008.

Banerjee, Sumanta. *Memoirs of Roads: Calcutta from Colonial Urbanization to Global Modernization*. New Delhi: Oxford University Press, 2016.

Barthes, Roland. *Camera Lucida*. Translated from the French by Richard Howard. New York: Hill and Wang, 1981.

Baudelaire, Charles. *The Parisian Prowler*. Translated from the French by Edward K. Kaplan. Athens: University of Georgia Press, 1997.

Baviskar, Amita. *Uncivil City: Ecology, Equity and the Commons in Delhi*. New Delhi: Sage and Yoda Press, 2020.

Baviskar, Amita, and Raka Ray, eds. *Elite and Everyman: The Cultural Politics of the Indian Middle Classes*. New Delhi: Routledge, 2011.

Bear, Laura. *Lines of the Nation: Indian Railway Workers, Bureaucracy, and the Intimate Historical Self*. New York: Columbia University Press, 2007.

Benjamin, Walter. *The Arcades Project*. Translated from the German by Howard Eiland and Kevin McLaughlin. Cambridge, MA: Belknap Press of Harvard University Press, 1999.

Brosius, Christine. *India's Middle Class: New Forms of Urban Leisure, Consumption and Prosperity*. New Delhi: Routledge, 2010.

Butalia, Urvashi. "The Fear That Stalks: Gender-Based Violence in Public Spaces." In *The Fear That Stalks: Gender-Based Violence in Public Spaces*, edited by Sara Pilot and Lora Prabhu. New Delhi: Zubaan Books, 2014.

Butcher, Melissa. "Cultures of Commuting: The Mobile Negotiation of Space and Subjectivity on Delhi's Metro." *Mobilities* 6, no. 2 (2011): 237–54.

Caba, Susan. "Calcutta Metro Instills Pride and Cuts Commute." *Mass Transit* 14, no. 9 (1987): 88–89.

Caldeira, Teresa P.R. "Imprinting and Moving Around: New Visibilities and Configurations of Public Space." *Public Culture* 24, no. 2 (2012): 385–419.

Calvino, Italo. *Invisible Cities*. Translated from the Italian by William Weaver. New York: Harcourt, 1974.

Canetti, Elias. *Crowds and Power*. Translated from the German by Carol Stewart. New York: Noonday Press, 1962.

Chakrabarty, Dipesh. *Habitations of Modernity: Essays in the Wake of Subaltern Studies*. Chicago: University of Chicago Press, 2002.

Chatterjee, Pritha. "Embedded or Liberated? An Exploration into the Social

Milieu of Delhi." In *Marginalization in Globalizing Delhi: Issues of Land, Livelihoods and Health*, edited by Sanghmitra S. Acharya, Sucharita Sen, Milap Punia, and Sunita Reddy, 153–79. Delhi: Springer India, 2017.

Chatterji, Angana P., Thomas Blom Hansen, and Christophe Jaffrelot, eds. *Majoritarian State: How Hindu Nationalism Is Changing India*. New York: Oxford University Press, 2019.

Chaudhuri, Neel, dir. *Still and Still Moving*. Theatrical performance. Kamani Auditorium. March 24, 2015. New Delhi: Tadpole Repertory.

Chua, Jocelyn Lim. *In Pursuit of the Good Life: Aspiration and Suicide in Globalizing South India*. Berkeley: University of California Press, 2014.

Cody, Francis. "Publics and Politics." *Annual Review of Anthropology* 40 (2011): 37–52.

Coleman, Leo. "Inside and Outside the House: A Narrative of Mobility and Becoming in Delhi." *Journal of Contemporary Ethnography* 45, no. 6 (2016): 692–715.

Collier, Stephen J., and Aihwa Ong. "Global Assemblages, Anthropological Problems." In *Global Assemblages: Technology, Politics, and Ethics as Anthropological Problems*, edited by Aihwa Ong and Stephen J. Collier, 3–21. Malden, MA: Blackwell, 2004.

Dalakoglou, Dimitris, and Penny Harvey. "Roads and Anthropology: Ethnographic Perspectives on Space, Time, and (Im)mobility." *Mobilities* 7, no. 4 (2012): 459–65.

Das, Veena. *Life and Words: Violence and the Descent into the Ordinary*. Berkeley: University of California Press, 2007.

Datta, Sweta. "Platform Screen Doors for Automatic Ops, Not to Stop Suicides: DMRC." *Indian Express*, September 26, 2016. http://indianexpress.com/artic le/cities/delhi/platform-screen-doors-for-automatic-ops-not-to-stop-suicides -dmrc-3050071/

Dayal, Anuj. *25 Management Strategies for Delhi Metro's Success: The Sreedharan Way*. New Delhi: Delhi Metro Rail Corporation, 2012.

De Certeau, Michel. *The Practice of Everyday Life*. Translated from the French by Steven Randall. Berkeley: University of California Press, 1984.

Deleuze, Gilles, and Félix Guattari. *A Thousand Plateaus: Capitalism and Schizophrenia*. Translated from the French by Brian Massumi. Minneapolis: University of Minnesota Press, 1987.

Delhi High Court. Case WP (C) NO. 380/2012. *Nyaya Bhoomi versus Government of Delhi and ANR*. Judgement pronounced on October 18, 2012. New Delhi. http://lobis.nic.in/ddir/dhc/PNJ/judgement/18-10-2012/PNJ18102012 CW3802012.pdf

Delhi Metro Rail Corporation. *A Dream Revisited: An Archival Journey into the Making of the Delhi Metro Rail*. New Delhi: Delhi Metro Rail Corporation, 2003.

Delhi Metro Rail Corporation. *Towards New Horizons....* New Delhi: Delhi Metro Rail Corporation, n.d.

Dickey, Sara. *Living Class in Urban India.* New Brunswick, NJ: Rutgers University Press, 2016.

Dikshit, Sheila. *Citizen Delhi: My Times, My Life.* New Delhi: Bloomsbury, 2018.

Dumont, Jean-Paul. *Visayan Vignettes: Ethnographic Traces of a Philippine Island.* Chicago: University of Chicago Press, 1992.

Dupont, Véronique. "The Dream of Delhi as a Global City." *International Journal of Urban and Regional Research* 35, no. 3 (May 2011): 533–54.

———. "Slum Demolitions in Delhi since the 1990s: An Appraisal." *Economic and Political Weekly*, July 12, 2008, 79–87.

Evenson, Norma. *The Indian Metropolis: A View toward the West.* New Haven, CT: Yale University Press, 1989.

Feld, Steven. "Waterfalls of Song: An Acoustemology of Place Resounding in Bosavi, Papua New Guinea." In *Senses of Place*, edited by Steven Feld and Keith H. Basso, 91–135. Santa Fe, NM: School for Advanced Research Press, 1996.

Fernandes, Leela. "The Politics of Forgetting: Class Politics, State Power and the Restructuring of Urban Space in India." *Urban Studies* 41, no. 12 (2004): 2415–30.

Firth, Louis. "Urbanism as a Way of Life." *American Journal of Sociology* 44, no. 1 (July 1938): 1–24.

Fisch, Michael. *An Anthropology of the Machine: Tokyo's Commuter Train Network.* Chicago: University of Chicago Press, 2018.

Foucault, Michel. *Discipline and Punish: The Birth of the Prison.* Translated from the French by Alan Sheridan. 2nd ed. New York: Vintage Books, 1995.

Gentleman, Amelia. "Crackdown on 'Killer Buses' Strands Delhi Commuters." *New York Times*, July 14, 2007, A6.

Ghertner, D. Asher. *Rule by Aesthetics: World-Class City Making in Delhi.* New York: Oxford University Press, 2015.

Graham, Stephen, and Colin McFarlane. *Infrastructural Lives: Urban Infrastructure in Context.* New York: Routledge, 2014.

Goswami, Manu. *Producing India: From Colonial Economy to National Space.* Chicago: University of Chicago Press, 2004.

Government of India. *Delhi Master Plan 2021: Reader Friendly.* Delhi: Rupa, 2007.

Government of National Capital Territory of Delhi. *Statistical Abstract of Delhi 2016.* Delhi: Directorate of Economics and Statistics, 2016. https://delhi.gov.in.

Gupta, Narayani. *Delhi between Two Empires 1803–1931: Society, Government, and Urban Growth.* New Delhi: Oxford University Press, 1981.

Gupta, Shekhar. "Even in an Empty Delhi Metro Coach, Middle-Class Indians Make the Maids Sit on the Floor." *The Print*, E-paper, January 22, 2018.

https://theprint.in/2018/01/22/maid-middle-class-india-class-new-caste-ev en-metro-coach/

Hadlaw, Janin. "The London Underground Map: Imagining Time and Space." *Design Issues* 19, no. 1 (Winter 2003): 25–36.

Harvey, David. *The Condition of Postmodernity: An Enquiry into the Origins of Cultural Change.* Cambridge, MA: Blackwell, 1990.

Haslam, Nick. "Notes from the Underground—Metropolis." *Financial Times*, June 6, 1998.

Hayden, Dolores. *The Power of Place.* Cambridge, MA: MIT Press, 1995.

Hazards Centre. *Delhi Metro Rail: A New Mode of "Public" Transport?* New Delhi: Hazards Centre, 2006.

Heiman, Rachel, Mark Liechty, and Carla Freeman. "Charting an Anthropology of the Middle Classes." In *The Global Middle Classes: Theorizing through Ethnography*, edited by Rachel Heiman, Carla Freeman, and Mark Liechty, 3–29. Santa Fe, NM: School for Advanced Research Press, 2012.

Holston, James, and Arjun Appadurai. "Cities and Citizenship." *Public Culture* 8, no. 2. (1996): 187–204.

Hull, Matthew. "Communities of Place, Not Kind: American Technologies of Neighborhood in Postcolonial Delhi." *Comparative Studies in Society and History* 53, no. 4 (2011): 757–90.

Jacobs, Jane. *The Death and Life of American Cities.* New York: Vintage Books, 1961.

Jameson, Fredric. *Postmodernism, or, The Cultural Logic of Late Capitalism.* Durham, NC: Duke University Press, 1991.

Joshi, Poornima, and A.M. Jigeesh. "Anatomy of a Riot in North East Delhi." *Hindu Business Line.* Chatham: Newstex, 2020.

Joyce, Patrick. *The Rule of Freedom: Liberalism and the Modern City.* London: Verso, 2003

Kashyup, Anurag, dir. *Dev.D.* Feature film. Mumbai: UTV Motion Pictures, 2009.

Kaviraj, Sudipta. "Filth and the Public Sphere: Concepts and Practices of Space in Calcutta." *Public Culture* 10, no. 1 (1997): 83–113.

Khilnani, Sunil. *The Idea of India.* New Delhi: Penguin, 1997.

Kleinman, Julie. *Adventure Capital: Migration and the Making of an African Hub in Paris.* Berkeley: University of California Press, 2019.

Krishnan, Kavita. *Fearless Freedom.* Delhi: Penguin, 2019.

Larkin, Brian. "The Politics and Poetics of Infrastructure." *Annual Review of Anthropology* 42 (2013): 327–43.

Latour, Bruno. *Aramis, or the Love of Technology.* Translated from the French by Catherine Porter. Cambridge, MA: Harvard University Press, 1996.

———. "From Realpolitik to Dingpolitik, or How to Make Things Public." In

Making Things Public: Atmospheres of Democracy, edited by Bruno Latour and Peter Weibel. Cambridge, MA: MIT Press, 2005.

Lee, Anru. "Subways as a Space of Cultural Intimacy: The Mass Rapid Transit System in Taipei, Taiwan." *China Journal*, no. 58 (July 2007).

Lefebvre, Henri. *The Production of Space*. Translated from the French by Donald Nicholson-Smith. Oxford: Blackwell, 1991.

———. *Writings on Cities*. Translated from the French by Eleonore Kofman and Elizabeth Lebas. Oxford: Blackwell, 1996.

Legg, Stephen. *Spaces of Colonialism: Delhi's Urban Governmentalities*. Oxford: Wiley-Blackwell, 2007.

Lemon, Alaina. "Talking Transit and Spectating Transition: The Moscow Metro." In *Altering States: Ethnographies of Transition in Eastern Europe and the Former Soviet Union*, edited by Daphne Berdahl, Matti Bunzl, and Martha Lampland, 14–39. Ann Arbor: University of Michigan Press, 2000.

Liechty, Mark. *Suitably Modern: Making Middle-Class Culture in a New Consumer Society*. Princeton, NJ: Princeton University Press, 2003.

Low, Adam. *The Strange Luck of V.S. Naipaul*. Documentary Film. London: Lone Star Productions for BBC Arena, 2008.

Low, Setha. *Spatializing Culture: The Ethnography of Space and Place*. New York: Routledge, 2017.

Luiselli, Valeria. *Sidewalks*. Translated from the Spanish by Christina MacSweeney. Minneapolis: Coffee House Press, 2014.

Lynch, Kevin. *The Image of the City*. Cambridge: MIT Press, 1960.

Mackey, Robert. "Beating of African Students by Mob in India Prompts Soul-Searching on Race." *New York Times*, September 30, 2014. www.nytimes.com /2014/10/01/world/asia/beating-of-african-students-by-mob-in-india-promp ts-soul-searching-on-race.html

Mann, Anupama. "A Megaproject Matrix: Ideology, Discourse, and Regulation in the Delhi Metro Rail." Unpublished doctoral thesis. University of Southern California, School of Policy, Planning, and Development, 2009.

Massey, Doreen. *For Space*. London: Sage, 2005.

Mehra, Rakeysh Omprakash, dir. *Delhi-6*. Feature Film. Mumbai: UTV Motion Pictures, 2009.

Mehrotra, Rahul. *Architecture in India: Since 1990s*. Berlin: Hatje Cantz Verlag, 2011.

———. "Negotiating the Static and Kinetic Cities: The Emergent Urbanism of Mumbai." In *Other Cities, Other Worlds: Urban Imaginaries in a Globalizing Age*, edited by Andreas Huyssen, 205–18. Durham, NC: Duke University Press, 2008.

Menon, A.G. Krishna. "Imagining the Indian City." *Economic and Political Weekly* 32, no. 46 (November 15, 1997).

Mitchell, Lisa. "'To Stop Train Pull Chain': Writing Histories of Contemporary

Political Practice." *Indian Economic and Social History Review* 48, no. 4 (2011): 469–95.

Mody, Sujata. "A Photo on Delhi Metro Sparked a Debate on Domestic Help. Now Pass a Law to Protect Them." *The Print*, E-paper, January 30, 2018. https://theprint.in/2018/01/30/delhi-metro-domestic-help-pass-law-protect-them/

Mohan, Dinesh. *Mythologies, Metros, and Future Urban Transport.* TRIPP Report Series. Delhi: Indian Institute of Technology, 2008.

Nader, Laura. "Up the Anthropologist: Perspectives Gained from Studying Up." In *Reinventing Anthropology*, edited by Dell Hymes, 284–311. New York: Pantheon Books, 1972.

Nair, Shalini. "Free Travel for Women Threatens Metro Survival, Sreedharan Writes to Modi." *Indian Express*, June 15, 2019. https://indianexpress.com/article/cities/delhi/free-travel-for-women-threatens-metro-survival-sreedharan-writes-to-modi-5781550/

Nigam, Chayyanika. "26 Fatal Leaps in 2019: Spike in Suicides at Metro." *India Today*, January 16, 2020. www.indiatoday.in/mail-today/story/26-fatal-leaps-in-2019-spike-in-suicides-at-metro-1637227-2020-01-16

Ojha, Sangeeta. "Delhi Metro Latest Update: Currently, 16 Stations Closed. Here Is Full List." *LiveMint*, E-paper, December 20, 2019. www.livemint.com/news/india/delhi-metro-latest-updates-stations-closed-11576829937881.html

Ong, Aihwa. "Worlding Cities or the Art of Being Global." In *Worlding Cities: Asian Experiments and the Art of Being Global*, edited by Ananya Roy and Aihwa Ong, 1–26. Oxford: Blackwell, 2011.

Onishi, Yumiko. *Breaking Ground: A Narrative on the Making of Delhi Metro.* Project Report. Tokyo: Japan International Cooperation Agency, 2016.

Pande, Mrinal. "Fellow Travelers" (Hum Safar). Translated from the Hindi by the author. In *Women Writing in India, Volume II: The 20th Century*, edited by Susie Tharu and K. Lalita, 548–56. New York: Feminist Press at the City University of New York.

Pandey, Shelly. "Reinterpreting Gender in Globalizing India: Afghan Sikh Refugees in Delhi City's Built Environment." In *The Routledge Companion to Modernity, Space and Gender*, edited by Alexandra Staub, 380–90. New York: Routledge, 2018.

Paul, John L. "Metro Man E. Sreedharan on Being a Guiding Force for Infrastructure Projects for More Than Five Decades." *The Hindu*, August 3, 2019. www.thehindu.com/news/national/metro-man-e-sreedharan-on-being-a-guiding-force-for-infrastructure-projects/article28806393.ece

Phadke, Shilpa. "Gendered Questions of Access in Mumbai." In *Transforming Asian Cities: Intellectual Impasse, Asianizing Space, and Emerging Translocalities*, edited by Nihal Perera and Wing Shing Tang. New York: Routledge, 2013.

Phadke, Shilpa, Sameera Khan, and Shilpa Ranade. *Why Loiter? Women and Risk on Mumbai Streets*. New Delhi: Penguin Books, 2011.

Poiesz, Pelle, Gert Jan Scholte, and Samme Vanderkaaij Gandhi, eds. *Learning from Delhi: Practising Architecture in Urban India*. Ahmedabad: Mapin, 2016.

Press Trust of India. "Women Gather Near Delhi's Jaffrabad Metro Station to Protest against CAA, NRC." NDTV. www.ndtv.com/delhi-news/citizenship-am endment-act-women-gather-near-delhis-jaffrabad-metro-station-to-protest -against-caa-nr-2184242

Ren, Xuefei. 2011. *Building Globalization: Transnational Architecture Production in Urban China*. Chicago: University of Chicago Press.

Ricoeur, Paul. "Narrative Time." *Critical Inquiry* 7, no. 1 (Autumn 1980): 169–90.

RITES. *Integrated Multi-Modal Mass Rapid Transport System for Delhi (Modified First Phase)*. Detailed Project Report (Summary). Government of National Capital Territory of Delhi, May 1995.

Rizvi, Andrea, and Elliott Sclar. "Implementing Bus Rapid Transit: A Tale of Two Indian Cities." *Research in Transportation Economics* 48 (2014): 194–204.

Robinson, Jennifer. *Ordinary Cities: Between Modernity and Development*. New York: Routledge, 2006.

Rose, Gillian. *Feminism and Geography: The Limits of Geographical Knowledge*. Cambridge: Polity Press, 1993.

Roy, Dunu. "Whose City?" *Seminar*, no. 648 (2013). www.india-seminar.com/20 13/648/648_dunu_roy.htm

Sadana, Rashmi. *English Heart, Hindi Heartland: The Political Life of Literature in India*. Berkeley: University of California Press, 2012.

Saidi-Sharouz, Mina. "Le Métro de Téhéran: Une gestion publique des relations de genre." Paper presented at "Ethnographies of Mass Transportation in a Globalized World," Workshop. Center for International Research in the Humanities and Social Sciences, New York University, May 26–27, 2016.

Sanyal, Bish. "Calcutta's Metro: Desperate Symbol of Middle-Class Hope." *The Statesman*, July 12, 1987, 4.

Sarkar, Jayanta. "Calcutta's Metro." *Far Eastern Economic Review* 156, no. 11 (March 18, 1993): 31.

Sarkar, Sreela. "Women at Work and Home: New Technologies and Labor among Minority Women in Seelampur." *Journal of Community Informatics* 5, no. 3 (2009) and 6, no. 1 (2010), special double issue, "Gender in Community Informatics."

Saxena, Astha. "Common Man to Top Leaders Come Out for Final Journey." *Indian Express*, July 22, 2019, 4.

Schivelbusch, Wolfgang. *The Railway Journey: The Industrialization of Time and Space in the 19th Century*. Berkeley: University of California Press, 1977.

Schrag, Zachary M. *The Great Society Subway: A History of the Washington Metro.* Baltimore: Johns Hopkins University Press, 2006.

Schwetman, John. "Harry Beck's London Underground Map: A Convex Lens for the Global City." *Transfers* 4, no. 2 (2014): 86–103.

Searle, Llerena Guiu. *Landscapes of Accumulation: Real Estate and the Neoliberal Imagination in Contemporary India.* Chicago: University of Chicago Press, 2016.

Sen, Aveek. "Notes from the Underground—Private Faces in Public Places." *The Telegraph*, February 16, 2003.

Sheikh, Shahana, and Ben Mandelkern. "The Delhi Development Authority: Accumulation without Development." A report of the "Cities of Delhi" project. New Delhi: Centre for Policy Research, 2014.

Shelly, Tara. "Private Space in Public Transport: Locating Gender in the Delhi Metro." *Economic and Political Weekly* 67, no. 51 (December 17, 2011): 71–74.

Siemiatycki, Matti. "Message in a Metro: Building Urban Rail Infrastructure and Image in Delhi, India." *International Journal of Urban and Regional Research* 30, no. 2 (2006): 277–92.

Singh, Upinder. *Ancient Delhi.* New Delhi: Oxford University Press, 1999.

Solnit, Rebecca, and Joshua Jelly-Schapiro. *Nonstop Metropolis: A New York City Atlas.* Berkeley: University of California Press, 2016.

Sontag, Susan. *On Photography.* New York: Dell, 1977.

Spain, Daphne. *Gendered Spaces.* Chapel Hill: University of North Carolina Press, 1992.

Spear, Percival. *Delhi: Its Monuments and History.* New Delhi: Oxford University Press, 1994.

Srivastava, Sanjay. *Entangled Urbanism: Slum, Gated Community, and Shopping Mall in Delhi and Gurgaon.* New Delhi: Oxford University Press, 2015.

Stewart, Kathleen. *Ordinary Affects.* Durham, NC: Duke University Press, 2007.

Strassler, Karen. *Demanding Images: Democracy, Mediation, and the Image-Event in Indonesia.* Durham, NC: Duke University Press, 2020.

Sundaram, Ravi. *Pirate Modernity: Delhi's Media Urbanism.* New Delhi: Routledge, 2010.

Tarlo, Emma. *Unsettling Memories: Narratives of the Emergency in Delhi.* Berkeley: University of California Press, 2003.

Taylor, Charles. *Modernity and the Rise of the Public Sphere.* The Tanner Lectures on Human Values. Delivered at Stanford University, February 25, 1992.

Tiwari, Geetam. "Metro Rail and the City: Derailing Public Transport." *Economic and Political Weekly* 48 (November 30, 2013): 65–76.

Tonnelat, Stéphane, and William Kornblum. *International Express: New Yorkers on the 7 Train.* New York: Columbia University Press, 2017.

Trivedi, Mitali, and Gagandeep Singh, dirs. *Please Mind the Gap.* Documentary

Film. Bengaluru: Public Service Broadcasting Trust and Human Capability Foundation, 2018.

United Nations, Department of Economic and Social Affairs, Population Division. *World Urbanization Prospects: The 2018 Revision* (ST/ESA/SER.A/420). New York: United Nations, 2019.

Vertesi, Janet. "Mind the Gap: The London Underground Map and Users' Representations of Urban Space." *Social Studies of Science* 38, no. 1 (2008): 7–33.

Virilio, Paul. *Speed and Politics: An Essay on Dromology.* Translated from the French by Mark Polizzotti. Los Angeles: Semiotext(e), 2006.

Viswanath, Kalpana, and Surabhi Tandon Mehrotra. "'Shall we go out?' Women's Safety in Public Spaces in Delhi." *Economic and Political Weekly* 42, no. 17 (April 28–May 4, 2007): 1542–48.

Von Schnitzler, Antina. "Citizenship Prepaid: Water, Calculability, and Techno-Politics in South Africa." *Journal of Southern African Studies* 34, no. 4 (2008): 899–917.

Warner, Michael. "Publics and Counterpublics." *Public Culture* 14, no. 1 (Winter 2002): 49–90.

Wilson, Elizabeth. "The Invisible Flâneur." *New Left Review* I/191 (January–February 1992).

Index

Page numbers followed by n denote notes. Page numbers in italics denote illustrations.

metro fare hike, 190; negotiation with
Delhi metro workers, 153; network map,
216n4; as "non-place," 222n34; policies of,
155–56; property development by, 219n16;
and protests, 47–48; publications, 41, 68,
228n20; role as property developer,
219n15; on suicide attempts on metro
tracks, 174–75; underpasses and walls,
221n28; videos, 54; work culture in,
41–43, 91–92
Delhi Statistical Abstract 2016, 220n19
Delhi Urban Arts Commission, 38
Demanding Images (Strassler), 232n6
Democracy Now, 221n27
Dickey, Sara, 218n13, 231n22
Dikshit, Sheila, 45, 98–102, 107, 116, 144, 186,
228n29, 229n7, 229n8
Dilli Haat, 35–36, 195–97
disability in public space, 195–97
displacement of residents, 30, 100, 121
driverless trains, 150
DTC (Delhi Transport Corporation) buses,
19–20, 200
Dumont, Jean-Paul, 223–24n45
Dupont, Véronique, 227n13, 227n14
Dwarka Sector 9 station, 43

East Center mall, 75
Economic and Political Weekly, 38–39
elevated tracks, 72, 89
elevators, 32, 40–41, 63
Elite and Everyman (Baviskar and Ray),
222n30
English Heart, Hindi Heartland (Sadana),
230n12
Entangled Urbanism (Srivastava), 218n12,
219n14
e-rickshaws, 136, 185–88
ethnography, 21–22, 203–4, 223n45, 233n2
European architects, 108–9
Evenson, Norma, 217n7

fares: metro fare hike, 190–92; metro versus
bus, 11, 102, 161, 164, 181, 184, 222n33
Fearless Freedom (Krishnan), 215n2
feedback, customer, 154
feeder buses, 165
Feld, Steven, 225n5
Fernandes, Leela, 228n28
financing, 9, 92, 142
Firth, Louis, 221n25
Fisch, Michael, 223n36, 232n10
Ford Foundation, 38, 229n10

For Space (Massey), 223n34
Freeman, Carla, 222n30
French National Railways (SNCF), 229n3

Gammon India, blacklisting of, 107
Gandhi, Indira, 69
Gandhi, Samme Vanderkaaij, 226n7
Gandhi, Sandeep, 144
Gandhi Nagar market, 71
gangway as ethnographic space, 88–89, 91,
163–64
Gautam Nagar, 117–18
gaze: female, 2, 14, 167–68; unwanted, 106
gendered liberation, 35–37, 76–77
Gendered Spaces (Spain), 218n10
gender equality, 60–61
gender identity, personal negotiation of, 91
Gentleman, Amelia, 223n43
Ghertner, Asher, 227n13
Ghevra station, 134, 201
The Global Middle Classes (Heiman, Free-
man, and Liechty), 222n30
Gole Market, 39
Goodman, Amy, 221n27
Goswain, Naresh, 52
Goswami, Manu, 220n20, 220n21
Government of India 2011 census website,
215n1
Graham, Stephen, 225n47
Greater Kailash station, 161
The Great Society Subway (Schrag), 222n31
Green Line, *128*, 132–36, 201
greenway project, 166
Grey Line, 150
Guattari, Felix, 224n46
Gupta, Akhil, 218n13
Gupta, Shekhar, 168, 232n5
Gurgaon to Gurugram, name change, 217n6

Hadlaw, Janin, 216n4
handicapped access, 184–85, 196–97
Hansen, Thomas Blom, 219n17
Harkesh Nagar, 49
Harvey, David, 218n10
Harvey, Penny, 218n13
Haryana: caste conflicts in, 112–14, 130–31;
Gurgaon to Gurugram, name change,
217n6; metro extension in, 3, 123, 133;
ratio of women in, 215n1; women's safety
in, 1–2
Haslam, Nick, 223n39
Hauz Khas station, 123, 184
Hayden, Dolores, 225n4

Founded in 1893,
UNIVERSITY OF CALIFORNIA PRESS
publishes bold, progressive books and journals
on topics in the arts, humanities, social sciences,
and natural sciences—with a focus on social
justice issues—that inspire thought and action
among readers worldwide.

The UC PRESS FOUNDATION
raises funds to uphold the press's vital role
as an independent, nonprofit publisher, and
receives philanthropic support from a wide
range of individuals and institutions—and from
committed readers like you. To learn more, visit
ucpress.edu/supportus.

www.ingramcontent.com/pod-product-compliance
Lightning Source LLC
Chambersburg PA
CBHW020848270326
41928CB00006B/600